Keto Diet for Beginners

800 Simple and Delicious Recipes| 30-Day Meal Prep| Lose up to 30 Pounds in 4 Weeks

Dr Stacy Wader

Table of contents

Introduction

This book guides you to all about the ketogenic diet from basics. You can also know how the diet works and what are the different health benefits provided by the keto diet. 8 important tips guide you during your keto journey.

To follow the keto diet successfully you should understand about very basics of the keto diet. In this book, we have to discuss one of the most successful diet plan popularly known as ketogenic diet plan. I hope this book will help you in your weight loss efforts and guide you on how to implement a successful keto diet. Basically, the keto diet is low carb, high fat and a moderate amount of protein diet. Keto is not just only a diet plan but also it is one of the healthy eating habits provides you numerous health benefits. Keto diet has proven by many scientific studies and researches it not only just diet it also helps to treat various medical conditions.

My goal here is that provides you all the information about the keto diet with its health benefits. You must know the science behind the ketogenic diet. There are various books available in the market on this subject so thanks for choosing my book and enjoy delicious recipes.

Chapter 1: The Basics of the Keto Diet

What Is the Keto Diet

The keto diet is basically low in carbohydrates, high in fats and moderate in protein. To perform daily activities our body needs energy. These energies are coming in the form of carbohydrates, fats, and proteins.

When you consume less amount of carbs daily (less than 50 grams) your body burns fats and proteins for energy instead of glucose (carbohydrates). This state of your body is called ketosis. When your body is in the state of ketosis it effectively burns fats from your body. Due to this your body weight is reduced rapidly. Keto diet is very effective on weight loss and it also helps to treat certain medical conditions like epilepsy, Alzheimer's and Parkinson's. It not only improves your physical health but also improve your mental health.

How to Is different from Another Diet

- The main difference of the keto diet is that it is very effective on rapid weight loss to compare to any other diet. If you want to lose your weight you must follow the keto diet.

- Keto diet is more carbohydrate restrictive diet compare to another diet like the Atkin diet.

- Normally our body uses glucose (carbohydrates) as a primary source of energy but while you are on a keto diet your body will push into the state of ketosis in which your body breaks down fats from the liver for energy instead of glucose (carbohydrates).

- Keto diet is not only just a diet plan it also helps to treat certain medical conditions like Alzheimer's, Parkinson's, high blood pressure, type-2 diabetes, heart disease and it also very effective on epilepsy conditions.

How Does the Ketogenic Diet Work?

The main purpose of a keto diet is to put and keep your body in the metabolic state called ketosis. Normally our bodies use glucose (carbohydrates) as a primary source of energy. Glucose is stored in our body muscles and tissues. Excess glucose is converted and stored in the form of glycogens to our body. When the glycogen level into our body increases then excess glycogens are converted into the form of fats and these fats are stored into our liver. Keto diet is carb restrictive diet when you reduce carb intake your glycogen storage also reduces and hormonal insulin level into your body is decreased. In this process, the fatty acid is released from your stored body fats. Your liver converts these fatty acids into ketones. Ketones are one kind of chemical products in your liver when your body burns fats for energy. Reducing carb intake will help to push your body into a metabolic state called ketosis.

How to Know when You Are in Ketosis

There are various signs and symptoms during a ketogenic diet confirms whether you are in ketosis or not. Some of them are given below.

- Rapid weight loss: During the first several weeks you have noticed that your weight decreases rapidly. This is happening due to a decrease in calories and you will lose your water weight first. Rapid weight loss is one of the signs that indicate you are in ketosis.

- Bad Breath: One of the most common side effects occur due to acetones. When your body breaks down fat for energy acetones are released during the fat breaking process. These acetones are released through your mouth due to this you have to face bad breath problem during the first week of the ketogenic diet. Bad breath sign indicates that you are in the ketosis.

- Dry Mouth and Increase Thirst: During keto diet carb intake is very low due to this insulin level is decreased in your body. Decrease insulin level into your body will allow your kidney to release sodium and water from your body. This is also one of the common side effects occurs during a keto diet. Due to all these conditions, your body dehydrates rapidly and you will face issues like dry mouth and increase thirst. This is one of the sign indicates that you are in ketosis.

- Headaches: This is also one of the common side effect noticed in the first week of the ketogenic diet. This is happening due to lower the intake of carbohydrates. Electrolytes imbalance and dehydration is also one of the causes of headache. Headache is also one of the symptoms occurs during the ketogenic diet and this sign indicates that you are in ketosis.

- Frequent Urination: Frequent urination symptoms are detected during the first week of the ketogenic diet. When your body loses the glycogen store it also loses water in it. Due to this, you have noticed frequent urination during a ketogenic diet. This symptom indicates that you are in ketosis.

The Health Benefits of Keto Diet

Keto diet provides you various health benefits which are described as follows

- Weight loss: Compare to another diet ketogenic diet is very effective on weight loss. It gives you long term weight loss benefits.Normally our body uses glucose as a primary energy source. When you are on a ketogenic diet your body breaks down fats for energy instead of glucose. When you consume a moderate amount of protein during keto diet means it doesn't feel you a hungry compared to another diet. This will reduce your body weight rapidly and you will get long term weight loss benefits during a ketogenic diet.

- Maintain Blood sugar level: Basically keto diet is low carb diet due to this it helps to reduce your blood sugar level and insulin level. One of the scientific research and study proves that a keto diet is very effective in treating type-2 diabetes. To transport into your body cells glucose needs insulin and also increase insulin sensitivity. On the other side, ketones don't need insulin to transport into a body cell. Due to this your blood sugar level are maintain and stable throughout the day.

- Improves Brain function: Keto diet is low carb diet which will decrease your blood glucose and insulin level. During the fat breaking process, fatty acids are released and your liver produces ketones from fatty acids. These ketones full fill 70 percent of your brain energy needs. Scientific research and study prove that a keto diet is very effective to treat a brain-related disease like epilepsy, Alzheimer's and Parkinson's disease.

- Increase HDL cholesterol and Improve LDL cholesterol level: Keto diet is low carb and high-fat diet helps to increase good HDL (High-density lipoprotein)cholesterol level in blood. Smaller bad LDL particles are leads to you towards heart disease. Low carb diet helps to increase the size of bad LDL particles. Which help to reduce the number of total LDL particles in the bloodstream. Lowering carb intake helps to improve your heart function and reduce the risk of heart disease.

- Work on various disease: While you are on a keto diet your body uses ketones for energy. Ketones are antioxidant and anti-inflammatory properties. It helps to treat some brain conditions like Alzheimer's, Parkinson's and epilepsy. It is also effective for type-2 diabetes, cancer, and heart-related disease.

Helpful Tips for the Keto Journey

- Limit carb consumption: Keto diet is a low carb diet it recommends to consume below 25 grams of carbs daily. Eating low carb will keep your body in the state of ketosis.

- Stay your body hydrated: During a ketogenic diet, your body lose glycogen store and these glycogens hold some water release through urination. Drinking tea, coffee, smoothie and plenty of plain water may help you to stay hydrated.

- Use MCT oils: Medium Chain Triglycerides (MCTs) are one of the healthy fat found in coconut oil. These healthy fats are quickly absorbed by your liver and convert it into ketones. It helps to maintain the level of ketosis in your body.

- Sleep enough: While you are on keto diet enough sleep is very important. Sleep in a dark and cool room where temperature maintains at 65 F and sleep at least 7 hours daily at night.

- Consume adequate amount of protein daily: Normally when you are on a keto diet your body burns fats for energy instead of a carb. In this process your body losses some muscles and fats. Maintaining your muscle mass, you just need to consume an adequate amount of protein daily.

- Do exercise regularly: Regular exercise helps to maintain your blood sugar level and also reduce your weight. When you are doing exercise during keto diet your ketones level are increased.

- Add extra salt to your diet: When you are on keto diet due to low carb consumption your blood insulin level decreases and it allows your kidney to release water and sodium from your body. Adding an extra 3 to 5 grams of sodium in your diet will also help to avoid electrolyte imbalance.

- Clear out your kitchen of carbohydrates: Most of the people consume their favorite carb loaded food just because they fail to remove them from their kitchen. You must clean all carbohydrates from your kitchen pantry includes sodas, pasta, candy, bread, and rice.

Chapter 2: Smoothies & Breakfast

Creamy Raspberry Smoothie

Preparation Time: 5 minutes; Cooking Time: 5 minutes; Serve: 2

Ingredients:

- 1 cup unsweetened almond milk
- 1/2 tsp vanilla
- 1 tbsp cream cheese, softened
- 2 tbsp swerve
- 1/4 cup fresh raspberries
- 4 tbsp heavy cream
- 1 cup ice

Directions:

1. Add all ingredients into the blender and blend until smooth and creamy.
2. Serve and enjoy.

Nutritional Value (Amount per Serving):

Calories 157; Fat 14.7 g; Carbohydrates 5.9 g; Sugar 0.9 g; Protein 1.7 g; Cholesterol 47 mg

Energy Booster Breakfast Smoothie

Preparation Time: 5 minutes; Cooking Time: 5 minutes; Serve: 1

Ingredients:

- 1 cup unsweetened almond milk
- 1/2 cup ice
- 1 1/2 tsp maca powder
- 1 tbsp almond butter
- 1 tbsp MCT oil

Directions:

1. Add all ingredients into the blender and blend until smooth.
2. Serve and enjoy.

Nutritional Value (Amount per Serving):

Calories 248; Fat 26.5 g; Carbohydrates 6.5 g; Sugar 1.2 g; Protein 4.9 g; Cholesterol 0 mg

Blackberry Smoothie

Preparation Time: 5 minutes; Cooking Time: 5 minutes; Serve: 2

Ingredients:

- 1 cup unsweetened almond milk
- 1/2 cup ice
- 1/2 tsp vanilla
- 1 tsp erythritol
- 2 oz cream cheese, softened
- 4 tbsp heavy whipping cream
- 2 oz fresh blackberries

Directions:

1. Add all ingredients into the blender and blend until smooth.
2. Serve and enjoy.

Nutritional Value (Amount per Serving):

Calories 238; Fat 22.9 g; Carbohydrates 7.9 g; Sugar 4.1 g; Protein 3.7 g; Cholesterol 72 mg

Choco Sunflower Butter Smoothie

Preparation Time: 5 minutes; Cooking Time: 5 minutes; Serve: 1
Ingredients:
- 1/3 cup unsweetened coconut milk
- 1/4 cup ice
- 1/2 tsp vanilla
- 1 tsp unsweetened cocoa powder
- 2/3 cup water
- 2 tbsp sunflower seed butter

Directions:
1. Add all ingredients into the blender and blend until smooth.
2. Serve and enjoy.

Nutritional Value (Amount per Serving):
Calories 379; Fat 34.6 g; Carbohydrates 13 g; Sugar 3 g; Protein 8.5 g; Cholesterol 0 mg

Cheese Blueberry Smoothie

Preparation Time: 5 minutes; Cooking Time: 5 minutes; Serve: 1
Ingredients:
- 1 cup unsweetened almond milk
- 1/2 cup ice
- 1/4 tsp vanilla
- 5 drops liquid stevia
- 1 scoop vanilla protein powder
- 1/3 cup blueberries
- 2 oz cream cheese

Directions:
1. Add all ingredients into the blender and blend until smooth.
2. Serve and enjoy.

Nutritional Value (Amount per Serving):
Calories 380; Fat 23.5 g; Carbohydrates 11.1 g; Sugar 5.3 g; Protein 32.7 g; Cholesterol 64 mg

Delicious Cinnamon Smoothie

Preparation Time: 5 minutes; Cooking Time: 5 minutes; Serve: 1
Ingredients:
- 1/4 cup vanilla protein powder
- 1 tbsp ground chia seeds
- 1/2 tsp cinnamon
- 1 tbsp coconut oil
- 1/2 cup water
- 1/4 cup ice
- 1/2 cup unsweetened coconut milk

Directions:
1. Add all ingredients into the blender and blend until smooth.
2. Serve and enjoy.

Nutritional Value (Amount per Serving):
Calories 439; Fat 43 g; Carbohydrates 12.8 g; Sugar 9 g; Protein 6.8 g; Cholesterol 6 mg

Tasty Berry Smoothie

Preparation Time: 5 minutes; Cooking Time: 5 minutes; Serve: 4

Ingredients:
- 1/2 cup blackberries
- 2/3 cup strawberries
- 2/3 cup raspberries
- 1 1/2 cups unsweetened almond milk
- 1/2 cup unsweetened coconut milk
- 1 tbsp heavy cream

Directions:
1. Add all ingredients into the blender and blend until smooth.
2. Serve and enjoy.

Nutritional Value (Amount per Serving):
Calories 123; Fat 10.1 g; Carbohydrates 8.5 g; Sugar 4 g; Protein 1.8 g; Cholesterol 5 mg

Coconut Avocado Smoothie

Preparation Time: 5 minutes; Cooking Time: 5 minutes; Serve: 1
Ingredients:
- 1 cup unsweetened coconut milk
- 1 tsp chia seeds
- 1 tsp lime juice
- 5 spinach leaves
- 1/2 avocado
- 1 tsp ginger

Directions:
1. Add all ingredients into the blender and blend until smooth.
2. Serve and enjoy.

Nutritional Value (Amount per Serving):
Calories 104; Fat 7.6 g; Carbohydrates 7.1 g; Sugar 0.3 g; Protein 2.6 g; Cholesterol 0 mg

Healthy Green Smoothie

Preparation Time: 5 minutes; Cooking Time: 5 minutes; Serve: 2
Ingredients:
- 1 cup avocado
- 1/2 lemon, peeled
- 1 cucumber, peeled
- 1 tsp ginger, peeled
- 1/2 cup cilantro
- 1 cup baby spinach
- 1 cup of water

Directions:
1. Add all ingredients into the blender and blend until smooth.
2. Serve and enjoy.

Nutritional Value (Amount per Serving):
Calories 179; Fat 14.5 g; Carbohydrates 13.1 g; Sugar 3 g; Protein 3 g; Cholesterol 0 mg

Cinnamon Coconut Smoothie

Preparation Time: 5 minutes; Cooking Time: 5 minutes; Serve: 1
Ingredients:
- 1/2 tsp cinnamon
- 1 scoop vanilla protein powder
- 1 tbsp shredded coconut
- 3/4 cup unsweetened almond milk
- 1/4 cup unsweetened coconut milk

Directions:
1. Add all ingredients into the blender and blend until smooth.
2. Serve and enjoy.

Nutritional Value (Amount per Serving):
- Calories 300; Fat 18.7 g; Carbohydrates 7 g; Sugar 2.6 g; Protein 29.3 g; Cholesterol 2 mg

Cranberry Coconut Smoothie

Preparation Time: 5 minutes; Cooking Time: 5 minutes; Serve: 1
Ingredients:
- 1 cup unsweetened coconut milk
- 1 tbsp MCT oil
- 1 tsp erythritol
- 1/2 cup fresh cranberries

Directions:
1. Add all ingredients into the blender and blend until smooth.
2. Serve and enjoy.

Nutritional Value (Amount per Serving):
- Calories 175; Fat 18 g; Carbohydrates 12 g; Sugar 7 g; Protein 0 g; Cholesterol 0 mg

Creamy Strawberry Avocado Smoothie

Preparation Time: 5 minutes; Cooking Time: 5 minutes; Serve: 2
Ingredients:
- 2/3 cup strawberries
- 1/2 cup ice
- 5 drops liquid stevia
- 1 tbsp lime juice
- 1 1/2 cups unsweetened coconut milk
- 1 avocado

Directions:
1. Add all ingredients into the blender and blend until smooth.
2. Serve and enjoy.

Nutritional Value (Amount per Serving):
Calories 243; Fat 21.7 g; Carbohydrates 13.3 g; Sugar 2.9 g; Protein 2.2 g; Cholesterol 0 mg

Choco Macadamia Smoothie

Preparation Time: 5 minutes; Cooking Time: 5 minutes; Serve: 1
Ingredients:
- 1 tbsp unsweetened cocoa powder
- 2 tbsp chia seed
- 1 tbsp coconut butter
- 1 tsp MCT oil
- 2 tbsp macadamia nuts
- 1 cup unsweetened almond milk

Directions:
1. Add all ingredients into the blender and blend until smooth.
2. Serve and enjoy.

Nutritional Value (Amount per Serving):
Calories 368; Fat 35.2 g; Carbohydrates 13.7 g; Sugar 1.8 g; Protein 7.5 g; Cholesterol 0 mg

Apple Ginger Blueberry Smoothie

Preparation Time: 5 minutes; Cooking Time: 5 minutes; Serve: 2
Ingredients:

- 1/2 apple
- 1 tsp MCT oil
- 1/2 tbsp collagen powder
- 1 tsp ginger
- 1 cup unsweetened coconut milk
- 1/2 cup coconut yogurt
- 15 blueberries

Directions:

1. Add all ingredients into the blender and blend until smooth.
2. Serve and enjoy.

Nutritional Value (Amount per Serving):
Calories 169; Fat 15 g; Carbohydrates 5 g; Sugar 2 g; Protein 4 g; Cholesterol 5 mg

Strawberry Protein Smoothie

Preparation Time: 5 minutes; Cooking Time: 5 minutes; Serve: 1
Ingredients:

- 1/3 cup strawberries
- 1/3 cup water
- 1/2 cup unsweetened almond milk
- 1/2 scoop vanilla protein powder
- 1 tbsp almond butter

Directions:

1. Add all ingredients into the blender and blend until smooth.
2. Serve and enjoy.

Nutritional Value (Amount per Serving):
Calories 189; Fat 10.9 g; Carbohydrates 7.9 g; Sugar 3.2 g; Protein 17.7 g; Cholesterol 1 mg

Coconut Breakfast Smoothie

Preparation Time: 5 minutes; Cooking Time: 5 minutes; Serve: 1
Ingredients:

- 2 tbsp coconut butter
- 1/2 cup unsweetened coconut milk
- 8 drops liquid stevia
- 1/4 cup whey protein powder
- 1 tbsp coconut oil
- 1 tsp vanilla
- 1/4 cup water
- 1/2 cup ice

Directions:

1. Add all ingredients into the blender and blend until smooth.
2. Serve and enjoy.

Nutritional Value (Amount per Serving):
Calories 560; Fat 45 g; Carbohydrates 12 g; Sugar 6 g; Protein 27 g; Cholesterol 63 mg

Kiwi Cucumber Smoothie

Preparation Time: 5 minutes; Cooking Time: 5 minutes; Serve: 6

Ingredients:

- 4 cups water
- 1 tbsp erythritol
- 2 tbsp fresh parsley
- 1/3 cup pineapple, chopped
- 1 cup romaine lettuce
- 1/2 avocado
- 1/2 cup kiwi
- 1 cup cucumber, sliced
- 1 tbsp fresh ginger

Directions:

1. Add all ingredients into the blender and blend until smooth.
2. Serve and enjoy.

Nutritional Value (Amount per Serving):

Calories 52; Fat 2 g; Carbohydrates 5 g; Sugar 2 g; Protein 0.9 g; Cholesterol 0 mg

Coconut Chocolate Smoothie

Preparation Time: 5 minutes; Cooking Time: 5 minutes; Serve: 1

Ingredients:

- 1/4 cup heavy cream
- 1/4 cup unsweetened coconut milk
- 1/2 cup unsweetened almond milk
- 1 tsp liquid stevia
- 1/2 tbsp unsweetened cocoa powder

Directions:

1. Add all ingredients into the blender and blend until smooth.
2. Serve and enjoy.

Nutritional Value (Amount per Serving):

Calories 201; Fat 18 g; Carbohydrates 6 g; Sugar 2.5 g; Protein 3 g; Cholesterol 11 mg

Creamy Protein Green Smoothie

Preparation Time: 5 minutes; Cooking Time: 5 minutes; Serve: 1

Ingredients:

- 1/2 tsp liquid stevia
- 1/4 cup heavy cream
- 1/2 cup coconut milk
- 1/2 scoop protein powder
- 1/4 avocado, chopped
- 1/2 cucumber, chopped
- ½ cup ice cubes

Directions:

1. Add all ingredients into the blender and blend until smooth.
2. Serve and enjoy.

Nutritional Value (Amount per Serving):

Calories 270; Fat 20 g; Carbohydrates 10 g; Sugar 2 g; Protein 12 g; Cholesterol 42 mg

Chia Strawberry Spinach Smoothie

Preparation Time: 5 minutes; Cooking Time: 5 minutes; Serve: 1

Ingredients:

- 1 tsp chia seeds
- 1/2 cup spinach

- 3 fresh strawberries
- 1 tbsp erythritol
- 2 tbsp unsweetened almond butter

Directions:

1. Add all ingredients into the blender and blend until smooth.
2. Serve and enjoy.

Nutritional Value (Amount per Serving):

Calories 242; Fat 18 g; Carbohydrates 10 g; Sugar 2.5 g; Protein 9 g; Cholesterol 0 mg

Mocha Cocoa Smoothie

Preparation Time: 5 minutes; Cooking Time: 5 minutes; Serve: 3

Ingredients:

- 1 avocado
- 1 1/2 cups unsweetened almond milk
- 1/2 cup unsweetened coconut milk
- 3 tbsp unsweetened cocoa powder
- 2 tsp instant coffee
- 3 tbsp erythritol
- 1 tsp vanilla

Directions:

1. Add all ingredients into the blender and blend until smooth.
2. Serve and enjoy.

Nutritional Value (Amount per Serving):

Calories 200; Fat 16 g; Carbohydrates 12 g; Sugar 0.5 g; Protein 3 g; Cholesterol 0 mg

Breakfast Smoothie Bowl

Preparation Time: 5 minutes; Cooking Time: 5 minutes; Serve: 1

Ingredients:

- 1/4 cup erythritol
- 3/4 cup unsweetened coconut milk
- 1/2 avocado
- 2 tbsp fresh lemon juice
- 1/4 cup ice
- 1 cup spinach
- 1/2 scoop MCT oil powder
- 1/2 scoop perfect Keto collagen

Directions:

1. Add all ingredients into the blender and blend until smooth.
2. Pour smoothie in a bowl and top with chia seeds.
3. Serve and enjoy.

Nutritional Value (Amount per Serving):

Calories 320; Fat 25 g; Carbohydrates 14 g; Sugar 2.1 g; Protein 10 g; Cholesterol 0 mg

Easy Lemon Blueberry Smoothie

Preparation Time: 5 minutes; Cooking Time: 5 minutes; Serve: 2

Ingredients:

- 1/2 cup fresh blueberries
- 1 tbsp fresh lemon juice
- 14 oz unsweetened coconut milk
- 1/2 tsp vanilla

Directions:

1. Add all ingredients into the blender and blend until smooth.
2. Serve and enjoy.

Nutritional Value (Amount per Serving):

Calories 55; Fat 3.5 g; Carbohydrates 6 g; Sugar 4 g; Protein 0.7 g; Cholesterol 0 mg

Anti-inflammatory Spinach Ginger Smoothie

Preparation Time: 5 minutes; Cooking Time: 5 minutes; Serve: 2

Ingredients:

- 1 oz spinach
- 2 tbsp lime juice
- 2/3 cup water
- 1/3 cup unsweetened coconut milk
- 2 tsp fresh ginger, grated

Directions:

1. Add all ingredients into the blender and blend until smooth.
2. Serve and enjoy.

Nutritional Value (Amount per Serving):

Calories 102; Fat 10 g; Carbohydrates 5.2 g; Sugar 2 g; Protein 1.5 g; Cholesterol 0 mg

Strawberry Avocado Almond Smoothie

Preparation Time: 5 minutes; Cooking Time: 5 minutes; Serve: 5

Ingredients:

- 1 lb strawberries
- 1/4 cup erythritol
- 1 avocado
- 1 1/2 cups unsweetened almond milk

Directions:

1. Add all ingredients into the blender and blend until smooth.
2. Serve and enjoy.

Nutritional Value (Amount per Serving):

Calories 105; Fat 7 g; Carbohydrates 11 g; Sugar 3.5 g; Protein 1 g; Cholesterol 0 mg

Turmeric Avocado Smoothie

Preparation Time: 5 minutes; Cooking Time: 5 minutes; Serve: 2

Ingredients:

- 1/2 avocado
- 1/2 tsp turmeric
- 1 tsp ginger, grated
- 1/4 cup unsweetened almond milk
- 3/4 cup unsweetened coconut milk
- 1 cup ice cube, crushed
- 1 tsp fresh lemon juice

Directions:

1. Add all ingredients to the blender and blend until smooth.
2. Serve and enjoy.

Nutritional Value (Amount per Serving):

- Calories 222; Fat 22 g; Carbohydrates 7 g; Sugar 1.5 g; Protein 2 g; Cholesterol 0 mg

Coconut Chia Blueberry Smoothie

Preparation Time: 5 minutes; Cooking Time: 5 minutes; Serve: 4
Ingredients:
- 2 tbsp chia seed
- 2 tbsp coconut oil
- 1 cup unsweetened almond milk
- 1/2 cup coconut cream
- 1 cup unsweetened coconut milk
- 1 cup blueberries
- 2 tbsp swerve

Directions:
1. Add all ingredients to the blender and blend until smooth.
2. Serve and enjoy.

Nutritional Value (Amount per Serving):
Calories 250; Fat 20 g; Carbohydrates 10 g; Sugar 4.5 g; Protein 6 g; Cholesterol 18 mg

Pumpkin Chia Smoothie

Preparation Time: 5 minutes; Cooking Time: 5 minutes; Serve: 1
Ingredients:
- 1 cup unsweetened almond milk
- 1/4 cup pumpkin puree
- 1 tbsp chia seeds
- 1 tsp vanilla
- 1/2 scoop whey protein powder
- 1 tsp pumpkin pie spice

Directions:
1. Add all ingredients to the blender and blend until smooth.
2. Serve and enjoy.

Nutritional Value (Amount per Serving):
Calories 175; Fat 7 g; Carbohydrates 12 g; Sugar 3 g; Protein 15 g; Cholesterol 32 mg

Blackcurrant Chia Smoothie

Preparation Time: 5 minutes; Cooking Time: 5 minutes; Serve: 2
Ingredients:
- 2 tbsp chia seeds
- 1/2 cup water
- 1/4 cup unsweetened coconut milk
- 2 strawberries
- 1/2 cup black currants
- 5 drops liquid stevia
- 1/2 tsp vanilla

Directions:
1. Add all ingredients to the blender and blend until smooth.
2. Serve and enjoy.

Nutritional Value (Amount per Serving):
Calories 100; Fat 4.5 g; Carbohydrates 13 g; Sugar 7 g; Protein 1.8 g; Cholesterol 0 mg

Celery Cucumber Smoothie

Preparation Time: 5 minutes; Cooking Time: 5 minutes; Serve: 2

Ingredients:

- 1/2 lime juice
- 1 small cucumber
- 4 celery stalks
- 1/2 cup ice cubes
- 1/2 cup water

Directions:

1. Add all ingredients to the blender and blend until smooth.
2. Serve and enjoy.

Nutritional Value (Amount per Serving):

Calories 30; Fat 0.2 g; Carbohydrates 7 g; Sugar 3 g; Protein 1 g; Cholesterol 0 mg

Cilantro Mint Avocado Smoothie

Preparation Time: 5 minutes; Cooking Time: 5 minutes; Serve: 2
Ingredients:

- 3 sprigs cilantro
- 5 fresh mint leaves
- 10 drops liquid stevia
- 1/2 cup unsweetened almond milk
- 3/4 cup unsweetened coconut milk
- 1/2 avocado
- 1 1/2 cups ice
- 1/4 tsp vanilla
- 1 lime juice

Directions:

1. Add all ingredients to the blender and blend until smooth.
2. Serve and enjoy.

Nutritional Value (Amount per Serving):

Calories 180; Fat 14 g; Carbohydrates 10 g; Sugar 2 g; Protein 3 g; Cholesterol 0 mg

Cherry Coconut Smoothie

Preparation Time: 5 minutes; Cooking Time: 5 minutes; Serve: 3
Ingredients:

- 1 can unsweetened coconut milk
- 1/4 tsp turmeric
- 1/2 avocado
- 1 cup ice cubes
- 1 cup frozen cherries
- 1/4 cup cocoa powder

Directions:

1. Add all ingredients to the blender and blend until smooth.
2. Serve and enjoy.

Nutritional Value (Amount per Serving):

Calories 125; Fat 9 g; Carbohydrates 12 g; Sugar 5 g; Protein 2 g; Cholesterol 0 mg

Green Tea Cucumber Smoothie

Preparation Time: 5 minutes; Cooking Time: 5 minutes; Serve: 2
Ingredients:

- 1/2 cup ice
- 1/2 tsp liquid stevia
- 1 tsp fresh lemon juice
- 2 oz avocado

- 1 cucumber, sliced
- 1 1/2 tsp matcha green tea powder
- 8 oz water

Directions:
1. Add all ingredients to the blender and blend until smooth.
2. Serve and enjoy.

Nutritional Value (Amount per Serving):
Calories 81; Fat 5.7 g; Carbohydrates 8 g; Sugar 2.7 g; Protein 1.5 g; Cholesterol 0 mg

Cucumber Celery Smoothie

Preparation Time: 5 minutes; Cooking Time: 5 minutes; Serve: 1
Ingredients:
- 1 tsp matcha powder
- 1 tbsp MCT oil
- 1/2 avocado
- 1 celery stalk
- 1 small cucumber
- 1/2 cup unsweetened almond milk

Directions:
1. Add all ingredients into the blender and blend until smooth.
2. Serve and enjoy.

Nutritional Value (Amount per Serving):
Calories 198; Fat 18 g; Carbohydrates 13 g; Sugar 5 g; Protein 3 g; Cholesterol 0 mg

Keto Golden Smoothie

Preparation Time: 5 minutes; Cooking Time: 5 minutes; Serve: 1
Ingredients:
- 1/4 tsp cinnamon
- 1/2 tsp turmeric
- 1 tbsp MCT oil
- 1/2 tsp vanilla
- 2 tbsp water
- 1 cup unsweetened coconut milk
- Pinch of salt

Directions:
1. Add all ingredients into the blender and blend until smooth.
2. Serve and enjoy.

Nutritional Value (Amount per Serving):
Calories 156; Fat 18 g; Carbohydrates 3 g; Sugar 0.3 g; Protein 0.1 g; Cholesterol 0 mg

Simple Egg Muffins

Preparation Time: 10 minutes; Cooking Time: 25 minutes; Serve: 6
Ingredients:
- 6 eggs
- 2 green onion, sliced
- 1/2 cup cheddar cheese, shredded
- 1 tomato, chopped
- 1/2 cup fresh spinach, chopped
- 1/4 cup unsweetened almond milk
- Pepper
- Salt

Directions:

1. Preheat the oven to 350 F.
2. In a mixing bowl, whisk eggs with milk, pepper, and salt.
3. Stir in green onions, cheese, tomatoes, and spinach.
4. Pour egg mixture into the greased muffin tray and bake for 20-25 minutes.
5. Serve and enjoy.

Nutritional Value (Amount per Serving):

Calories 107; Fat 7.7 g; Carbohydrates 1.4 g; Sugar 0.8 g; Protein 8.2 g; Cholesterol 174 mg

Cauliflower Breakfast Casserole

Preparation Time: 10 minutes; Cooking Time: 45 minutes; Serve: 6
Ingredients:

- 10 eggs
- 10 oz bacon, cooked and crumbled
- 1/2 cup heavy cream
- 1 tsp paprika
- 8 oz cheddar cheese, shredded
- 4 cups cauliflower rice
- 1/4 tsp pepper
- 1 tsp salt

Directions:
1. Preheat the oven to 350 F.
2. Spread cauliflower rice in a greased casserole dish.
3. Top with half cheddar cheese.
4. In a bowl, whisk eggs with heavy cream, paprika, pepper, and salt.
5. Pour egg mixture over cauliflower mixture.
6. Top with bacon and remaining cheese and bake for 45 minutes.
7. Serve and enjoy.

Nutritional Value (Amount per Serving):

Calories 565; Fat 43.4 g; Carbohydrates 5 g; Sugar 2 g; Protein 37 g; Cholesterol 378 mg

Almond Porridge

Preparation Time: 10 minutes; Cooking Time: 5 minutes; Serve: 2
Ingredients:

- 3/4 cup coconut cream
- 1/8 tsp cloves
- 1 tsp liquid stevia
- 1/2 cup ground almonds
- 1/8 tsp cardamom
- 1/8 tsp nutmeg
- 1/2 tsp ground cinnamon

Directions:
1. Add coconut cream in saucepan and heat over medium heat until it forms a liquid.
2. Add stevia and ground almonds and stir well for 5 minutes.
3. Add cinnamon, cloves, nutmeg, and cardamom. Stir well.
4. Serve and enjoy.

Nutritional Value (Amount per Serving):

Calories 350; Fat 33 g; Carbohydrates 10 g; Sugar 4 g; Protein 7 g; Cholesterol 0 mg

Spinach Quiche

Preparation Time: 10 minutes; Cooking Time: 4 hours; Serve: 4

Ingredients:

- 4 eggs
- 4 oz feta cheese
- 2 cups unsweetened almond milk
- 10 oz frozen spinach, chopped and thawed
- 1/4 tsp salt

Directions:

1. In a large bowl, whisk together all ingredients.
2. Spray slow cooker with cooking spray.
3. Pour egg mixture into the slow cooker.
4. Cover and cook on low for 4 hours.
5. Serve and enjoy.

Nutritional Value (Amount per Serving):

Calories 431; Fat 39 g; Carbohydrates 10 g; Sugar 2 g; Protein 14 g; Cholesterol 189 mg

Simple Egg Tomato Scramble

Preparation Time: 10 minutes; Cooking Time: 10 minutes; Serve: 2

Ingredients:

- 6 eggs, lightly beaten
- 3 tbsp fresh parsley, chopped
- 14 oz tomatoes, diced
- 1 tbsp olive oil
- Pepper
- Salt

Directions:

1. Heat oil in a pan over medium heat.
2. Add tomatoes and cook for 4 minutes.
3. Add beaten eggs and stir until eggs are cooked.
4. Add parsley and stir well to mix. Season with pepper and salt.
5. Serve and enjoy.

Nutritional Value (Amount per Serving):

Calories 285; Fat 20 g; Carbohydrates 9 g; Sugar 6 g; Protein 18 g; Cholesterol 491 mg

Kale Muffins

Preparation Time: 10 minutes; Cooking Time: 30 minutes; Serve: 8

Ingredients:

- 1 cup kale, chopped
- 1/4 cup chives, chopped
- 6 large eggs
- 1/2 cup unsweetened coconut milk
- Pepper
- Salt

Directions:

1. Preheat the oven to 350 F.
2. Add all ingredients into the bowl and whisk well.
3. Pour mixture into the greased muffin tray and bake for 30 minutes.
4. Serve and enjoy.

Nutritional Value (Amount per Serving):

Calories 90; Fat 7 g; Carbohydrates 2 g; Sugar 1 g; Protein 5 g; Cholesterol 140 mg

Cauliflower Frittata

Preparation Time: 10 minutes; Cooking Time: 5 minutes; Serve: 1

Ingredients:

- 1 egg
- 1 tbsp olive oil
- 1/4 cup cauliflower rice
- 1/8 tsp black pepper
- 1/4 tsp turmeric
- 1/2 tbsp onion, diced
- Salt

Directions:

1. In a bowl, whisk all ingredients except oil.
2. Heat oil in a pan over medium heat.
3. Pour egg mixture in the hot oil pan and cook for 3-4 minutes or until lightly golden brown.
4. Serve and enjoy.

Nutritional Value (Amount per Serving):

Calories 192; Fat 18 g; Carbohydrates 3 g; Sugar 2 g; Protein 6.3 g; Cholesterol 164 mg

Cinnamon Flaxseed Muffin

Preparation Time: 5 minutes; Cooking Time: 5 minutes; Serve: 1

Ingredients:

- 1 egg, lightly beaten
- 2 tsp erythritol
- 1/4 cup ground flaxseed
- 1 tsp butter, melted
- 1/2 tsp baking powder
- 1/2 tsp ground cinnamon

Directions:

1. Spray microwave-safe mug with cooking spray.
2. Add all ingredients to the mug and mix well.
3. Place mug in microwave and microwave for 45 seconds.
4. Serve and enjoy.

Nutritional Value (Amount per Serving):

Calories 250; Fat 17 g; Carbohydrates 10 g; Sugar 1 g; Protein 10.9 g; Cholesterol 174 mg

Asparagus Quiche

Preparation Time: 10 minutes; Cooking Time: 45 minutes; Serve: 8

Ingredients:

- 2 lbs asparagus, trimmed and cut the ends
- 10 eggs
- 1 tsp salt
- 2 tbsp olive oil
- Pepper
- Salt

Directions:

1. Preheat the oven to 425 F.
2. Place asparagus in greased baking tray and roast in preheated oven for 15 minutes.
3. Meanwhile, in a bowl, whisk together eggs, oil, pepper, and salt until smooth.
4. Place roasted asparagus in a quiche pan.
5. Pour egg mixture over the asparagus and bake for 30 minutes.
6. Serve and enjoy.

Nutritional Value (Amount per Serving):

Calories 141; Fat 10.5 g; Carbohydrates 5 g; Sugar 2.6 g; Protein 9.4 g; Cholesterol 208 mg

Pecan Porridge

Preparation Time: 10 minutes; Cooking Time: 5 minutes; Serve: 2

Ingredients:

- 1/4 cup pecans, chopped
- 3/4 cup unsweetened almond milk
- 1/4 cup unsweetened coconut milk
- 2 tbsp chia seeds
- 1/2 tsp cinnamon
- 1/4 cup unsweetened coconut
- 2 tbsp hemp seeds
- 1 tbsp coconut oil
- 1/4 cup almond butter

Directions:

1. Add oil, almond butter, almond milk, and coconut milk in a saucepan and simmer over medium heat.
2. Once porridge mixture is hot then remove from heat.
3. Add toasted coconut, pecans, hemp seeds, chia seeds, and cinnamon and stir well.
4. Serve and enjoy.

Nutritional Value (Amount per Serving):

Calories 485; Fat 47.9 g; Carbohydrates 14 g; Sugar 3.9 g; Protein 11.2 g; Cholesterol 0 mg

Chia Vanilla Pudding

Preparation Time: 5 minutes; Cooking Time: 5 minutes; Serve: 2

Ingredients:

- 2 cups unsweetened coconut milk
- 5 tbsp chia seeds
- 1/2 tsp vanilla
- Blueberries

Directions:

1. Add vanilla, coconut milk, and chia seeds in a glass jar.
2. Seal jar tightly and shake well and place in the fridge for overnight.
3. Top with blueberries and serve.

Nutritional Value (Amount per Serving):

Calories 220; Fat 12 g; Carbohydrates 15 g; Sugar 2 g; Protein 10 g; Cholesterol 0 mg

Squash Casserole

Preparation Time: 10 minutes; Cooking Time: 25 minutes; Serve: 6

Ingredients:

- 2 cups spaghetti squash, cooked
- 12 eggs, lightly beaten
- 1/4 cup butter, melted
- 1 bell pepper, diced
- 1 cup cheddar cheese, shredded
- 1 cup heavy cream
- Pepper
- Salt

Directions:

1. Preheat the oven to 350 F.

2. Spray a baking dish with cooking spray and set aside.
3. In a large bowl, add all ingredients and mix until well combined.
4. Pour mixture into the prepared baking dish.
5. Bake for 25 minutes or until done.
6. Serve and enjoy.

Nutritional Value (Amount per Serving):
Calories 430; Fat 37 g; Carbohydrates 5 g; Sugar 1.3 g; Protein 18 g; Cholesterol 395 mg

Almond Pancakes

Preparation Time: 10 minutes; Cooking Time: 10 minutes; Serve: 1
Ingredients:
- 1 egg
- 2 tbsp water
- 1 scoop vanilla protein powder
- 1 tbsp almond flour

Directions:
1. Add all ingredients into the bowl and mix well.
2. Heat pan over medium heat.
3. Once the pan is hot pour tablespoons of batter into pan and cook pancakes for 2 minutes on each side.
4. Serve and enjoy.

Nutritional Value (Amount per Serving):
Calories 252; Fat 10.8 g; Carbohydrates 12 g; Sugar 2.6 g; Protein 29.8 g; Cholesterol 224 mg

Creamy Egg Scrambled

Preparation Time: 5 minutes; Cooking Time: 5 minutes; Serve: 1
Ingredients:
- 2 eggs
- 1 tbsp heavy whipping cream
- 1 tbsp chives, chopped
- 1 oz cheddar cheese, shredded
- 1 oz butter
- 1/4 tsp pepper
- 1/2 tsp salt

Directions:
1. Melt butter in a pan over medium heat.
2. Whisk eggs together with heavy whipping cream, pepper, and salt.
3. Pour the egg mixture into the pan and stir for 3-4 minutes.
4. Add cheddar cheese and stir until cheese is melted.
5. Garnish with chopped chives and serve.

Nutritional Value (Amount per Serving):
Calories 495; Fat 45 g; Carbohydrates 2 g; Sugar 1 g; Protein 17 g; Cholesterol 439 mg

Cauliflower Bread

Preparation Time: 10 minutes; Cooking Time: 45 minutes; Serve: 8
Ingredients:
- 4 large eggs
- 1 1/2 tbsp garlic powder
- 1 tbsp psyllium husk powder
- 5 tbsp coconut flour

- 4 cups cauliflower rice
- 1/2 tsp baking powder
- 1 tbsp onion powder
- 1 tsp salt

Directions:

1. Preheat the oven to 400 F.
2. Add all ingredients into the large bowl and mix until well combined.
3. Pour batter into the greased pan and bake for 45 minutes.
4. Slice and serve.

Nutritional Value (Amount per Serving):

Calories 117; Fat 4.7 g; Carbohydrates 10 g; Sugar 3.9 g; Protein 7 g; Cholesterol 93 mg

Chapter 3: Poultry Recipes

Baked Chicken Fajitas

Preparation Time: 10 minutes; Cooking Time: 18 minutes; Serve: 6

Ingredients:

- 1 1/2 lbs chicken tenders
- 2 tbsp fajita seasoning
- 2 tbsp olive oil
- 1 onion, sliced
- 2 bell pepper, sliced
- 1 lime juice
- 1 tsp kosher salt

Directions:

1. Preheat the oven to 400 F.
2. Add all ingredients in a large mixing bowl and toss well.
3. Transfer bowl mixture on a baking tray and bake in preheated oven for 15-18 minutes.
4. Serve and enjoy.

Nutritional Value (Amount per Serving):

Calories 286; Fat 13 g; Carbohydrates 6.8 g; Sugar 2.8 g; Protein 33 g; Cholesterol 101 mg

Baked Chicken Wings

Preparation Time: 10 minutes; Cooking Time: 50 minutes; Serve: 4

Ingredients:

- 2 lbs chicken wings
- 1 tbsp lemon pepper seasoning
- 2 tbsp butter, melted
- 4 tbsp olive oil

Directions:

1. Preheat the oven to 400 F.
2. Toss chicken wings with olive oil.
3. Arrange chicken wings on a baking tray and bake for 50 minutes.
4. In a small bowl, mix together lemon pepper seasoning and butter.
5. Remove wings from oven and brush with butter and seasoning mixture.
6. Serve and enjoy.

Nutritional Value (Amount per Serving):

Calories 606; Fat 36 g; Carbohydrates 1 g; Sugar 0 g; Protein 65 g; Cholesterol 217 mg

Chicken with Spinach Broccoli

Preparation Time: 10 minutes; Cooking Time: 10 minutes; Serve: 4

Ingredients:

- 1 lb chicken breasts, cut into pieces
- 4 oz cream cheese
- 1/2 cup parmesan cheese, shredded
- 2 cups baby spinach
- 2 cup broccoli florets
- 1 tomato, chopped
- 2 garlic cloves, minced
- 1 tsp Italian seasoning
- 2 tbsp olive oil
- Pepper
- Salt

Directions:

1. Heat oil in a saucepan over medium-high heat.
2. Add chicken, season with pepper, Italian seasoning, and salt and sauté for 5 minutes or until chicken cooked through.
3. Add garlic and sauté for a minute.
4. Add cream cheese, parmesan cheese, spinach, broccoli, and tomato and cook for 3-4 minutes more.
5. Serve and enjoy.

Nutritional Value (Amount per Serving):

Calories 444; Fat 28 g; Carbohydrates 5.9 g; Sugar 1.4 g; Protein 40 g; Cholesterol 140 mg

Delicious Bacon Chicken

Preparation Time: 10 minutes; Cooking Time: 40 minutes; Serve: 6

Ingredients:

- 2 1/2 lbs chicken breasts, cut in half
- 4 oz cheddar cheese, shredded
- 1/2 lb bacon, cut into strips
- 1/2 tsp paprika
- 1/2 tsp onion powder
- 1/2 tsp garlic powder
- Pepper
- Salt

Directions:

1. Preheat the oven to 400 F.
2. In a small bowl, mix together paprika, onion powder, garlic powder, pepper, and salt.
3. Rub chicken with spice mixture.
4. Place chicken on a baking tray and top each with bacon piece.
5. Bake for 30 minutes. Remove from oven and sprinkle with cheese and bake for 10 minutes more.
6. Serve and enjoy.

Nutritional Value (Amount per Serving):

Calories 642; Fat 36 g; Carbohydrates 1.2 g; Sugar 0.3 g; Protein 73 g; Cholesterol 230 mg

Mexican Chicken

Preparation Time: 10 minutes; Cooking Time: 25 minutes; Serve: 6

Ingredients:

- 2 cups chicken, cooked and shredded
- 1/2 cup Monterey jack cheese
- 1 1/2 cup cheddar cheese
- 3/4 cup chicken broth
- 2 tsp taco seasoning
- 12 oz cauliflower rice
- 14 oz Rotel tomatoes
- 2 garlic cloves, minced
- 1/3 cup green pepper, diced
- 1 onion, diced
- 1 tbsp butter

Directions:

1. Melt butter in a pan over medium heat.
2. Add garlic, pepper, and onion and sauté until softened.
3. Steam cauliflower rice according to packet instructions.
4. Add seasoning, broth, cauliflower rice, and Rotel to the pan.
5. Stir well and cook for 10 minutes.
6. Add chicken and cook for 5 minutes.
7. Top with cheese and cook until cheese is melted.

8. Serve and enjoy.

Nutritional Value (Amount per Serving):
Calories 270; Fat 15 g; Carbohydrates 8.1 g; Sugar 2.5 g; Protein 24 g; Cholesterol 79 mg

Chicken Casserole

Preparation Time: 10 minutes; Cooking Time: 40 minutes; Serve: 8

Ingredients:
- 2 lbs chicken, cooked and shredded
- 5 oz cream cheese, softened
- 4 oz butter, melted
- 5 oz ham, cut into small pieces
- 5 oz Swiss cheese
- 1 oz fresh lemon juice
- 3/4 tbsp Dijon mustard
- ½ tsp salt

Directions:
1. Preheat the oven to 350 F.
2. Add chicken in a baking dish then top with ham pieces.
3. Add butter, lemon juice, mustard, cream cheese, and salt into the blender and blend until smooth.
4. Pour butter mixture over chicken and ham mixture.
5. Arrange cheese slices on top and bake for 40 minutes.
6. Serve and enjoy.

Nutritional Value (Amount per Serving):
Calories 450; Fat 30 g; Carbohydrates 2 g; Sugar 1 g; Protein 40 g; Cholesterol 171 mg

Stuffed Jalapenos

Preparation Time: 10 minutes; Cooking Time: 15 minutes; Serve: 12

Ingredients:
- 1/2 cup chicken, cooked and shredded
- 6 jalapenos, halved
- 3 tbsp green onion, sliced
- 1/4 cup cheddar cheese, shredded
- 1/2 tsp dried basil
- 1/4 tsp garlic powder
- 3 oz cream cheese
- 1/2 tsp dried oregano
- 1/4 tsp salt

Directions:
1. Preheat the oven to 390 F.
2. Mix all ingredients in a bowl except jalapenos.
3. Stuff chicken mixture into each jalapeno halved and place on a baking tray.
4. Bake for 25 minutes.
5. Serve and enjoy.

Nutritional Value (Amount per Serving):
Calories 106; Fat 9 g; Carbohydrates 2 g; Sugar 1 g; Protein 7 g; Cholesterol 35 mg

Asian Garlic Chicken

Preparation Time: 10 minutes; Cooking Time: 4 Hours; Serve: 6
Ingredients:

- 1 1/2 lbs chicken breasts, skinless and boneless
- 2 tbsp water
- 2 tbsp soy sauce
- 1/2 onion, chopped
- 1 1/2 tsp red pepper flakes
- 2 garlic cloves, minced
- 1/2 tsp ground ginger

Directions:

1. Place chicken into the crockpot.
2. Add remaining ingredients on top of chicken.
3. Cover and cook on high for 4 hours.
4. Shred the chicken using a fork and serve.

Nutritional Value (Amount per Serving):

Calories 250; Fat 9 g; Carbohydrates 10 g; Sugar 6 g; Protein 34 g; Cholesterol 100 mg

Creamy Chicken Mushrooms

Preparation Time: 10 minutes; Cooking Time: 30 minutes; Serve: 4

Ingredients:

- 2 lbs chicken breasts, halved
- 1/4 cup sun-dried tomatoes
- 7.5 oz mushrooms, sliced
- ½ cup mayonnaise
- 1 tsp salt

Directions:

1. Preheat the oven to 400 F.
2. Place chicken breasts into the greased baking dish and top with sun-dried tomatoes, mushrooms, mayonnaise, and salt. Mix well.
3. Bake in the oven for 30 minutes.
4. Serve and enjoy.

Nutritional Value (Amount per Serving):

Calories 561; Fat 27 g; Carbohydrates 10 g; Sugar 4 g; Protein 68 g; Cholesterol 210 mg

Cheese Bacon Chicken

Preparation Time: 10 minutes; Cooking Time: 6 Hours 4 minutes; Serve: 8

Ingredients:

- 6 chicken breasts, skinless and boneless
- 3/4 cup chicken broth
- 1 tsp garlic, minced
- 1/4 tsp thyme
- 1/2 tsp Rosemary
- 1/2 tsp poultry seasoning
- 3/4 cup cheddar cheese
- 2 oz cream cheese
- 2/3 cup heavy cream
- 2 bacon pieces, cooked and crumbled
- 3 tbsp butter
- Pepper
- Salt

Directions:

1. Add chicken, broth, garlic, thyme, rosemary, poultry seasoning, and butter into the crock pot.
2. Add bacon on top of chicken.
3. Cover and cook on low for 6 hours.
4. Add cream cheese and cream and stir well to combine.
5. Shred the chicken using fork into the crock pot.
6. Transfer chicken mixture into the greased casserole dish.

7. Top with cheddar cheese and broil for 4 minutes.

8. Serve and enjoy.

Nutritional Value (Amount per Serving):

Calories 301; Fat 25 g; Carbohydrates 4 g; Sugar 2.5 g; Protein 18 g; Cholesterol 150 mg

Yummy Chicken Tenders

Preparation Time: 10 minutes; Cooking Time: 15 minutes; Serve: 4

Ingredients:

- 1 ½ lbs chicken tenders
- 1 tsp chicken seasoning
- 1 tbsp olive oil
- 2 tbsp BBQ sauce, unsweetened

Directions:

1. Add all ingredients except oil in a zip-lock bag.
2. Seal bag shakes well and place in the fridge for 2-3 hours.
3. Heat oil in a pan over medium heat.
4. Cook chicken tenders in a pan until completely cooked.
5. Serve and enjoy.

Nutritional Value (Amount per Serving):

Calories 364; Fat 17 g; Carbohydrates 3 g; Sugar 3 g; Protein 50 g; Cholesterol 150 mg

Parmesan Chicken

Preparation Time: 10 minutes; Cooking Time: 35 minutes; Serve: 4

Ingredients:

- 1 lb chicken breasts, skinless and boneless
- ½ cup parmesan cheese, grated
- 1/2 cup mayonnaise
- 1 tsp garlic powder
- 1 tsp poultry seasoning
- ¼ tsp onion powder
- Pepper

Directions:

1. Preheat the oven to 375 F.
2. In a small bowl, mix together mayonnaise, garlic powder, onion powder, poultry seasoning, and pepper.
3. Place chicken in greased baking dish.
4. Spread mayonnaise mixture over chicken then sprinkles cheese.
5. Bake for 35 minutes.
6. Serve and enjoy.

Nutritional Value (Amount per Serving):

Calories 391; Fat 24 g; Carbohydrates 12 g; Sugar 2.5 g; Protein 34 g; Cholesterol 110 mg

Curried Coconut Chicken

Preparation Time: 10 minutes; Cooking Time: 6 Hours; Serve: 8

Ingredients:

- 6 chicken thighs
- 14.5 oz coconut milk
- ½ tbsp curry powder
- 3 garlic cloves, minced
- 1 onion, sliced
- 1 tbsp olive oil
- 2 green onion, sliced
- 3 tbsp fresh cilantro, chopped

- 3 cups chicken broth
- 1/4 tsp pepper
- 1 tsp salt

Directions:

1. Add oil into the crockpot.
2. Add all ingredients except green onion and cilantro into the crock pot and stir well.
3. Cover and cook on high for 6 hours.
4. Serve and enjoy.

Nutritional Value (Amount per Serving):

Calories 332; Fat 25 g; Carbohydrates 8 g; Sugar 3 g; Protein 24 g; Cholesterol 65 mg

Roasted Pepper Chicken

Preparation Time: 10 minutes; Cooking Time: 15 minutes; Serve: 4

Ingredients:

- 4 chicken breasts, skinless and boneless
- 1 1/2 tsp Italian seasoning
- 2/3 cup red peppers, roasted and chopped
- 3/4 cup heavy cream
- 3 garlic cloves, minced
- 4 tbsp olive oil
- 1/2 tsp salt

Directions:

1. Add pepper, garlic, oil, 1 teaspoon Italian seasoning, pepper, and salt into the blender and blend until smooth.
2. Season chicken with remaining seasoning and cook in a pan over medium heat for 7-8 minutes on each side.
3. Transfer chicken to a plate.
4. Pour red pepper mixture into the pan and cook for 2 minutes.
5. Add heavy cream and stir well.
6. Return chicken to the pan stir well to coat with sauce.
7. Serve and enjoy.

Nutritional Value (Amount per Serving):

Calories 520; Fat 37 g; Carbohydrates 5 g; Sugar 2 g; Protein 42 g; Cholesterol 10 mg

Asparagus Pesto Chicken

Preparation Time: 10 minutes; Cooking Time: 15 minutes; Serve: 3

Ingredients:

- 1 lb chicken thighs, skinless, boneless, and cut into pieces
- 3/4 lb asparagus, trimmed and cut in half
- 2 tbsp olive oil
- 1 3/4 cups grape tomatoes, halved
- 1/4 cup basil pesto
- Pepper
- Salt

Directions:

1. Heat oil in a pan over medium heat.
2. Add chicken to the pan and season with pepper and salt and cook for 5-8 minutes.
3. Add pesto and asparagus and cook for 2-3 minutes.
4. Remove pan from heat and add tomatoes and stir well.
5. Serve and enjoy.

Nutritional Value (Amount per Serving):

Calories 415; Fat 21 g; Carbohydrates 10 g; Sugar 5 g; Protein 48 g; Cholesterol 136 mg

Caper Chicken

Preparation Time: 15 minutes; Cooking Time: 15 minutes; Serve: 4
Ingredients:

- 8 chicken thighs, skinless and boneless
- 1 thyme sprig
- 2 garlic cloves, crushed
- 2 tbsp capers, drained
- ½ cup dry white wine
- 2 tbsp fresh parsley, chopped
- 1 tbsp butter
- 2 tbsp fresh lemon juice
- 1 cup chicken stock
- 3 tbsp olive oil
- ¼ tsp pepper
- ½ tsp kosher salt

Directions:

1. Season chicken with pepper and salt.
2. Heat 1 tbsp of oil in a pan over medium-high heat.
3. Add chicken and cook for 5 minutes.
4. Turn chicken to another side.
5. Add thyme, garlic, capers, and wine and cook for 2 minutes.
6. Add stock and remaining oil. Bring to boil. Turn heat to medium and cook for 8 minutes.
7. Remove from heat and add butter and lemon juice. Stir well.
8. Garnish with parsley and serve.

Nutritional Value (Amount per Serving):
Calories 700; Fat 36 g; Carbohydrates 3 g; Sugar 1 g; Protein 84 g; Cholesterol 68 mg

Simple Mushroom Chicken

Preparation Time: 10 minutes; Cooking Time: 15 minutes; Serve: 4
Ingredients:

- 4 chicken breasts, boneless and skinless
- 1 1/2 cups mushrooms, sliced
- 1 tbsp olive oil
- ½ cup chicken stock
- 2 garlic cloves, minced
- 1 onion, chopped
- ¼ tsp pepper
- ½ tsp salt

Directions:

1. Season chicken with pepper and salt.
2. Heat oil in a pan over medium heat.
3. Add chicken and cook for 5-6 minutes on each side.
4. Transfer chicken on a plate.
5. Add onion and mushrooms to the pan and sauté for 2-3 minutes.
6. Add garlic and sauté for a minute.
7. Add stock and bring to boil. Stir well and cook for 1-2 minutes.
8. Pour pan mixture over chicken and serve.

Nutritional Value (Amount per Serving):
Calories 330; Fat 15 g; Carbohydrates 5 g; Sugar 2 g; Protein 44 g; Cholesterol 75 mg

Flavorful Baked Fajitas

Preparation Time: 10 minutes; Cooking Time: 30 minutes; Serve: 4

Ingredients:

- 2 chicken breasts, cut into chunks
- 2 carrots, cut into strips
- 2 zucchini, cut into strips
- 2 bell peppers, cut into strips
- 1 tbsp olive oil
- ½ tsp dried oregano
- 1/2 tsp ground cumin
- 1 tbsp dried chives
- 1 1/2 tbsp paprika
- ¼ tsp pepper
- 1 ½ tsp salt

Directions:

1. Preheat the oven to 400 F.
2. Add all ingredients into the large bowl and toss well.
3. Transfer bowl mixture on baking tray spread well.
4. Bake in the oven for 30 minutes or until chicken is cooked.
5. Serve and enjoy.

Nutritional Value (Amount per Serving):

Calories 256; Fat 10 g; Carbohydrates 12 g; Sugar 7 g; Protein 25 g; Cholesterol 65 mg

Creamy Herb Chicken

Preparation Time: 10 minutes; Cooking Time: 4 Hours; Serve: 4

Ingredients:

- 1 lb chicken breasts, skinless and boneless
- 3 garlic cloves, minced
- 2 tbsp olive oil
- 1 tsp chicken bouillon
- 1/2 cup water
- 1/2 cup ricotta cheese
- 3.5 oz cream cheese
- 1/2 tsp ground pepper
- 1 tsp oregano, dried
- 1/4 tsp thyme, dried
- 1/2 tsp rosemary, dried

Directions:

1. Place chicken into the crockpot.
2. Top with cream cheese and ricotta cheese.
3. Pour water, oregano, thyme, basil, thyme, rosemary, garlic, oil, bouillon, and pepper over the chicken.
4. Cover and cook on high for 4 hours.
5. Serve and enjoy.

Nutritional Value (Amount per Serving):

Calories 425; Fat 28 g; Carbohydrates 4 g; Sugar 1 g; Protein 39 g; Cholesterol 140 mg

Tasty Chicken Curry

Preparation Time: 10 minutes; Cooking Time: 20 minutes; Serve: 6

Ingredients:

- 1 ½ lbs chicken thighs, skinless, boneless, and cut into pieces
- 1 tbsp jalapeno pepper, minced
- 1 1/2 tbsp ginger, diced
- 2 tbsp olive oil
- ¼ cup fresh cilantro, chopped
- 2 tbsp fresh lemon juice
- 1 1/2 tsp cayenne
- 2 tsp garam masala
- 2 tsp turmeric

- 3/4 cup tomatoes, chopped

Directions:

1. Heat oil in a pan over medium heat.
2. Add jalapenos and ginger and sauté for 2-3 minutes.
3. Add chicken and sear chicken from both sides.
4. Add tomatoes and stir well.
5. Add all spices and stir well and cook until chicken is completely cooked.
6. Add lemon juice and stir well.
7. Garnish with cilantro and serve.

Nutritional Value (Amount per Serving):

Calories 270; Fat 14 g; Carbohydrates 4 g; Sugar 1 g; Protein 34 g; Cholesterol 100 mg

Easy Greek Chicken

Preparation Time: 10 minutes; Cooking Time: 6 Hours; Serve: 4

Ingredients:

- 4 chicken breasts, skinless and boneless
- 1 1/2 cups hot water
- 2 1/2 tbsp lemon juice
- 3 tbsp Greek Rub
- 4 garlic cloves, minced
- 2 chicken bouillon cubes, crumbled

Directions:

1. Spray slow cooker with cooking spray.
2. Rub chicken with Greek rub and garlic.
3. Place chicken into the crock pot and pour lemon juice over the chicken.
4. Stir crumble chicken bouillon cubes into the 1 1/2 cups hot water. Pour over chicken.
5. Cover and cook on low for 6 hours.
6. Serve and enjoy.

Nutritional Value (Amount per Serving):

Calories 290; Fat 11 g; Carbohydrates 2 g; Protein 43 g; Sugar 2 g; Cholesterol 130 mg

Cheese Pesto Chicken

Preparation Time: 10 minutes; Cooking Time: 10 minutes; Serve: 6

Ingredients:

- 2 lbs chicken breasts, skinless, boneless, and slice
- 3/4 cup pesto
- 3/4 cup mozzarella cheese, shredded
- Pepper
- Salt

Directions:

1. Season chicken with pepper and salt.
2. Add chicken and pesto in a bowl mix until well coated.
3. Place in the fridge for 2-3 hours.
4. Grill chicken over medium heat until cooked.
5. Top with cheese and serve.

Nutritional Value (Amount per Serving):

Calories 300; Fat 14 g; Carbohydrates 1 g; Sugar 1 g; Protein 40 g; Cholesterol 120 mg

Delicious Chicken Wings

Preparation Time: 10 minutes; Cooking Time: 30 minutes; Serve: 6

Ingredients:

- 1 1/2 lbs chicken wings
- 1 egg, beaten
- 1 tsp cayenne pepper
- 5 tbsp olive oil
- 3/4 cup apple cider vinegar
- 2 garlic cloves, minced
- 1/2 tsp pepper
- 3/4 tsp salt

Directions:

1. Add all ingredients except chicken in a bowl and mix well.
2. Add chicken wings mix until well coated and set aside for 20 minutes.
3. Preheat the oven to 450 F.
4. Place marinated wings in a greased baking dish and bake for 30 minutes.
5. Serve and enjoy.

Nutritional Value (Amount per Serving):

Calories 355; Fat 24 g; Carbohydrates 1 g; Sugar 2 g; Protein 34 g; Cholesterol 130 mg

Chicken Stir Fry

Preparation Time: 10 minutes; Cooking Time: 20 minutes; Serve: 6
Ingredients:

- 1 lb chicken thighs, skinless and boneless, cut into pieces
- 2 carrots, cut into strips
- 2 cups broccoli florets
- 1 tbsp coconut oil
- 1/2 tbsp sesame seeds
- 1 tsp coconut amino
- 1 tsp fresh ginger, minced
- 1 tsp sesame oil
- 1/2 cup chicken broth
- 1/4 tsp red pepper flakes
- 2 garlic cloves, minced
- 1 tsp salt

Directions:

1. Heat oil in a pan over high heat.
2. Add chicken and sauté for 8 minutes.
3. Stir in carrots, ginger, garlic, broccoli, broth, red pepper flakes, and salt.
4. Cover and cook for 5 minutes.
5. Remove pan from heat and stir in sesame seeds, coconut amino, and sesame oil.
6. Serve and enjoy.

Nutritional Value (Amount per Serving):

Calories 200; Fat 10 g; Carbohydrates 6 g; Sugar 2 g; Protein 24 g; Cholesterol 68 mg

Easy Grilled Chicken

Preparation Time: 10 minutes; Cooking Time: 25 minutes; Serve: 4
Ingredients:

- 2 lbs chicken breasts
- 6 tbsp olive oil
- ¼ cup fresh lemon juice
- 2 tsp dried oregano
- 1 1/2 tsp paprika
- 4 garlic cloves, minced
- ½ cup fresh parsley, chopped
- Pepper
- Salt

Directions:

1. Add lemon juice, oregano, paprika, garlic, parsley, and olive oil to a large zip-lock bag.
2. Pierce chicken with knife or fork and season with pepper and salt.
3. Add chicken into the zip-lock bag.
4. Seal bag and shake well and place in the fridge for 20 minutes.
5. Preheat the grill over medium-high heat.
6. Remove chicken from bag and grill for 4-6 minutes per side.
7. Serve and enjoy.

Nutritional Value (Amount per Serving):
Calories 628; Fat 39 g; Carbohydrates 3 g; Sugar 1 g; Protein 62 g; Cholesterol 200 mg

Broiled Chicken

Preparation Time: 10 minutes; Cooking Time: 10 minutes; Serve: 4
Ingredients:
- 2 chicken breasts
- 1 1/2 tsp dry thyme
- 1 tsp soy sauce
- 2 tsp white wine
- 1/8 tsp pepper
- 2 tsp dry basil
- 2 tbsp olive oil

Directions:
1. Preheat the oven to broil-high.
2. Add all ingredients except chicken into the bowl and mix well.
3. Add chicken into the bowl and coat well.
4. Place coated chicken on broiler rack and broil for 5 minutes then flip to other side and broil for 5 minutes more.
5. Serve and enjoy.

Nutritional Value (Amount per Serving):
Calories 146; Fat 8 g; Carbohydrates 1 g; Sugar 1 g; Protein 15 g; Cholesterol 40 mg

Paprika Chicken

Preparation Time: 10 minutes; Cooking Time: 35 minutes; Serve: 4
Ingredients:
- 4 chicken breasts, skinless and boneless, cut into pieces
- 2 tbsp paprika
- 3 tbsp olive oil
- 3 garlic cloves, minced
- 2 tbsp lemon juice
- Pepper
- Salt

Directions:
1. Preheat the oven to 350 F.
2. In a small bowl, mix together garlic, lemon juice, paprika, and olive oil.
3. Season chicken with pepper and salt.
4. Spread 1/3 garlic mixture in the casserole dish.
5. Place chicken into the casserole dish and rub with dish garlic mixture.
6. Pour remaining sauce on top of chicken.
7. Bake for 30-35 minutes.
8. Serve and enjoy.

Nutritional Value (Amount per Serving):
Calories 380; Fat 22 g; Carbohydrates 3 g; Sugar 1 g; Protein 43 g; Cholesterol 85 mg

Spicy Grilled Chicken

Preparation Time: 10 minutes; Cooking Time: 15 minutes; Serve: 4
Ingredients:

- 4 chicken breasts, skinless and boneless
- 2 tsp dried oregano
- 2 tsp paprika
- ½ tsp chili powder
- ¼ tsp garlic powder
- ¼ tsp onion powder
- 3 garlic cloves, minced
- 1/4 cup fresh parsley, minced
- ½ cup olive oil
- ½ cup fresh lemon juice
- Pepper
- Salt

Directions:
1. Add lemon juice, oregano, paprika, chili powder, garlic powder, onion powder, garlic, parsley, and olive oil to a large zip-lock bag.
2. Season chicken with pepper and salt and add to the zip-lock bag.
3. Seal bag and shake well and let marinade chicken in the fridge for 20 minutes.
4. Place marinated chicken on hot grill and cook for 5-6 minutes on each side.
5. Serve and enjoy.

Nutritional Value (Amount per Serving):
Calories 146; Fat 8 g; Carbohydrates 1 g; Sugar 0.5 g; Protein 13.5 g; Cholesterol 40 mg

Lemon Butter Chicken

Preparation Time: 10 minutes; Cooking Time: 4 Hours; Serve: 4
Ingredients:

- 20 oz chicken breasts, skinless, boneless, and cut into pieces
- 3/4 cup chicken broth
- 1 tsp dried parsley
- 2 tbsp olive oil
- 2 tbsp butter
- ½ cup fresh lemon juice
- 1/8 tsp dried thyme
- ¼ tsp dried basil
- ½ tsp dried oregano
- 1 tsp salt

Directions:
1. Heat butter and oil in a pan over medium-high heat.
2. Add chicken to the pan and cook until brown.
3. Transfer chicken to the crockpot. Add remaining ingredients on top of chicken.
4. Cover with lid and cook on low for 4 hours.
5. Serve and enjoy.

Nutritional Value (Amount per Serving):
Calories 420; Fat 24 g; Carbohydrates 7 g; Sugar 1 g; Protein 43 g; Cholesterol 68 mg

Asian Chicken Balls

Preparation Time: 10 minutes; Cooking Time: 50 minutes; Serve: 8
Ingredients:

- 2 lbs ground chicken
- 2 green onion, sliced

- 1 cup almond meal
- 2 tbsp fresh lemon juice
- 1/4 cup chili sauce

- 1/2 cup fresh cilantro, chopped
- 1 tbsp coriander powder
- Oil for frying

Directions:

1. Add all ingredients except oil into the large bowl and mix until well combined.
2. Make small balls from the mixture.
3. Heat oil in large pan over medium heat.
4. Add chicken balls in hot oil and fry until lightly golden browned.
5. Serve and enjoy.

Nutritional Value (Amount per Serving):

Calories 287; Fat 14 g; Carbohydrates 3 g; Protein 35 g; Sugar 0.8 g; Cholesterol 100 mg

Turkey Patties

Preparation Time: 10 minutes; Cooking Time: 10 minutes; Serve: 2

Ingredients:

- ½ lb ground turkey
- 1/2 tsp cumin
- 1 tsp paprika
- 1 tbsp cilantro, chopped
- 1 tbsp lime juice

- 1/2 shallot, peeled and minced
- 1/2 jalapeno pepper
- 2 tbsp olive oil
- 1/2 tsp pepper
- 1/2 tsp sea salt

Directions:

1. Add ground turkey, spices, herbs and lime juice in mixing bowl, mix well until combined.
2. Make two patties from the mixture.
3. Heat oil in a pan over medium-high heat.
4. Place patties and cook for about 5 minutes each side.
5. Serve and enjoy.

Nutritional Value (Amount per Serving):

Calories 225; Fat 13 g; Carbohydrates 2 g; Protein 31 g; Cholesterol 115 mg

CreamyRanch Chicken

Preparation Time: 10 minutes; Cooking Time: 4 Hours; Serve: 6

Ingredients:

- 2 lbs chicken breasts, skinless and boneless
- 3 tbsp ranch dressing
- ¼ tsp garlic powder
- ¼ tsp onion powder

- 4 oz cream cheese
- 3 tbsp butter
- Pepper
- Salt

Directions:

1. Place chicken into the slow cooker. Season with garlic powder, onion powder, pepper, and salt.
2. Add cream cheese and butter over chicken.
3. Sprinkle ranch dressing over chicken.
4. Cover and cook on high for 4 hours.
5. Shred chicken using a fork and serve.

Nutritional Value (Amount per Serving):

Calories 405; Fat 24 g; Carbohydrates 1 g; Protein 45 g; Cholesterol 170 mg

Quick Salsa Chicken

Preparation Time: 10 minutes; Cooking Time: 15 minutes; Serve: 8

Ingredients:

- 2 lbs chicken breasts, skinless and boneless
- ¼ tsp chili powder
- ¼ tsp garlic powder
- 1 1/2 cup salsa
- Pepper
- Salt

Directions:

1. Add all ingredients into the instant pot and stir well.
2. Seal pot with lid and cook on poultry mode for 15 minutes.
3. Release pressure using quick release method than open the lid.
4. Remove chicken from pot and shred using a fork.
5. Return shredded chicken to the pot and stir well.
6. Serve and enjoy.

Nutritional Value (Amount per Serving):

Calories 230; Fat 8 g; Carbohydrates 4 g; Protein 34 g; Sugar 2 g; Cholesterol 100 mg

Tasty Chili Lime Chicken

Preparation Time: 10 minutes; Cooking Time: 20 minutes; Serve: 2

Ingredients:

- 1 lb chicken thighs, skinless and boneless
- 1 tbsp chili powder
- 3 tbsp lime juice
- 1/2 cup chicken stock
- 4 garlic cloves, minced
- 1 tsp cumin
- 1/4 tsp pepper
- 1 tsp kosher salt

Directions:

1. Add all ingredients into the instant pot and stir well.
2. Cover pot with lid and cook on high pressure for 10 minutes.
3. Allow to release pressure naturally then open the lid.
4. Remove chicken from pot and shred using a fork.
5. Return shredded chicken to pot and stir well.
6. Serve and enjoy.

Nutritional Value (Amount per Serving):

Calories 471; Fat 18 g; Carbohydrates 6 g; Protein 69 g; Sugar 1 g; Cholesterol 200 mg

Hot Sauce Wings

Preparation Time: 10 minutes; Cooking Time: 20 minutes; Serve: 2

Ingredients:

- 1/2 lb chicken wings
- 1/4 cup hot sauce
- Pepper
- Salt

Directions:
1. Preheat the air fryer at 400 F for 5 minutes.
2. Place chicken wings in the air fryer basket season with pepper and salt and air fry for 12 minutes.
3. Turn and air fry for 10 minutes more.
4. Transfer wings into the bowl. Pour hot sauce over wings and toss well.
5. Serve and enjoy.

Nutritional Value (Amount per Serving):
Calories 220; Fat 8 g; Carbohydrates 0.5 g; Sugar 1 g; Protein 34 g; Cholesterol 100 mg

Herb Tomato Chicken

Preparation Time: 10 minutes; Cooking Time: 15 minutes; Serve: 6

Ingredients:
- 3 lbs chicken, cut into pieces
- 3 large tomatoes, sliced
- 1 tbsp ground oregano
- 1/2 tbsp ground rosemary
- 1/4 cup chicken broth
- 1 tbsp olive oil
- 1/2 tbsp ground sage
- Pepper
- Salt

Directions:
1. Add oil into the pressure cooker.
2. Add sliced chicken and sprinkle with sage, oregano, rosemary, pepper, and salt.
3. Place chicken onto a tomato slices.
4. Pour broth over the chicken.
5. Seal pressure cooker with lid and cook on chicken/meat mode for 15 minutes.
6. Release pressure using quick release method then open the lid.
7. Serve and enjoy.

Nutritional Value (Amount per Serving):
Calories 381; Fat 10 g; Carbohydrates 3 g; Sugar 2 g; Protein 67 g; Cholesterol 174 mg

Smoky Chicken Legs

Preparation Time: 10 minutes; Cooking Time: 30 minutes; Serve: 4

Ingredients:
- 4 whole chicken legs, bone-in and skin-on
- 1 tsp garlic powder
- 1 tsp liquid smoke
- 1 cup chicken broth
- 1/4 tsp pepper
- 1/4 tsp salt

Directions:
1. Place trivet in the pressure cooker.
2. Add liquid smoke and broth.
3. Season chicken with garlic powder, pepper, and salt and place on a trivet.
4. Seal pressure cooker with lid and cook on chicken mode for 20 minutes.
5. Release pressure using quick release method then open the lid.
6. Place chicken on baking tray and broil for 10 minutes.
7. Serve and enjoy.

Nutritional Value (Amount per Serving):
Calories 220; Fat 14 g; Carbohydrates 1 g; Sugar 1 g; Protein 23 g; Cholesterol 94 mg

Pesto Chicken

Preparation Time: 10 minutes; Cooking Time: 30 minutes; Serve: 4

Ingredients:

- 4 chicken breasts, skinless, boneless, and cut into pieces
- 1/2 cup mozzarella cheese, grated
- 1 tsp chili flakes, crushed
- 1/3 tsp garlic powder
- ¼ tsp cayenne
- 1/2 cup basil pesto
- Pepper
- Salt

Directions:

1. Preheat the oven to 375 F.
2. Add 1/4 cup basil pesto in baking dish and spread well.
3. Season chicken with garlic powder, cayenne, pepper, and salt.
4. Place chicken on top of pesto and top with remaining pesto.
5. Cover dish and bake for 25-30 minutes.
6. Sprinkle grated cheese on top of chicken and cook for 5 minutes more.
7. Serve and enjoy.

Nutritional Value (Amount per Serving):

Calories 289; Fat 12 g; Carbohydrates 1 g; Sugar 1 g; Protein 44 g; Cholesterol 130 mg

Baked Chicken

Preparation Time: 10 minutes; Cooking Time: 45 minutes; Serve: 6

Ingredients:

- 6 chicken breasts
- 2 tbsp lemon juice
- 1/2 cup olive oil
- 3 tbsp cup soy sauce
- 1 tsp garlic salt
- 3/4 tbsp oregano

Directions:

1. Add all ingredients into the zip-lock bag and shake well and place in fridge for 4 hours.
2. Preheat the oven to 350 F.
3. Remove chicken from zip-lock bag and place onto a baking dish.
4. Bake for 45 minutes.
5. Serve and enjoy.

Nutritional Value (Amount per Serving):

Calories 430; Fat 28 g; Carbohydrates 2 g; Sugar 0.5 g; Protein 43 g; Cholesterol 131 mg

Yummy Chicken Curry

Preparation Time: 10 minutes; Cooking Time: 25 minutes; Serve: 6

Ingredients:

- 1 lb chicken breast sliced
- 14.5 oz coconut milk
- 1/4 cup cilantro, chopped
- 2 tbsp curry powder
- 1/2 cup onion
- 6 tbsp olive oil
- 2 tsp garlic paste
- 2 tsp ginger, chopped
- Salt

Directions:

1. Heat oil in a saucepan over medium heat.
2. Add onion and curry powder and sauté until onion softened.
3. Add chicken and sauté.
4. Add garlic and ginger and stir well.
5. Add coconut milk and water and stir well.
6. Cook curry for 10 minutes or until thickened.
7. Garnish with cilantro and serve.

Nutritional Value (Amount per Serving):
Calories 466; Fat 34 g; Carbohydrates 6 g; Sugar 3 g; Protein 25 g; Cholesterol 64 mg

Chicken Patties

Preparation Time: 10 minutes; Cooking Time: 10 minutes; Serve: 6
Ingredients:

- 2 cups chicken, cooked and shredded
- 1/2 cup almond meal
- 1/3 cup mayonnaise
- 2 tbsp olive oil
- 2 tbsp lemon juice
- 3 green onions, chopped
- Pinch of pepper

Directions:
1. In a bowl, add mayonnaise, almond meal, chicken, lemon juice, onion and pepper mix well until combine.
2. Make six patties from mixture.
3. Heat oil in large pan and fry patties over the medium heat for 3 minutes on each side.
4. Serve and enjoy.

Nutritional Value (Amount per Serving):
Calories 190; Fat 12 g; Carbohydrates 7 g; Sugar 2 g; Protein 14 g; Cholesterol 40 mg

Turkey with Cabbage

Preparation Time: 10 minutes; Cooking Time: 15 minutes; Serve: 4
Ingredients:

- 1 lb turkey sausage, sliced
- 1 onion, diced
- 1 medium cabbage head, sliced
- 1 tbsp olive oil
- 2 tsp Dijon mustard
- 2 garlic cloves, minced
- Pepper
- Salt

Directions:
1. Add oil into the instant pot and set pot on sauté mode.
2. Add onions and cook sausage until browned.
3. Add remaining ingredients and cabbage and sauté until cabbage cooked.
4. Serve and enjoy

Nutritional Value (Amount per Serving):
Calories 430; Fat 35 g; Carbohydrates 3.2 g; Sugar 1.2 g; Protein 22 g; Cholesterol 95 mg

Simple Shredded Turkey

Preparation Time: 10 minutes; Cooking Time: 8 Hours; Serve: 24
Ingredients:

- 4 lbs turkey breast, skinless, boneless, and halves
- 1 packet onion soup mix
- 1/2 cup butter, cubed

- 12 oz chicken stock
- ¼ tsp garlic powder
- Pepper
- Salt

Directions:
1. Place turkey breast into the crock pot. Season with pepper and salt.
2. Combine together butter, chicken stock, garlic powder, and onion soup mix and pour over turkey breast.
3. Cover crock pot with lid and cook on low for 8 hours.
4. Shred the turkey with fork and serve.

Nutritional Value (Amount per Serving):
Calories 110; Fat 5 g; Carbohydrates 3 g; Sugar 2 g; Protein 13 g; Cholesterol 40 mg

Juicy & Tender Turkey Breast

Preparation Time: 10 minutes; Cooking Time: 4 Hours; Serve: 12
Ingredients:
- 6 lbs turkey breast, bone-in
- 3 rosemary sprigs
- 2 garlic cloves, peeled

- 1/2 cup water
- Pepper
- Salt

Directions:
1. Place turkey breast into the slow cooker.
2. Add water, garlic, and rosemary on top. Season with pepper and salt.
3. Cover slow cooker with lid and cook on low for 4 hours.
4. Serve and enjoy.

Nutritional Value (Amount per Serving):
Calories 238; Fat 4 g; Carbohydrates 100 g; Sugar 7 g; Protein 39 g; Cholesterol 95 mg

Turkey Meatballs

Preparation Time: 10 minutes; Cooking Time: 10 minutes; Serve: 4
Ingredients:
- 1 ½ lbs ground turkey
- 1 egg, lightly beaten
- 1 bell pepper, chopped
- 2 garlic cloves, minced
- 2 tbsp onion, chopped

- 2 tbsp fresh coriander, chopped
- 3 tbsp fresh parsley, chopped
- Pepper
- Salt

Directions:
1. Preheat the air fryer to 400 F.
2. In a bowl, mix together all ingredients until well combined.
3. Make balls from meat mixture.
4. Place meatballs in air fryer basket and air fry for 8-10 minutes. Shake halfway through.
5. Serve and enjoy.

Nutritional Value (Amount per Serving):
Calories 355; Fat 20 g; Carbohydrates 2 g; Sugar 2 g; Protein 48 g; Cholesterol 215 mg

Veggie Turkey Meatballs

Preparation Time: 10 minutes; Cooking Time: 12 minutes; Serve: 4

Ingredients:

- 1 egg
- 1 lb ground turkey
- 1/4 cup carrots, grated
- 2 tbsp coconut flour
- 2 garlic clove, minced
- 2 tbsp green onion, chopped
- 1/4 cup celery, chopped
- ¼ tsp garlic powder
- ¼ tsp chili powder
- Pepper
- Salt

Directions:

1. Preheat the air fryer at 400 F.
2. Add all ingredients into the large bowl and mix until well combined.
3. Make small balls from meat mixture.
4. Place meatballs into the air fryer basket and air fry for 12 minutes. Turn halfway through.
5. Serve and enjoy.

Nutritional Value (Amount per Serving):

Calories 275; Fat 15 g; Carbohydrates 6 g; Sugar 1 g; Protein 34 g; Cholesterol 67 mg

Spicy Creamy Chicken

Preparation Time: 10 minutes; Cooking Time: 6 Hours; Serve: 5

Ingredients:

- 1 lb chicken thighs, boneless, skinless, cut into chunks
- 1 ½ tbsp garam masala
- 3 tbsp tomato paste
- 1/2 tbsp ginger, grated
- 2 garlic cloves, minced
- 2 tsp onion powder
- 2 tbsp olive oil
- 1 tsp guar gum
- 1 cup coconut milk
- 3/4 cup heavy cream
- 13.5 oz tomatoes, diced
- 2 tsp paprika

Directions:

1. Add chicken into the crock pot.
2. Add ginger over the chicken then add all spices.
3. Add tomatoes, tomato paste, and olive oil. Stir well.
4. Add half cup coconut milk and stir well.
5. Cover and cook on low for 6 hours.
6. Add heavy cream, guar gum, and remaining coconut milk and stir well.
7. Serve and enjoy.

Nutritional Value (Amount per Serving):

Calories 445; Fat 32 g; Carbohydrates 11 g; Sugar 4 g; Protein 30 g; Cholesterol 115 mg

Meatloaf

Preparation Time: 10 minutes; Cooking Time: 40 minutes; Serve: 8

Ingredients:

- 2 eggs
- 2 lbs ground turkey
- ½ cup marinara sauce, sugar-free and homemade

- 3/4 cup cottage cheese
- 1 lb mozzarella cheese, cut into hunks
- 2 tsp Italian seasoning
- ¼ cup basil pesto

- ½ cup parmesan cheese, grated
- ¼ tsp pepper
- 1 tsp salt

Directions:
1. Preheat the oven to 400 F.
2. Add all ingredients into the large bowl and mix until well combined.
3. Transfer bowl mixture to the greased casserole dish and bake for 40 minutes.
4. Serve and enjoy.

Nutritional Value (Amount per Serving):
Calories 351; Fat 19 g; Carbohydrates 4 g; Sugar 2 g; Protein 43 g; Cholesterol 180 mg

Spicy Chili Chicken

Preparation Time: 10 minutes; Cooking Time: 6 Hours 30 minutes; Serve: 6

Ingredients:
- 6 chicken thighs, skinless, boneless and thawed
- 4.5 oz green chilies

- 2 tbsp tomato paste
- 2 tsp garlic salt

Directions:
1. Add chicken into the crock pot and cook on low for 6 hours.
2. Drain juices from slow cooker.
3. Mix together garlic salt, tomato paste, and green chilies and pour over chicken.
4. Cover crock pot with lid and cook on high for 30 minutes.
5. Shred chicken using a fork and serve.

Nutritional Value (Amount per Serving):
Calories 285; Fat 11 g; Carbohydrates 2 g; Sugar 1 g; Protein 43 g; Cholesterol 131 mg

Tasty Harissa Chicken

Preparation Time: 10 minutes; Cooking Time: 4 Hours; Serve: 4

Ingredients:
- 1 lb chicken breasts, skinless and boneless
- 3/4 cup harissa sauce
- 1/4 tsp garlic powder

- 1/2 tsp ground cumin
- ¼ onion powder
- 1/2 tsp kosher salt

Directions:
1. Season chicken with onion powder, garlic powder, cumin, and salt.
2. Place chicken to the crock pot.
3. Pour harissa sauce over the chicken.
4. Cover and cook on low for 4 hours.
5. Remove chicken from crock pot and shred using a fork.
6. Return shredded chicken to the pot and stir well.
7. Serve and enjoy.

Nutritional Value (Amount per Serving):
Calories 230; Fat 10 g; Carbohydrates 1 g; Sugar 0.5 g; Protein 33 g; Cholesterol 100 mg

Feta Lemon Chicken

Preparation Time: 10 minutes; Cooking Time: 45 minutes; Serve: 8

Ingredients:

- 8 chicken breasts, skinless and boneless
- 1/2 tbsp oregano leaves
- 3 tbsp lemon juice
- 2 tbsp green onion, chopped
- 3.5 oz feta cheese, crumbled
- 1/4 tsp pepper
- Salt

Directions:

1. Preheat the oven to 350 F.
2. Place chicken in greased baking dish.
3. Drizzle with lemon juice.
4. Sprinkle with oregano and pepper.
5. Top with green onion and feta cheese.
6. Bake in for 45 minutes.
7. Serve and enjoy.

Nutritional Value (Amount per Serving):

Calories 245; Fat 11 g; Carbohydrates 1 g; Sugar 0.5 g; Protein 35 g; Cholesterol 110 mg

Italian Pepper Chicken

Preparation Time: 10 minutes; Cooking Time: 4 Hours 5 minutes; Serve: 4

Ingredients:

- 4 chicken breasts, skinless and boneless
- 3 garlic cloves, minced
- 2 1/2 tbsp lemon juice
- 2 1/2 tsp Italian seasoning
- 1 tbsp capers
- 3/4 cup roasted red peppers, chopped
- ½ cup olives
- 1 onion, chopped
- Pepper
- Salt

Directions:

1. Season chicken with pepper and salt.
2. Cook chicken in a large pan over medium-high heat for 1-2 minutes on each side.
3. Transfer chicken into the crock pot.
4. Add remaining ingredients over the chicken.
5. Cover and cook on low for 4 hours.
6. Serve and enjoy.

Nutritional Value (Amount per Serving):

Calories 355; Fat 16 g; Carbohydrates 9 g; Sugar 4 g; Protein 44 g; Cholesterol 130 mg

Yummy Chicken Shawarma

Preparation Time: 10 minutes; Cooking Time: 15 minutes; Serve: 4

Ingredients:

- 8 chicken thighs, skinless
- 1/2 tbsp cardamom
- 1 tbsp coriander, chopped
- 1/2 tbsp cumin
- 3 garlic cloves, minced
- 3 tbsp olive oil
- 2 tbsp lemon juice
- 1 tsp cayenne pepper
- 1 1/2 tsp paprika
- 1/4 tsp pepper
- 2 tsp salt

Directions:

1. In a bowl, add all ingredients except chicken and coat well.
2. Place chicken into the large zip-lock bag and pour seal bag and shake well.
3. Place chicken into the fridge for overnight.
4. Heat grill over medium-high heat.
5. Place chicken on hot grill and cook for 6-7 minutes on each side.
6. Serve and enjoy.

Nutritional Value (Amount per Serving):
Calories 660; Fat 33 g; Carbohydrates 3 g; Sugar 0.5 g; Protein 85 g; Cholesterol 261 mg

Cheesy Jalapeno Chicken Casserole

Preparation Time: 10 minutes; Cooking Time: 40 minutes; Serve: 8
Ingredients:
- 2 lbs chicken breast, skinless and boneless
- ¾ lb jalapeno peppers, cut into strips and remove seeds
- 7.5 oz cream cheese, softened
- 1/2 tsp garlic powder
- 1/2 cup bacon, cooked and crumbled
- 4.5 oz cheddar cheese, grated
- ¼ tsp onion powder

Directions:
1. Preheat the oven to 375 F.
2. Place chicken in a casserole dish and season with garlic powder and onion powder.
3. Pour cream cheese over chicken.
4. Top with jalapeno and cheddar cheese.
5. Bake in for 40 minutes.
6. Top with crumbled bacon and return dish in oven bake for 5 minutes more.
7. Serve and enjoy.

Nutritional Value (Amount per Serving):
Calories 350; Fat 24 g; Carbohydrates 4 g; Sugar 1 g; Protein 32 g; Cholesterol 120 mg

Balsamic Herb Chicken

Preparation Time: 10 minutes; Cooking Time: 4 Hours; Serve: 10
Ingredients:
- 6 chicken breasts, skinless and boneless
- 14.5 oz can tomatoes, diced
- 1/2 tsp dried basil
- 1/2 tsp dried rosemary
- 1 tbsp olive oil
- 1/2 cup balsamic vinegar
- 3/4 tsp thyme
- 1/2 tsp dried oregano
- 2 garlic cloves
- 1 onion, sliced
- Pepper
- Salt

Directions:
1. Add all ingredients into the crock pot and stir well.
2. Cover and cook on high for 4 hours.
3. Stir well and serve.

Nutritional Value (Amount per Serving):
Calories 195; Fat 7 g; Carbohydrates 4 g; Sugar 2 g; Protein 26 g; Cholesterol 84 mg

Tomato Olive Chicken

Preparation Time: 10 minutes; Cooking Time: 15 minutes; Serve: 2
Ingredients:

- 2 chicken breasts, skinless and boneless
- 1 1/2 tsp Italian seasoning
- 2 cup cherry tomatoes, cut in half
- 3/4 cup olives
- 2 tbsp olive oil
- ¼ tsp pepper
- ¼ tsp salt

Directions:

1. Season chicken with Italian seasoning, pepper, and salt.
2. Heat oil in a pan over medium heat.
3. Place chicken to the pan and cook for 4-6 minutes on each side.
4. Transfer chicken to a plate.
5. Add olives and tomatoes to the pan and cook for 2-4 minutes.
6. Pour olive and tomato mixture on top of chicken and serve.

Nutritional Value (Amount per Serving):

Calories 469; Fat 30 g; Carbohydrates 8 g; Sugar 4 g; Protein 44 g; Cholesterol 84 mg

Baked Wings

Preparation Time: 10 minutes; Cooking Time: 55 minutes; Serve: 4
Ingredients:

- 2 lbs chicken wings
- 1 tsp Worcestershire sauce
- 1/3 cup cayenne pepper sauce
- 2 tbsp butter
- Pepper
- Salt

Directions:

1. Preheat the oven to 400 F.
2. Season chicken wings with pepper and salt and place on a baking tray and bake for 45-50 minutes.
3. Meanwhile, in a small saucepan, mix together Worcestershire sauce, butter, and cayenne pepper sauce. Bring to boil.
4. Remove saucepan from heat and let it cool.
5. Place chicken wings in a large mixing bowl.
6. Pour prepared sauce over chicken wings and coat well.
7. Serve and enjoy.

Nutritional Value (Amount per Serving):

Calories 535; Fat 24 g; Carbohydrates 11 g; Sugar 0.5 g; Protein 68 g; Cholesterol 68 mg

Delicious Bacon Chicken

Preparation Time: 10 minutes; Cooking Time: 8 Hours; Serve: 4
Ingredients:

- 5 chicken breasts
- 1 1/2 tbsp dried thyme
- 10 bacon slices, chopped
- 5 tbsp olive oil
- 1/2 tbsp dried rosemary
- 3/4 tbsp dried oregano
- 1 tbsp salt

Directions:

1. Add all ingredients into the crock pot and stir well.
2. Cover and cook on low for 8 hours.
3. Shred the chicken using fork and serve.

Nutritional Value (Amount per Serving):
Calories 620; Fat 29 g; Carbohydrates 2 g; Sugar 0.5 g; Protein 55 g; Cholesterol 145 mg

Mustard Chicken Thighs

Preparation Time: 10 minutes; Cooking Time: 50 minutes; Serve: 4
Ingredients:
- 1 ½ lbs chicken thighs, skinless and boneless
- ¼ cup French mustard
- 2 tsp olive oil
- 2 tbsp Dijon mustard

Directions:
1. Preheat the oven to 375 F.
2. In a mixing bowl, mix together olive oil, Dijon mustard, and French mustard.
3. Add chicken to the bowl and coat well.
4. Arrange chicken on baking tray and bake for 45-50 minutes.
5. Serve and enjoy.

Nutritional Value (Amount per Serving):
Calories 400; Fat 15 g; Carbohydrates 14 g; Sugar 10 g; Protein 50 g; Cholesterol 75 mg

Coconut Creamy Chicken Curry

Preparation Time: 10 minutes; Cooking Time: 6 Hours; Serve: 6
Ingredients:
- 1 ½ lbs chicken thighs, boneless
- ½ cup chicken broth
- 2 tbsp curry powder
- 3 tbsp fresh ginger, chopped
- 14.5 oz can coconut milk
- ½ tsp red pepper, crushed
- ½ tsp coriander, crushed
- ½ tsp pepper
- 1 tsp kosher salt

Directions:
1. Add all ingredients into the crock pot and stir well.
2. Seal and cook on low for 6 hours.
3. Serve and enjoy.

Nutritional Value (Amount per Serving):
Calories 373; Fat 23 g; Carbohydrates 6 g; Sugar 0.7 g; Protein 35 g; Cholesterol 100 mg

Curried Chicken Wings

Preparation Time: 10 minutes; Cooking Time: 6 Hours; Serve: 6
Ingredients:
- 3 lbs chicken wings
- 1 tbsp coconut milk
- 2 oz basil, minced
- 7.5 oz green curry paste
- 2 tbsp fresh cilantro, minced
- 1/2 tbsp fresh ginger, minced

Directions:
1. Add chicken wings into the crock pot.

2. In a bowl, whisk together coconut milk, cilantro, ginger, basil, and curry paste.
3. Pour coconut milk mixture over chicken wings and stir well.

4. Cover and cook on low for 6 hours.
5. Serve and enjoy.

Nutritional Value (Amount per Serving):
Calories 320; Fat 14 g; Carbohydrates 6 g; Sugar 0.5 g; Protein 40 g; Cholesterol 120 mg

Zucchini Tomato Dill Chicken

Preparation Time: 10 minutes; Cooking Time: 30 minutes; Serve: 6
Ingredients:
- 2 lbs chicken tenders
- 2 dill sprigs
- 1 zucchini, sliced
- 3/4 cup grape tomatoes
- 2 tbsp olive oil
- For topping:
- 1 tbsp olive oil
- 2 tbsp feta cheese, crumbled
- 2 tbsp fresh dill, chopped
- 2 tbsp fresh lemon juice

Directions:
1. Preheat the oven to 400 F.
2. Drizzle the olive oil on a baking tray then place chicken, zucchini, dill, and tomatoes on the tray. Season with salt.
3. Bake for 30 minutes.
4. Meanwhile, in a small bowl, stir together all topping ingredients.
5. Place chicken plate and top with vegetable. Remove dill sprigs.
6. Sprinkle topping on top of chicken and vegetables.
7. Serve and enjoy.

Nutritional Value (Amount per Serving):
Calories 555; Fat 27 g; Carbohydrates 5 g; Sugar 2 g; Protein 68 g; Cholesterol 205 mg

Creamy Taco Chicken

Preparation Time: 10 minutes; Cooking Time: 6 Hours; Serve: 6
Ingredients:
- 2 lbs chicken breasts
- 1/2 cup chicken stock
- 3/4 cup sour cream
- 2 tsp taco seasoning
- 14.5 oz can tomato

Directions:
1. Add all ingredients into the crock pot and stir well.
2. Cover and cook on low for 6 hours.
3. Stir well and serve.

Nutritional Value (Amount per Serving):
Calories 264; Fat 12 g; Carbohydrates 4 g; Protein 34 g; Sugar 1 g; Cholesterol 115 mg

Green Bean Chicken Curry

Preparation Time: 10 minutes; Cooking Time: 20 minutes; Serve: 4
Ingredients:

- 1 lb chicken thighs, boneless
- 2 cans coconut milk
- 3 tbsp butter
- 1 onion, chopped
- 3.5 oz green beans, chopped
- 3/4 lb broccoli, chopped
- 1/2 tbsp ginger, grated
- 1 red chili pepper, chopped
- 2 tbsp curry powder
- Pepper
- Salt

Directions:
1. Melt butter in pan over medium heat.
2. Add ginger, chili pepper, and onion in pan sauté for 2-3 minutes.
3. Add chicken and curry powder and cook for 10 minutes.
4. Add green beans and broccoli and stir well.
5. Add coconut milk and simmer for 15 minutes.
6. Serve and enjoy.

Nutritional Value (Amount per Serving):
Calories 340; Fat 18 g; Carbohydrates 10 g; Sugar 2 g; Protein 36 g; Cholesterol 125 mg

Creamy Cheese Chicken

Preparation Time: 10 minutes; Cooking Time: 10 minutes; Serve: 4
Ingredients:
- 4 chicken breasts, cut into chunks
- 2/3 cup chicken stock
- 4 creamy swiss cheese wedges
- 1 tsp olive oil
- Pepper
- Salt

Directions:
1. Season chicken with pepper and salt.
2. Heat oil in a pan over medium-high heat.
3. Add chicken to pan and browned for 2-3 minutes on each side.
4. Add stock, cheese and stir well.
5. Turn heat to medium-low and cook until cheese melted, about 5 minutes.
6. Serve and enjoy.

Nutritional Value (Amount per Serving):
Calories 386; Fat 23 g; Carbohydrates 2 g; Sugar 0 g; Protein 40 g; Cholesterol 123 mg

Skillet Greek Chicken

Preparation Time: 10 minutes; Cooking Time: 15 minutes; Serve: 4
Ingredients:
- 1 1/2 lbs chicken thighs
- 1 1/2 cup marinated artichokes
- 1 1/2 cups cherry tomatoes
- 10 fresh basil leaves
- 3 tbsp balsamic vinegar
- 1/4 tsp dried thyme
- 1/2 tsp dried oregano
- 1/4 tsp pepper
- 1/2 tsp salt

Directions:
1. Heat skillet over medium-high heat.
2. Sear chicken in hot skillet for 3 minutes on each side.
3. Add tomatoes, marinated artichokes, balsamic vinegar, and seasoning in a chicken skillet.
4. Turn heat to medium.

5. Cover and simmer for 10 minutes.
6. Turn heat to high and cook until all liquid reduce.

7. Cook chicken until lightly browned.
8. Garnish with basil and serve.

Nutritional Value (Amount per Serving):

Calories 395; Fat 17 g; Carbohydrates 6 g; Sugar 3 g; Protein 51 g; Cholesterol 150 mg

Rosemary Orange Chicken Roast

Preparation Time: 10 minutes; Cooking Time: 35 minutes; Serve: 4

Ingredients:

- 16 oz chicken breasts, skinless
- 1/4 cup orange juice
- 2 garlic cloves, chopped
- 1/2 tsp olive oil
- 1 tsp rosemary, chopped
- Pepper
- Salt

Directions:

1. Preheat the oven to 450 F.
2. Rub chicken with garlic and oil. Season with rosemary, pepper, and salt.
3. Place chicken in prepared baking dish.
4. Pour orange juice over chicken and bake for 25 minutes.
5. Turn chicken to other side and bake for 10 minutes.
6. Serve and enjoy.

Nutritional Value (Amount per Serving):

Calories 231; Fat 9 g; Carbohydrates 2 g; Sugar 2 g; Protein 30 g; Cholesterol 100 mg

Turkey with Mushrooms

Preparation Time: 10 minutes; Cooking Time: 6 Hours; Serve: 6

Ingredients:

- 1 1/2 lbs turkey breast cutlets
- 1 tsp sage, minced
- 8 oz mushrooms, sliced
- 1 medium onion, sliced
- 1/4 cup water
- 1/4 tsp pepper
- 1 tsp butter
- 1/8 Tsp salt

Directions:

1. Melt butter in a pan over medium heat.
2. Add mushrooms and onion in a pan and sauté until softened.
3. Add half mushroom and onion mixture into the crock pot.
4. Add turkey into the crock pot and sprinkle with pepper, sage, and salt.
5. Add remaining mushroom and onion mixture over turkey. Pour water into the crock pot.
6. Cover and cook on low for 6 hours.
7. Serve and enjoy.

Nutritional Value (Amount per Serving):

Calories 140; Fat 1 g; Carbohydrates 3 g; Sugar 1 g; Protein 30 g; Cholesterol 45 mg

Spicy Jamaican Chicken Curry

Preparation Time: 10 minutes; Cooking Time: 30 minutes; Serve: 6

Ingredients:

- 2 lbs chicken legs, wash and clean
- 2 tbsp green onion, sliced
- 2 tbsp Jamaican curry powder
- 1 thyme sprig
- ¼ tsp rosemary
- 1 small onion, sliced
- 1 tbsp garlic salt

Directions:

1. Season chicken with garlic salt.
2. Spray pan with cooking spray and heat over medium heat.
3. Add curry powder, thyme, onion, and green onion to the pan and stir well.
4. Add chicken to the pan and cook until chicken is brown, about 10 minutes on high heat.
5. Add 2 cups water and stir well.
6. Cover and simmer for 30 minutes.
7. Serve and enjoy.

Nutritional Value (Amount per Serving):

Calories 290; Fat 10 g; Carbohydrates 1 g; Sugar 1 g; Protein 44 g; Cholesterol 136 mg

Chicken with Onion Mushrooms

Preparation Time: 10 minutes; Cooking Time: 6 Hours; Serve: 2

Ingredients:

- 2 chicken breasts, skinless and boneless
- 3/4 cup mushrooms, sliced
- 1 cup chicken broth
- 1 onion, sliced
- ¼ tsp oregano
- 1/4 tsp thyme, dried
- Pepper
- Salt

Directions:

1. Add all ingredients into the crock pot.
2. Cover and cook on low for 6 hours.
3. Serve and enjoy.

Nutritional Value (Amount per Serving):

Calories 325; Fat 11 g; Carbohydrates 7 g; Protein 45 g; Sugar 1 g; Cholesterol 130 mg

Cheese Spinach Chicken

Preparation Time: 10 minutes; Cooking Time: 20 minutes; Serve: 4

Ingredients:

- 4 chicken breasts, skinless and boneless
- 2 tbsp pecans, chopped
- 2 tbsp green onion, sliced
- 3/4 cup mushrooms, sliced
- 3 cups fresh spinach
- 2 cheese slices
- 1/2 tsp chicken seasoning
- 1 tsp olive oil

Directions:

1. Heat oil in pan over medium heat.
2. Add onion, pecans, mushrooms, and spinach and sauté until tender. Set aside.
3. Season chicken with chicken seasoning.
4. Cook chicken on hot grill for 5 minutes on each side.

5. Top with cheese and grill until cheese is melted.

6. Pour spinach mixture on top of chicken and serve.

Nutritional Value (Amount per Serving):
Calories 295; Fat 15 g; Carbohydrates 3 g; Sugar 1 g; Protein 38 g; Cholesterol 115 mg

Flavors Garlic Dump Chicken

Preparation Time: 10 minutes; Cooking Time: 35 minutes; Serve: 8
Ingredients:
- 6 chicken breasts
- 2 tbsp fresh lemon juice
- 2 tbsp fresh parsley flakes
- 4 tbsp olive oil
- 2 tsp garlic, minced

Directions:
1. Add all ingredients into the mixing bowl and place in refrigerator for 1 hour.
2. Pour marinated chicken in baking dish and bake at 350 F for 35 minutes.
3. Serve and enjoy.

Nutritional Value (Amount per Serving):
Calories 255; Fat 11 g; Carbohydrates 1 g; Sugar 0.5 g; Protein 36 g; Cholesterol 108 mg

Spicy Drumsticks

Preparation Time: 10 minutes; Cooking Time: 40 minutes; Serve: 4
Ingredients:
- 32 oz chicken drumsticks
- 2 tbsp vinegar
- 2 tbsp olive oil
- 2 tbsp Tabasco
- 1 tsp paprika
- 1 tbsp tomato paste
- 1 tsp salt

Directions:
1. Preheat the oven to 450 F.
2. In large mixing bowl, add all ingredients and mix well to coat.
3. Place coated chicken drumsticks on greased baking dish and bake for 30 minutes.
4. Serve and enjoy.

Nutritional Value (Amount per Serving):
Calories 451; Fat 21 g; Carbohydrates 1 g; Sugar 0.5 g; Protein 63 g; Cholesterol 200 mg

Mediterranean Chicken

Preparation Time: 10 minutes; Cooking Time: 6 Hours; Serve: 8
Ingredients:
- 3 lbs chicken breasts, skinless and boneless
- 3/4 cup olives, pitted and chopped
- 1 onion, chopped
- 1 1/2 cups chicken stock
- 14 oz can artichoke hearts, drained
- 28 oz can whole tomatoes, drained and chopped
- 1/4 cup fresh parsley, chopped
- 1 1/2 tsp dried thyme

- 1 1/2 tsp dried basil
- 1 tbsp curry powder
- 1/4 cup vinegar
- 1 tsp pepper
- 1 tsp kosher salt

Directions:
1. Add all ingredients into the crock pot and stir well.
2. Cover and cook on low for 6 hours.
3. Shred the chicken using fork.
4. Stir well and serve.

Nutritional Value (Amount per Serving):
Calories 380; Fat 14 g; Carbohydrates 8 g; Sugar 4 g; Protein 52 g; Cholesterol 150 mg

Caper Olive Chicken

Preparation Time: 10 minutes; Cooking Time: 20 minutes; Serve: 4
Ingredients:
- 4 chicken breasts, boneless
- 3 tbsp capers, rinsed and drained
- 1 1/2 cups cherry tomatoes
- 3 tbsp olive oil
- 15 olives, pitted and halved
- Pepper
- Salt

Directions:
1. Preheat the oven to 475 F.
2. In a bowl, toss together 2 tablespoons olive oil, capers, olives, and tomatoes. Set aside.
3. Heat remaining oil in skillet over medium-high heat.
4. Place chicken in skillet and cook until brown, about 4 minutes.
5. Turn chicken. Add olive and tomato mixture.
6. Place in oven and roast for 18 minutes.
7. Serve and enjoy.

Nutritional Value (Amount per Serving):
Calories 402; Fat 22 g; Carbohydrates 5 g; Sugar 2 g; Protein 44 g; Cholesterol 129 mg

Yummy Chicken Fajitas

Preparation Time: 10 minutes; Cooking Time: 10 minutes; Serve: 6
Ingredients:
- 4 chicken breasts, skinless and boneless
- 1/2 cup water
- 1 packet fajita seasoning
- 1 onion, sliced
- 2 bell pepper, sliced

Directions:
1. Add all ingredients into the instant pot and stir well.
2. Seal pot with lid and cook on high for 10 minutes.
3. Release pressure using quick release method than open the lid.
4. Shred the chicken using fork and serve.

Nutritional Value (Amount per Serving):
Calories 190; Fat 7 g; Carbohydrates 2 g; Sugar 1 g; Protein 28 g; Cholesterol 84 mg

Chicken Chili Casserole

Preparation Time: 10 minutes; Cooking Time: 40 minutes; Serve: 8
Ingredients:

- 2 lbs cooked chicken, shredded
- 4 oz Swiss cheese
- 3 oz green chili
- 2 tbsp fresh lemon juice
- 1 ½ tbsp Dijon mustard
- 5 oz cream cheese, softened
- 4 oz butter, melted
- 5 oz ham, cut into small pieces
- ½ tsp salt

Directions:
1. Preheat the oven to 350 F.
2. Place chicken in the baking dish then top with green chili and ham.
3. Add butter, lemon juice, cream cheese, mustard, and salt into the blender and blend until a thick sauce.
4. Pour sauce over chicken mixture.
5. Arrange cheese slices on top.
6. Bake in for 40 minutes.
7. Serve and enjoy.

Nutritional Value (Amount per Serving):
Calories 450; Fat 30 g; Carbohydrates 3 g; Sugar 0.5 g; Protein 42 g; Cholesterol 85 mg

Moroccan Chicken

Preparation Time: 10 minutes; Cooking Time: 6 Hours; Serve: 8
Ingredients:

- 3 lbs chicken thighs, skinless and boneless
- ¼ cup fresh parsley, chopped
- 1 lb Moroccan stew sauce

Directions:
1. Add all ingredients into the crock pot and stir well.
2. Cover and cook on low for 6 hours.
3. Serve and enjoy.

Nutritional Value (Amount per Serving):
Calories 265; Fat 11 g; Carbohydrates 6 g; Sugar 1 g; Protein 33 g; Cholesterol 45 mg

Caprese Meatloaf

Preparation Time: 10 minutes; Cooking Time: 60 minutes; Serve: 6
Ingredients:

- 1 egg, lightly beaten
- 1 lb ground chicken
- 2 garlic cloves, minced
- 4 oz mozzarella cheese, diced
- 2 tbsp basil, chopped
- ½ cup tomatoes, diced
- ½ cup almond flour

Directions:
1. Preheat the oven to 350 F.
2. Add all ingredients into the mixing bowl and mix until well combined.
3. Transfer loaf mixture into the greased loaf pan and bake for 60 minutes.
4. Slice and serve.

Nutritional Value (Amount per Serving):

Calories 265; Fat 14 g; Carbohydrates 3.7 g; Sugar 0.8 g; Protein 30 g; Cholesterol 105 mg

Yummy Mozzarella Chicken

Preparation Time: 10 minutes; Cooking Time: 20 minutes; Serve: 4

Ingredients:

- 4 chicken breasts, skinless and boneless
- 3/4 cup mozzarella cheese, shredded
- 1/4 cup Italian dressing
- 1 zucchini, chopped
- 1 onion, sliced
- 3/4 cup olives, pitted
- 1/2 cup cherry tomatoes

Directions:

1. Heat pan over medium-high heat.
2. Add chicken in a pan and cover and cook for 5-7 minutes on each side.
3. Add zucchini and onions and cook for 4-5 minutes.
4. Add olives, tomatoes, and Italian dressing and cover and cook for 2 minutes.
5. Top with shredded cheese cover for 2 minutes.
6. Serve and enjoy.

Nutritional Value (Amount per Serving):

Calories 385; Fat 18 g; Carbohydrates 8 g; Sugar 4 g; Protein 46 g; Cholesterol 144 mg

Chicken Skewers

Preparation Time: 10 minutes; Cooking Time: 20 minutes; Serve: 4

Ingredients:

- 1 chicken breast, cut into cubes
- 3 tbsp olive oil
- 1 tsp oregano
- 3 garlic cloves, minced
- 2 tbsp lemon juice
- 1/2 tsp pepper
- 1 tsp kosher salt

Directions:

1. Add all ingredients into the bowl and mix well. Cover and place in fridge for 1 hour.
2. Preheat the oven to 425 F.
3. Slide chicken onto skewers and place on baking tray and bake for 10 minutes.
4. Turn to other side and bake for 10 minutes more.
5. Serve and enjoy.

Nutritional Value (Amount per Serving):

Calories 115; Fat 10 g; Carbohydrates 1 g; Sugar 0.5 g; Protein 4 g; Cholesterol 10 mg

Delicious Chicken Thighs

Preparation Time: 10 minutes; Cooking Time: 55 minutes; Serve: 4

Ingredients:

- 8 chicken thighs
- ¼ cup capers, drained
- 10 oz jar roasted red peppers, drained and sliced
- 2 cups cherry tomatoes
- 3 tbsp fresh parsley, chopped
- 1 tsp dried oregano
- 5 garlic cloves, crushed

- 4 tbsp olive oil
- Pepper
- Salt

Directions:

1. Preheat the oven to 400 F.
2. Season chicken with pepper and salt.
3. Heat 2 tablespoons oil in a pan over medium heat.
4. Add chicken to the pan and sear until brown from all the side.
5. Transfer chicken onto a baking tray.
6. Add tomato, capers, oregano, garlic, and red peppers around the chicken. Season with pepper and salt and drizzle with remaining olive oil.
7. Bake for 45-55 minutes.
8. Garnish with parsley and serve.

Nutritional Value (Amount per Serving):

Calories 475; Fat 24 g; Carbohydrates 5 g; Sugar 2.4 g; Protein 57 g; Cholesterol 173 mg

Basil Olive Chicken

Preparation Time: 10 minutes; Cooking Time: 16 minutes; Serve: 4

Ingredients:

- 2 lbs chicken
- 1 tbsp olive oil
- 1/2 tsp oregano
- 3 garlic cloves, minced
- 2 tbsp vinegar
- 1/3 cup chicken stock
- 4 oz Capers
- 4.5 oz olives
- 1/4 cup fresh basil
- 1/8 tsp pepper
- 1/4 tsp salt

Directions:

1. Add oil to the instant pot and set the pot on sauté mode.
2. Add chicken to the pot and sauté for 3-4 minutes.
3. Add remaining ingredients and stir well.
4. Seal pot with lid and cook on manual mode for 12 minutes.
5. Release pressure using quick release method than open the lid.
6. Serve and enjoy.

Nutritional Value (Amount per Serving):

Calories 430; Fat 15 g; Carbohydrates 5 g; Sugar 0.5 g; Protein 67 g; Cholesterol 94 mg

Turkey Soup

Preparation Time: 10 minutes; Cooking Time: 3 Hours 20 minutes; Serve: 8

Ingredients:

- 2 cups turkey, cooked and chopped
- 4 cups chicken stock
- 8 oz tomato sauce
- 2 cups zucchini, sliced
- 7.5 oz frozen green beans
- 3 oz cream cheese, softened
- 1 tsp Worcestershire sauce
- 1 tbsp chicken bouillon granules
- 1 onions, chopped
- 1/8 tsp black pepper
- 1/4 tsp salt

Directions:

1. Add all ingredients except cream cheese into the crock pot and stir well.
2. Cover and cook on high for 3 hours.
3. Blend 1 cup soup with cream cheese and return to the crock pot.
4. Stir well and cook for 20 minutes more.
5. Serve and enjoy.

Nutritional Value (Amount per Serving):
Calories 121; Fat 6 g; Carbohydrates 6 g; Sugar 2 g; Protein 13 g; Cholesterol 40 mg

Jerk Chicken Wings

Preparation Time: 10 minutes; Cooking Time: 5 Hours; Serve: 4
Ingredients:
- 20 oz chicken breasts
- 1 tsp cayenne pepper
- 1 tbsp paprika
- 1 1/2 tsp garlic powder
- 2 tsp white pepper
- 2 tsp thyme
- 2 tsp onion powder
- 1 tsp pepper
- 2 tsp salt

Directions:
1. In a small bowl, combine together all spices and rub over chicken.
2. Place chicken into the crock pot.
3. Cover and cook on low for 5 hours.
4. Serve and enjoy.

Nutritional Value (Amount per Serving):
Calories 290; Fat 10 g; Carbohydrates 4 g; Sugar 1 g; Protein 40 g; Cholesterol 120 mg

Garlicky Chicken

Preparation Time: 10 minutes; Cooking Time: 40 minutes; Serve: 4
Ingredients:
- 2 lbs chicken drumsticks
- 8 garlic cloves
- 2 tbsp olive oil
- 4 tbsp butter
- 2 tbsp parsley, chopped
- 2 tbsp lemon juice
- Pepper
- Salt

Directions:
1. Preheat the oven to 450 F.
2. Place chicken on baking tray. Season with pepper and salt.
3. Sprinkle the parsley and garlic over the chicken.
4. Drizzle with lemon juice and olive oil and bake for 35-40 minutes.
5. Serve and enjoy.

Nutritional Value (Amount per Serving):
Calories 559; Fat 32 g; Carbohydrates 3 g; Sugar 0.5 g; Protein 63 g; Cholesterol 231 mg

Coconut Zucchini Chicken Casserole

Preparation Time: 10 minutes; Cooking Time: 35 minutes; Serve: 8
Ingredients:

- 2 ½ lbs chicken breasts, boneless and cubed
- 12 oz roasted red peppers, drained and chopped
- 8 garlic cloves
- 2/3 cup mayonnaise
- 5 zucchini, cut into cubes
- 1 tsp xanthan gum
- 1 tbsp tomato paste
- 6 oz coconut cream
- 1 tsp salt

Directions:
1. Preheat the oven to 400 F.
2. Add zucchini and chicken to a casserole dish. Cover with foil.
3. Bake for 25 minutes. Stir well and cook for 10 minutes more.
4. Meanwhile, in a bowl, stir together remaining ingredients.
5. Pour bowl mixture over chicken and zucchini and broil for 5 minutes.
6. Serve and enjoy.

Nutritional Value (Amount per Serving):
Calories 232; Fat 15 g; Carbohydrates 11 g; Sugar 5 g; Protein 17 g; Cholesterol 49 mg

Simple Shredded Chicken

Preparation Time: 10 minutes; Cooking Time: 6 Hours; Serve: 4
Ingredients:
- 16 oz chicken breasts, skinless and boneless
- 1/2 cup chicken stock
- 1 tsp dried oregano
- 1 tsp onion powder
- 1 tsp garlic powder
- 1/2 tsp pepper
- 1 tsp salt

Directions:
1. Season chicken with pepper and salt.
2. Place chicken into the crock pot.
3. Sprinkle oregano, garlic powder, and onion powder over the chicken.
4. Pour chicken stock into the crock pot.
5. Cover and cook on low for 6 hours.
6. Shred the chicken using a fork.
7. Serve and enjoy.

Nutritional Value (Amount per Serving):
Calories 220; Fat 8 g; Carbohydrates 2 g; Sugar 0.5 g; Protein 34 g; Cholesterol 100 mg

Herb Chicken Thighs

Preparation Time: 10 minutes; Cooking Time: 4 Hours; Serve: 6
Ingredients:
- 2 lbs chicken thighs, skinless and boneless
- 1 1/2 tbsp fresh oregano, minced
- 1 onion, sliced
- 1 tbsp fresh thyme
- 2 garlic cloves, minced
- 1 tbsp fresh basil, minced
- Pepper
- Salt

Directions:
1. Season chicken with pepper and salt.
2. Add chicken, thyme, garlic, basil, and oregano into the mixing bowl and place in fridge for 1 hour.
3. Add onion to the crock pot.
4. Add marinated chicken into the crock pot.
5. Cover and cook on high for 4 hours.

6. Serve and enjoy.

Nutritional Value (Amount per Serving):

Calories 300; Fat 12 g; Carbohydrates 3 g; Sugar 1 g; Protein 44 g; Cholesterol 134 mg

Chili Lime Chicken Carnitas

Preparation Time: 10 minutes; Cooking Time: 4 Hours; Serve: 10

Ingredients:

- 2 1/2 lbs chicken breasts, skinless and boneless
- 1 tbsp garlic, minced
- 2 tsp cumin powder
- 1/4 cup cilantro, chopped
- 3 tbsp fresh lime juice
- 1 tbsp chili powder
- 1/2 tsp salt

Directions:

1. Place chicken into the crock pot.
2. Add remaining ingredients over the chicken.
3. Cover and cook on high for 4 hours.
4. Shred the chicken using fork and serve.

Nutritional Value (Amount per Serving):

Calories 220; Fat 9 g; Carbohydrates 1 g; Sugar 0.5 g; Protein 33 g; Cholesterol 100 mg

Easy Chicken Tacos

Preparation Time: 10 minutes; Cooking Time: 4 Hours; Serve: 8

Ingredients:

- 2 lbs chicken breasts, skinless and boneless
- 2 tbsp lime juice
- ½ tsp cumin powder
- ½ tsp garlic powder
- ¼ tsp oregano
- 1 tsp paprika
- 1 tsp chili powder
- 1/4 cup fresh cilantro, chopped
- 14 oz salsa

Directions:

1. Place chicken into the crock pot.
2. Add remaining ingredients on top of chicken.
3. Cover and cook on high for 4 hours.
4. Shred the chicken using fork and serve.

Nutritional Value (Amount per Serving):

Calories 235; Fat 9 g; Carbohydrates 5 g; Sugar 2 g; Protein 34 g; Cholesterol 100 mg

Mayo Cheese Chicken

Preparation Time: 10 minutes; Cooking Time: 4 Hours; Serve: 8

Ingredients:

- 2 lbs chicken breasts, skinless, boneless and halves
- 1 tsp paprika
- 2 tsp oregano, dried
- 1 cup mayonnaise
- 1/2 cup parmesan cheese, grated
- 1/2 cup chicken stock
- 1/4 tsp pepper
- Salt

Directions:

1. Place chicken and stock into the crock pot.
2. Cover and cook on high for 2 hours.
3. Combine remaining ingredients and pour over the chicken.
4. Cover and cook on high for 2 hours.
5. Serve and enjoy.

Nutritional Value (Amount per Serving):
Calories 390; Fat 22 g; Carbohydrates 8 g; Sugar 2 g; Protein 39 g; Cholesterol 125 mg

Lemon Dill Chicken

Preparation Time: 10 minutes; Cooking Time: 4 Hours; Serve: 4

Ingredients:

- 16 oz chicken breasts, skinless, boneless and halves
- 1/2 tsp lemon zest
- 1 small onion, sliced
- ¼ tsp garlic powder
- 1 tsp lemon pepper seasoning
- 2 tbsp fresh dill, minced
- 1 cup sour cream

Directions:

1. In a bowl, combine together lemon zest, garlic powder, lemon pepper seasoning, dill, onion, and sour cream.
2. Pour half bowl mixture into the crock pot.
3. Place chicken into the crock pot then pour remaining bowl mixture on top of chicken.
4. Cover and cook on low for 4 hours.
5. Serve and enjoy.

Nutritional Value (Amount per Serving):
Calories 340; Fat 21 g; Carbohydrates 3 g; Sugar 0.1 g; Protein 35 g; Cholesterol 125 mg

Turkey Breast

Preparation Time: 10 minutes; Cooking Time: 8 Hours; Serve: 10

Ingredients:

- 6 lbs turkey breasts
- 1 tbsp mustard seeds
- 2 onions, sliced
- 1/2 tbsp celery flakes
- 1 tbsp parsley, dried
- 1/2 cup fresh thyme, minced
- 1/2 tbsp pepper
- 1/2 tbsp salt

Directions:

1. Add onion to the slow cooker.
2. Make a slit on turkey skin using knife and spread thyme over turkey.
3. In a small bowl, combine together mustard seeds, celery flakes, parsley, pepper, and salt and rub over turkey.
4. Place turkey into the slow cooker.
5. Cover and cook on low for 8 hours.
6. Serve and enjoy.

Nutritional Value (Amount per Serving):
Calories 480; Fat 13 g; Carbohydrates 4 g; Sugar 1 g; Protein 81 g; Cholesterol 202 mg

Chicken Fajita Casserole

Preparation Time: 10 minutes; Cooking Time: 20 minutes; Serve: 4
Ingredients:
- 1 lb chicken, cooked and shredded
- 1/3 cup mayonnaise
- 8oz cream cheese
- 8 oz cheddar cheese, shredded
- 1 1/2 tbsp tex-mex seasoning
- 1 onion, sliced
- 1 bell pepper, sliced
- Pepper
- Salt

Directions:
1. Preheat the oven to 400 F.
2. Mix all ingredients except 2 oz cheddar cheese in a prepared baking dish.
3. Spread remaining cheese on top and bake for 15 minutes.
4. Serve and enjoy.

Nutritional Value (Amount per Serving):
Calories 640; Fat 44 g; Carbohydrates 12 g; Sugar 4 g; Protein 50 g; Cholesterol 200 mg

Greek Turkey Breasts

Preparation Time: 10 minutes; Cooking Time: 60 minutes; Serve: 6
Ingredients:
- 1 lb turkey breasts
- 1 1/2 tbsp dried oregano
- 1/2 cup olive oil
- 1 cup fresh lemon juice
- 2 tbsp yellow mustard
- 3 garlic cloves, minced

Directions:
1. Preheat the oven to 350 F.
2. In a medium bowl, whisk together oregano, mustard, garlic, oil, and lemon juice.
3. Place turkey into mixing bowl and pour marinade over turkey.
4. Place marinated turkey in the fridge for overnight.
5. Bake in for 50-60 minutes.
6. Serve and enjoy.

Nutritional Value (Amount per Serving):
Calories 241; Fat 19 g; Carbohydrates 6 g; Sugar 4 g; Protein 14 g; Cholesterol 34 mg

Yummy Turkey Bowl

Preparation Time: 5 minutes; Cooking Time: 5 minutes; Serve: 2
Ingredients:
- 4 oz turkey, cooked and diced
- 1 artichoke hearts, diced
- 3 olives, diced
- 3 cherry tomato, halved
- 3 basil leaves
- 1 1/2 tbsp pesto
- Pepper
- Salt

Directions:
1. Add all ingredients into the heat-safe bowl and mix well.
2. Place bowl in microwave and heat until warm, about 1 minute.

3. Serve and enjoy.

Nutritional Value (Amount per Serving):

Calories 171; Fat 6 g; Carbohydrates 9 g; Sugar 1 g; Protein 20 g; Cholesterol 46 mg

Salsa Turkey

Preparation Time: 10 minutes; Cooking Time: 30 minutes; Serve: 6

Ingredients:

- 4 turkey breasts, skinless and boneless
- 5 black peppercorns, crushed
- 1 tbsp olive oil
- Salt

For salsa:

- 3 garlic cloves, chopped
- 1 onion, diced
- 6 tomatoes, chopped
- 2 tbsp basil, chopped
- 4 oz olives, pitted and chopped
- Pepper
- Salt

Directions:

1. Brush turkey with oil and season with crushed peppercorns and salt. Set aside for 20 minutes.
2. Heat grill over high heat.
3. Grill turkey breasts for 10 minutes. Turn once.
4. In a bowl, mix together all salsa ingredients.
5. Pour salsa on a serving plate and top with turkey breasts.
6. Serve and enjoy.

Nutritional Value (Amount per Serving):

Calories 150; Fat 5 g; Carbohydrates 10 g; Sugar 4 g; Protein 18 g; Cholesterol 87 mg

Indian Tandoori Chicken

Preparation Time: 10 minutes; Cooking Time: 15 minutes; Serve: 4

Ingredients:

- 1 ¼ lbs chicken breasts, skinless and boneless
- 1 tsp ground coriander
- 1 tbsp paprika
- 2 tbsp olive oil
- ½ cup of coconut milk
- 1 tsp turmeric powder
- 1 tsp ground ginger
- 1 tsp ground cumin
- 1 tsp salt

Directions:

1. In a large bowl, whisk together coconut milk, turmeric, ginger, cumin, coriander, paprika, olive oil, and salt.
2. Add chicken to the bowl and mix until well coated.
3. Cover and place in fridge for overnight.
4. Preheat the grill.
5. Place marinated chicken on hot grill and grill until cooked.
6. Serve and enjoy.

Nutritional Value (Amount per Serving):

Calories 405; Fat 25 g; Carbohydrates 3 g; Sugar 1 g; Protein 43 g; Cholesterol 85 mg

Delicious Butter Chicken

Preparation Time: 10 minutes; Cooking Time: 5 Hours; Serve: 5

Ingredients:

- 1 lb chicken thighs, boneless and skinless
- 1 lb chicken breasts, boneless and skinless
- ¼ cup tomato paste
- 1 tbsp ginger garlic paste
- 1 ½ tbsp garam masala
- 1 tbsp curry powder
- 1/3 cup heavy cream
- 2 tbsp butter
- ½ cup chicken broth
- ¾ tsp kosher salt

Directions:

1. Cut chicken into chunks and add in crock pot.
2. Add remaining ingredients except cream into the crock pot and stir well.
3. Seal with lid and cook on low for 5 hours.
4. Stir in cream and cover for 10 minutes.
5. Serve and enjoy.

Nutritional Value (Amount per Serving):

Calories 425; Fat 21 g; Carbohydrates 4 g; Sugar 2 g; Protein 54 g; Cholesterol 75 mg

Chapter 4: Pork, Beef & Lamb Recipes

Pan Fry Pork Chops

Preparation Time: 10 minutes; Cooking Time: 8 minutes; Serve: 4

Ingredients:

- 4 pork chops, boneless
- 2 tbsp olive oil
- 1/4 tsp onion powder
- 1/4 tsp garlic powder
- 1/4 tsp pepper
- Salt

Directions:

1. Heat oil in cast iron skillet over high heat.
2. Season pork chops with garlic powder, onion powder, pepper, and salt.
3. Sear pork chops in hot oil about 3-4 minutes on each side.
4. Serve and enjoy.

Nutritional Value (Amount per Serving):

Calories 317; Fat 26 g; Carbohydrates 0.3 g; Sugar 0.1 g; Protein 18 g; Cholesterol 69 mg

Juicy & Tender Baked Pork Chops

Preparation Time: 10 minutes; Cooking Time: 35 minutes; Serve: 4

Ingredients:

- 4 pork chops, boneless
- 2 tbsp olive oil
- ½ tsp Italian seasoning
- ½ tsp paprika
- ½ tsp garlic powder
- ¼ tsp pepper
- ½ tsp sea salt

Directions:

1. Preheat the oven to 375 F.
2. In a small bowl, mix together garlic powder, paprika, Italian seasoning, pepper, and salt.
3. Brush pork chops with oil and rub with garlic powder mixture.
4. Place pork chops onto a baking tray and bake in preheated oven for 30-35 minutes.
5. Serve and enjoy.

Nutritional Value (Amount per Serving):

Calories 320; Fat 27 g; Carbohydrates 0.5 g; Sugar 0.2 g; Protein 18 g; Cholesterol 69 mg

Grilled Cilantro Lime Pork Chops

Preparation Time: 10 minutes; Cooking Time: 15 minutes; Serve: 2

Ingredients:

- 2 pork chops, boneless
- ¼ cup fresh cilantro, chopped
- For marinade:
- 1 tsp erythritol
- ¼ tsp chili powder
- ½ tsp ground cumin
- 2 tbsp fresh lime juice
- Salt

Directions:

1. Add all marinade ingredients in a mixing bowl and mix well.
2. Add pork chops in marinade and mix well and place in refrigerator for 15 minutes.
3. Preheat the grill over medium heat.
4. Remove pork chops from marinade and place on hot grill and cook for 7 minutes.
5. Turn pork chops to other side and cook for 7 minutes more.
6. Top with cilantro and serve.

Nutritional Value (Amount per Serving):
Calories 259; Fat 20 g; Carbohydrates 0.5 g; Sugar 0.1 g; Protein 18 g; Cholesterol 69 mg

Simple Grilled Pork Tenderloin

Preparation Time: 10 minutes; Cooking Time: 30 minutes; Serve: 8
Ingredients:
- 2 lbs pork tenderloin
- 2 tbsp ranch dressing mix
- 2 tbsp olive oil

Directions:
1. Preheat the grill to 350 F.
2. Brush pork loin with oil and season with ranch dressing.
3. Place pork loin on hot grill and cook for 30 minutes. Turn tenderloin every 10 minutes.
4. Slice and serve.

Nutritional Value (Amount per Serving):
Calories 175; Fat 7 g; Carbohydrates 2 g; Sugar 2 g; Protein 23 g; Cholesterol 73 mg

Grilled Ranch Pork Chops

Preparation Time: 10 minutes; Cooking Time: 16 minutes; Serve: 4
Ingredients:
- 4 pork chops, boneless
- 2 tbsp fresh parsley, chopped
- 1 tbsp ranch seasoning
- 1 tbsp olive oil
- Pepper
- Salt

Directions:
1. Preheat the grill over medium-high heat.
2. Brush pork chops with oil and rub with ranch seasoning, pepper, and salt.
3. Place pork chops on hot grill and cook for 6-8 minutes.
4. Turn to other side and cook for 6-8 minutes more.
5. Garnish with parsley and serve.

Nutritional Value (Amount per Serving):
Calories 287; Fat 23 g; Carbohydrates 0.1 g; Sugar 0 g; Protein 18 g; Cholesterol 69 mg

Rosrmary Garlic Pork Chops

Preparation Time: 10 minutes; Cooking Time: 35 minutes; Serve: 4
Ingredients:
- 4 pork chops, boneless
- ¼ tsp onion powder
- 2 garlic cloves, minced
- 1 tsp dried rosemary, crushed

- ¼ tsp pepper
- ¼ tsp sea salt

Directions:

1. Preheat the oven to 425 F.
2. Season pork chops with onion powder, pepper and salt.
3. Mix together rosemary and garlic and rub over pork chops.
4. Place pork chops on baking tray and roast for 10 minutes.
5. Set temperature 350 F and roast for 25 minutes more.
6. Serve and enjoy.

Nutritional Value (Amount per Serving):

Calories 260; Fat 20 g; Carbohydrates 1 g; Sugar 0 g; Protein 19 g; Cholesterol 70 mg

Delicious Minced Pork

Preparation Time: 10 minutes; Cooking Time: 20 minutes; Serve: 3

Ingredients:

- 14 oz minced pork
- 1/4 cup green bell pepper, chopped
- 1/2 onion, chopped
- 2 tbsp water
- ¼ tsp cumin powder
- 3/4 cup ketchup, sugar-free
- 1/2 tbsp olive oil
- Pepper
- Salt

Directions:

1. Heat oil in pan over medium heat.
2. Add pepper and onion and sauté until soften.
3. Add meat, pepper, cumin powder, and salt and cook until browned.
4. Add water and ketchup and stir well. Bring to boil.
5. Serve and enjoy.

Nutritional Value (Amount per Serving):

Calories 275; Fat 7 g; Carbohydrates 14 g; Sugar 13 g; Protein 36 g; Cholesterol 95 mg

Flavorful Pork Chops

Preparation Time: 10 minutes; Cooking Time: 8 hours; Serve: 4

Ingredients:

- 4 pork chops, boneless
- 1/2 tbsp garlic powder
- 1 tbsp paprika
- 3 garlic cloves, minced
- 1 cup vegetable broth
- 1/4 cup olive oil
- 1/2 tsp dried basil
- 1/2 tsp dried oregano
- 1 tbsp Italian seasoning
- Pepper
- Salt

Directions:

1. In a bowl, whisk together basil, oregano, Italian seasoning, garlic powder, paprika, garlic, broth, and olive oil. Pour into the crock pot.
2. Season pork chops with pepper and salt and place into the crock pot.
3. Cover and cook on low for 8 hours.
4. Serve and enjoy.

Nutritional Value (Amount per Serving):

Calories 390; Fat 32 g; Carbohydrates 4 g; Sugar 1 g; Protein 20 g; Cholesterol 70 mg

Cinnamon Olive Pork Chops

Preparation Time: 10 minutes; Cooking Time: 30 minutes; Serve: 6
Ingredients:

- 6 pork chops, boneless and cut into thick slices
- 1/2 cup olives, pitted and sliced
- 7.5 oz ragu
- 1 tbsp olive oil
- 1/4 cup beef broth
- 3 garlic cloves, chopped
- 1/8 tsp ground cinnamon
- 1 large onion, sliced

Directions:

1. Heat oil in a pan over medium-high heat.
2. Add pork chops in a pan and cook until lightly brown and set aside.
3. Cook garlic and onion and cook until onion is softened.
4. Add broth and bring to boil.
5. Return pork chops to pan and stir in ragu and remaining ingredients.
6. Cover and simmer for 20 minutes.
7. Serve and enjoy.

Nutritional Value (Amount per Serving):
Calories 320; Fat 22 g; Carbohydrates 6 g; Sugar 1 g; Protein 20 g; Cholesterol 70 mg

Thyme Oregano Pork Roast

Preparation Time: 10 minutes; Cooking Time: 1 hour 40 minutes; Serve: 6
Ingredients:

- 3 lbs pork roast, boneless
- 1 cup chicken stock
- 1 onion, chopped
- 2 garlic cloves, chopped
- 1 rosemary sprig
- 3 fresh oregano sprigs
- 3 fresh thyme sprigs
- 1 tbsp pepper
- 1 tbsp olive oil
- 1 tbsp kosher salt

Directions:

1. Preheat the oven to 350 F.
2. Season meat with pepper and salt.
3. Heat olive oil in a stockpot and sear pork roast on each side, about 4 minutes on each side.
4. Add onion and garlic. Stir in the stock, oregano, and thyme and bring to boil for a minute.
5. Cover pot and roast in the preheated oven for 1 hour 30 minutes.
6. Serve and enjoy.

Nutritional Value (Amount per Serving):
Calories 501; Fat 24 g; Carbohydrates 3 g; Sugar 1 g; Protein 65 g; Cholesterol 194 mg

Italian Pork Chops

Preparation Time: 10 minutes; Cooking Time: 30 minutes; Serve: 4
Ingredients:

- 4 pork loin chops, boneless
- 2 garlic cloves, minced

- 1 tsp Italian seasoning
- 1 tbsp fresh rosemary, chopped
- 1/4 tsp black pepper
- 1/2 tsp kosher salt

Directions:

1. Season pork chops with pepper and salt.
2. In a small bowl, mix together garlic, Italian seasoning, and rosemary.
3. Rub Pork chops with garlic and rosemary mixture.
4. Place pork chops on a baking tray and roast in oven at 425 F for 10 minutes.
5. Turn temperature to 350 F and roast for 25 minutes more
6. Serve and enjoy.

Nutritional Value (Amount per Serving):

- Calories 261; Fat 19 g; Carbohydrates 2 g; Sugar 0 g; Protein 18 g; Cholesterol 68 mg

Lemon Pepper Pork Tenderloin

Preparation Time: 10 minutes; Cooking Time: 25 minutes; Serve: 4

Ingredients:

- 1 lb pork tenderloin
- 3/4 tsp lemon pepper
- 1 1/2 tsp dried oregano
- 1 tbsp olive oil
- 4 tbsp feta cheese, crumbled
- 2 1/2 tbsp olive tapenade

Directions:

1. Add pork, oil, lemon pepper, and oregano in a zip-lock bag. Seal bag and rub well and place in a refrigerator for 2 hours.
2. Remove pork from zip-lock bag.
3. Using a sharp knife make lengthwise cut through the center of the tenderloin.
4. Spread olive tapenade on half tenderloin and sprinkle with crumbled cheese.
5. Fold another half of meat over to the original shape of tenderloin.
6. Close pork tenderloin with twine at 2-inch intervals.
7. Grill for 20 minutes. Turn tenderloin during grilling.
8. Sliced and serve.

Nutritional Value (Amount per Serving):

Calories 215; Fat 10 g; Carbohydrates 1 g; Sugar 1 g; Protein 31 g; Cholesterol 90 mg

Roasmary Garlic Pork Roast

Preparation Time: 10 minutes; Cooking Time: 1 hour 10 minutes; Serve: 6

Ingredients:

- 4 lbs pork loin roast, boneless
- 4 garlic cloves, peeled
- 2 lemon juice
- 1/4 cup fresh sage leaves
- 1/3 cup fresh rosemary leaves
- 1 tbsp salt

Directions:

1. Add sage, rosemary, garlic, lemon juice, and salt into the blender and blend until smooth.
2. Rub herb paste all over roast and place on hot grill.
3. Grill for 1 hour.
4. Sliced and serve.

Nutritional Value (Amount per Serving):

Calories 655; Fat 30 g; Carbohydrates 5 g; Sugar 1 g; Protein 88 g; Cholesterol 246 mg

Pork Egg Roll Bowl

Preparation Time: 10 minutes; Cooking Time: 10 minutes; Serve: 6
Ingredients:
- 1 lb ground pork
- 3 tbsp soy sauce
- 1 tbsp sesame oil
- 1/2 onion, sliced
- 1 medium cabbage head, sliced
- 2 tbsp green onion, chopped
- 2 tbsp chicken broth
- 1 tsp ground ginger
- 2 garlic cloves, minced
- Pepper
- Salt

Directions:
1. Brown meat in a pan over medium heat.
2. Add oil and onion to the pan with meat. Mix well and cook over medium heat.
3. In a small bowl, mix together soy sauce, ginger, and garlic.
4. Add soy sauce mixture to the pan.
5. Add cabbage to the pan and toss to coat.
6. Add broth to the pan and mix well.
7. Cook over medium heat for 3 minutes.
8. Season with pepper and salt.
9. Garnish with green onion and serve.

Nutritional Value (Amount per Serving):
Calories 171; Fat 5 g; Carbohydrates 10 g; Sugar 5 g; Protein 23 g; Cholesterol 56 mg

Onion Paprika Pork Tenderloin

Preparation Time: 10 minutes; Cooking Time: 30 minutes; Serve: 6
Ingredients:
- 2 lbs pork tenderloin
- For rub:
- 1 1/2 tbsp smoked paprika
- 1 tbsp garlic powder
- 1 1/2 tbsp onion powder
- ½ tbsp salt

Directions:
1. Preheat the oven to 425 F.
2. In a small bowl, mix together all rub ingredients and rub over pork tenderloin.
3. Spray pan with cooking spray and heat over medium-high heat.
4. Sear pork on all sides until lightly golden brown.
5. Place pan into the oven and roast for about 25-30 minutes.
6. Sliced and serve.

Nutritional Value (Amount per Serving):
Calories 225; Fat 5 g; Carbohydrates 2 g; Sugar 1 g; Protein 41 g; Cholesterol 45 mg

Stuff Cheese Pork Chops

Preparation Time: 10 minutes; Cooking Time: 25 minutes; Serve: 4
Ingredients:
- 4 pork chops, boneless and thick cut
- 2 tbsp olives, chopped
- 2 tbsp sun-dried tomatoes, chopped
- ½ cup feta cheese, crumbled
- 2 garlic cloves, minced
- 2 tbsp fresh parsley, chopped

Directions:

1. Preheat the oven to 375 F.
2. In a bowl, mix together feta cheese, garlic, parsley, olives, and sun-dried tomatoes.
3. Stuff feta cheese mixture in the pork chops. Season with pepper and salt.
4. Bake for 35 minutes.
5. Serve and enjoy.

Nutritional Value (Amount per Serving):
Calories 316; Fat 25 g; Carbohydrates 2 g; Sugar 1 g; Protein 21 g; Cholesterol 75 mg

Herb Pork Chops

Preparation Time: 10 minutes; Cooking Time: 30 minutes; Serve: 4
Ingredients:
- 4 pork chops, boneless
- 1 tbsp olive oil
- 2 garlic cloves, minced
- 1 tsp dried rosemary, crushed
- 1 tsp oregano
- ½ tsp thyme
- 1 tbsp fresh rosemary, chopped
- ¼ tsp pepper
- ¼ tsp salt

Directions:
1. Preheat the oven 425 F.
2. Season pork chops with pepper and salt and set aside.
3. In a small bowl, mix together garlic, oil, rosemary, oregano, thyme, and fresh rosemary and rub over pork chops.
4. Place pork chops on baking tray and roast for 10 minutes.
5. Turn heat to 350 F and roast for 25 minutes more.
6. Serve and enjoy.

Nutritional Value (Amount per Serving):
Calories 260; Fat 22 g; Carbohydrates 2.5 g; Sugar 0 g; Protein 19 g; Cholesterol 65 mg

Greek Pork Chops

Preparation Time: 10 minutes; Cooking Time: 20 minutes; Serve: 4
Ingredients:
- 4 pork chops, boneless
- 1 cup feta cheese, crumbled
- 2 zucchini, sliced
- 1 cup chicken stock
- 2 tsp oregano
- 1 tbsp garlic, minced
- ¼ cup olives, cut in half
- 2 cups cherry tomatoes, halved
- ¼ cup olive oil

Directions:
1. Season pork chops with pepper and salt.
2. Heat 2 tablespoons of oil in a pan over medium heat.
3. Add pork chops to the pan and cook until lightly brown from both the sides, about 3-5 minutes. Transfer pork chops on a plate.
4. Add remaining oil to the pan.
5. Add zucchini and cook 5 minutes.
6. Add garlic and sauté for 30 seconds.
7. Add oregano and stock and simmer for 2 minutes.
8. Set zucchini one side of the pan.
9. Return pork chops to the pan and cook until chops are no longer pink.

10. Transfer zucchini and pork chops to a plate.
11. Add olive and tomatoes to the pan and stir for a minute.
12. Pour olive and tomatoes over pork chops.
13. Top with feta cheese and serve.

Nutritional Value (Amount per Serving):
Calories 510; Fat 41 g; Carbohydrates 11 g; Sugar 6 g; Protein 26 g; Cholesterol 85 mg

Flavors Baked Pork Tenderloin

Preparation Time: 15 minutes; Cooking Time: 35 minutes; Serve: 6
Ingredients:
- 2 lbs pork tenderloin
- 3 garlic cloves, chopped
- Pepper
- Salt
- For the spice mix:
- ½ tsp allspice
- 1 tsp cinnamon
- 1/2 tsp cumin
- 1/2 tsp coriander powder
- ¼ tsp cayenne
- 1/2 tsp oregano
- ¼ tsp cloves

Directions:
1. Preheat the oven to 375 F.
2. In a small bowl, mix together all spice ingredients and set aside.
3. Make slits on pork tenderloin using a knife and insert chopped garlic into each slit.
4. Rub spice mixture over pork tenderloin.
5. Place pork tenderloin on greased baking tray and bake for 30-35 minutes.
6. Slice and serve.

Nutritional Value (Amount per Serving):
Calories 220; Fat 6 g; Carbohydrates 2 g; Sugar 0.1 g; Protein 40 g; Cholesterol 74 mg

Dijon Pork Chops

Preparation Time: 10 minutes; Cooking Time: 20 minutes; Serve: 4
Ingredients:
- 4 pork chops, boneless
- ½ cup coconut milk
- ½ cup chicken stock
- 2 tsp arrowroot
- 2 tbsp onion, minced
- 2 tbsp olive oil
- 1 tbsp Dijon mustard
- Pepper
- Salt

Directions:
1. Heat 1 tablespoon of oil in a pan over medium heat.
2. Season chops with pepper and salt and place to the pan.
3. Cook pork chops for 3 minutes on each side. Transfer pork chops to a plate.
4. Whisk stock and arrowroot together. Add mustard and coconut milk and whisk well and set aside.
5. Heat remaining oil in a pan over medium heat.

6. Add onion to the pan and sauté until softened. Pour stock mixture and stir well. Bring to boil.
7. Return pork chops to the pan and cook until sauce thickened.
8. Serve and enjoy.

Nutritional Value (Amount per Serving):
    Calories 311; Fat 24 g; Carbohydrates 4 g; Sugar 2 g; Protein 20 g; Cholesterol 68 mg

Lemon Garlic Pork Medallions

Preparation Time: 10 minutes; Cooking Time: 15 minutes; Serve: 4

Ingredients:

- 2 lbs pork tenderloin, sliced into medallions
- 2 tbsp lemon juice
- 1 tsp lemon zest, grated
- 3 tbsp olive oil
- 1 tsp dried oregano
- 2 garlic cloves, minced
- 1 ½ tsp vinegar
- Pepper
- Salt

Directions:

1. Add all ingredients into the large zip-lock bag.
2. Seal bag and shake well and place in fridge for 2 hours.
3. Spray grill pan with cooking spray and heat over medium-high heat.
4. Place medallions in the pan and cook until lightly golden brown, about 4 minutes on each side.
5. Serve and enjoy.

Nutritional Value (Amount per Serving):
    Calories 425; Fat 19 g; Carbohydrates 3 g; Sugar 1 g; Protein 60 g; Cholesterol 47 mg

Herb Butter Pork Chops

Preparation Time: 10 minutes; Cooking Time: 1 hour 15 minutes; Serve: 4

Ingredients:

- 4 pork chops, boneless
- 1 tbsp olive oil
- ½ tsp dried sage
- ½ tsp dried parsley
- ½ cup chicken broth
- 1 tbsp butter
- 1 ½ tsp chives
- ¼ tsp pepper
- ¼ tsp salt

Directions:

1. Preheat the oven to 350 F.
2. Season pork chops with pepper and place in greased baking pan.
3. In a small bowl, mix together butter, oil, sage, parsley, and chives.
4. Rub herb butter mixture on top of each pork chops.
5. Add broth in pan around the pork chops.
6. Cover with foil and bake for 1 hour.
7. Uncover and bake for 15 minutes more.
8. Serve and enjoy.

Nutritional Value (Amount per Serving):
    Calories 315; Fat 27 g; Carbohydrates 1 g; Sugar 1 g; Protein 19 g; Cholesterol 68 mg

Tender Pork Tenderloin

Preparation Time: 10 minutes; Cooking Time: 35 minutes; Serve: 3

Ingredients:

- 1 lb pork tenderloin
- ½ tbsp dried rosemary
- ¼ tsp thyme
- 1 tbsp olive oil
- Pepper
- Salt

Directions:

1. Preheat the oven to 400 F.
2. Mix together rosemary, thyme, and olive oil and rub over pork tenderloin.
3. Place pork tenderloin on baking pan and roast for 35 minutes.
4. Season with pepper and salt. Slice and serve.

Nutritional Value (Amount per Serving):

Calories 255; Fat 10 g; Carbohydrates 1 g; Sugar 0 g; Protein 40 g; Cholesterol 75 mg

Flavors Grilled Pork Chops

Preparation Time: 10 minutes; Cooking Time: 10 minutes; Serve: 4

Ingredients:

- 4 pork chops, boneless
- 1 tsp ground cumin
- 1 tbsp olive oil
- 2 tbsp tahini
- ¼ cup yogurt
- ½ tsp allspice
- ½ tsp ground cinnamon
- 1 tsp paprika
- ½ tsp ground coriander
- ½ tsp salt

Directions:

1. In a mixing bowl, whisk together yogurt, allspice, cinnamon, paprika, coriander, cumin, olive oil, tahini, and salt.
2. Add pork chops in yogurt mixture and coat well and place in fridge for 4 hours.
3. Heat grill over medium-high heat.
4. Place pork chops on hot grill and cook for 3-4 minutes each side.
5. Serve and enjoy.

Nutritional Value (Amount per Serving):

Calories 360; Fat 29 g; Carbohydrates 8 g; Sugar 5 g; Protein 20 g; Cholesterol 95 mg

Italian Seasoned Pork Chops

Preparation Time: 10 minutes; Cooking Time: 3 Hours; Serve: 6

Ingredients:

- 6 pork chops, boneless
- 14.5 oz can tomatoes, diced
- 1 onion, chopped
- 1/4 cup water
- 1 1/2 tsp garlic powder
- 1 1/2 tsp Italian seasoning
- 1/3 cup olive oil

Directions:

1. Place pork chops into the instant pot.
2. Pour remaining ingredients over the pork chops.

3. Seal pot with lid and select slow cook mode and cook on low for 3 hours.

4. Allow to release pressure naturally then open the lid.
5. Serve and enjoy.

Nutritional Value (Amount per Serving):
    Calories 381; Fat 32 g; Carbohydrates 7 g; Sugar 4 g; Protein 19 g; Cholesterol 58 mg

Cheesy Meatballs

Preparation Time: 10 minutes; Cooking Time: 10 minutes; Serve: 3
Ingredients:
- 1 lb ground beef
- ½ tsp garlic powder
- ¼ cup parmesan cheese
- 1 cup mozzarella cheese, cut into cubes
- ½ tsp pepper
- ½ tsp salt

Directions:
1. In a large mixing bowl, mix together ground meat, parmesan cheese, garlic powder, pepper, and salt.
2. Wrap mozzarella cheese cubes in ground meat and make round ball.
3. Fry meatballs in a pan. Cover pan with lid during the cooking.
4. Serve and enjoy.

Nutritional Value (Amount per Serving):
    Calories 310; Fat 11 g; Carbohydrates 0.9 g; Sugar 0.1 g; Protein 48g; Cholesterol 140 mg

Easy Curry Bowl

Preparation Time: 10 minutes; Cooking Time: 10 minutes; Serve: 4
Ingredients:
- 1 ½ lbs ground beef
- 5 ½ cups spinach, chopped
- ½ cup coconut cream
- 2 tbsp curry powder
- 3 garlic cloves, minced
- 1 onion, chopped
- 1 tbsp olive oil

Directions:
1. Heat oil in a pan over medium heat.
2. Add onion to the pan and sauté until soften.
3. Add garlic and curry powder and sauté for minute.
4. Add meat and sauté until cooked.
5. Add coconut cream and stir well.
6. Add spinach and sauté until spinach is wilted.
7. Serve and enjoy.

Nutritional Value (Amount per Serving):
    Calories 450; Fat 21 g; Carbohydrates 8 g; Sugar 2.5 g; Protein 54 g; Cholesterol 152 mg

Perfect Beef Casserole

Preparation Time: 10 minutes; Cooking Time: 35 minutes; Serve: 8
Ingredients:
- 1 lb ground beef
- ½ cup mozzarella cheese, shredded

- ½ cup cheddar cheese, shredded
- 2 cans green beans, drained
- ½ tsp garlic powder
- ½ cup heavy cream
- ½ cup chicken broth
- 3 oz cream cheese
- ½ tsp pepper
- ½ tsp salt

Directions:

1. Preheat the oven to 350 F.
2. Brown meat in pan. Add cream cheese and stir until cheese is melted.
3. Add broth, garlic powder, heavy cream, pepper, and salt and stir well. Bring to boil.
4. Turn heat to medium and simmer until mixture thickened.
5. Add green beans then sprinkle cheese on top and bake in preheated oven for 25 minutes.
6. Serve and enjoy.

Nutritional Value (Amount per Serving):

Calories 280; Fat 20 g; Carbohydrates 4 g; Sugar 2 g; Protein 18 g; Cholesterol 88 mg

Mexican Beef with Zucchini

Preparation Time: 10 minutes; Cooking Time: 25 minutes; Serve: 6
Ingredients:

- 1 ½ lbs ground beef
- ¼ tsp red pepper flakes
- ½ tsp onion powder
- ½ tsp ground cumin
- ½ tbsp chili powder
- 10 oz salsa
- 2 garlic cloves, minced
- 2 zucchini, diced
- ½ tsp pepper
- 1 tsp salt

Directions:

1. Brown meat in pan with garlic, pepper, and salt.
2. Add tomatoes and spices and stir well.
3. Cover and simmer over low heat for 10 minutes.
4. Add remaining ingredients and cook for 10 minutes more.
5. Serve and enjoy.

Nutritional Value (Amount per Serving):

Calories 239; Fat 7.5 g; Carbohydrates 6.2 g; Sugar 2.7 g; Protein 36 g; Cholesterol 101 mg

Mexican Beef

Preparation Time: 10 minutes; Cooking Time: 9 Hours; Serve: 10
Ingredients:

- 3 lbs beef chuck roast
- ½ tsp red chili flakes
- 1 tsp dried oregano
- ½ tsp paprika
- 1 tsp cumin
- 1 tbsp chili powder
- 2 tbsp lemon juice
- 2 tbsp tomato paste
- 3 garlic cloves, minced
- 1 onion, diced
- 1 tsp kosher salt

Directions:

1. In a small bowl, mix together all spices and set aside.
2. Add onion, garlic, lemon juice, and tomato paste in slow cooker and stir well.
3. Place meat into the slow cooker and sprinkle spice mixture all over meat.
4. Cover and cook on low for 8 hours.
5. Remove meat from slow cooker and shred using fork.
6. Return shredded meat to the slow cooker and cook for 60 minutes more.
7. Serve and enjoy.

Nutritional Value (Amount per Serving):
Calories 507; Fat 38 g; Carbohydrates 2.7 g; Sugar 1 g; Protein 36 g; Cholesterol 140 mg

Asian Beef Stew

Preparation Time: 10 minutes; Cooking Time: 5 hours 15 minutes; Serve: 8
Ingredients:
- 3 lbs beef stew meat, trimmed
- 2 tsp ginger, minced
- 2 garlic cloves, minced
- 1/3 cup tomato paste
- 14.5 oz can coconut milk
- 1 medium onion, sliced
- 2 tbsp olive oil
- 2 cups carrots, julienned
- 2 cups broccoli florets
- 2 tsp fresh lime juice
- 2 tbsp soy sauce
- 1/2 cup curry paste
- 2 Tsp sea salt

Directions:
1. Heat 1 tbsp oil in a pan over medium-high heat.
2. Add meat and brown the meat on all sides.
3. Transfer meat to crock pot.
4. Add remaining oil in a pan and sauté ginger, garlic, and onion over medium-high heat for 5 minutes.
5. Add coconut milk and stir well.
6. Transfer pan mixture to the crock pot.
7. Add remaining ingredients except for carrots and broccoli into the crock pot.
8. Cover and cook on high for 5 hours.
9. Add carrots and broccoli during the last 30 minutes of cooking.
10. Serve and enjoy.

Nutritional Value (Amount per Serving):
Calories 535; Fat 28 g; Carbohydrates 12 g; Sugar 3 g; Protein 55 g; Cholesterol 150 mg

Beef Roast

Preparation Time: 10 minutes; Cooking Time: 5 Hours; Serve: 6
Ingredients:
- 2 1/2 lbs beef roast
- 1 tbsp ground coriander
- 1 tbsp garam masala
- 1 Serrano pepper, minced
- 1 tbsp ginger, grated
- 5 garlic cloves, minced
- 2 tbsp fresh lemon juice
- 20 curry leaves
- 1 tsp mustard seeds
- 2 tbsp coconut oil
- 1 large onion, chopped
- 1/4 cup coconut slices
- 1/2 tsp ground pepper
- 1 tsp turmeric
- 1 1/2 tsp chili powder
- 1 tsp salt

Directions:

1. Add oil, mustard seeds, onion, and salt into the crock pot and cook on high for 1 hour.
2. Add remaining ingredients except for coconut and cook on high for 3 hours.
3. Shred meat using a fork.
4. Add coconut slices and cook on high for 1 hour.
5. Serve and enjoy.

Nutritional Value (Amount per Serving):

Calories 445; Fat 19 g; Carbohydrates 7 g; Sugar 2 g; Protein 59 g; Cholesterol 170 mg

Almond Cinnamon Beef Meatballs

Preparation Time: 10 minutes; Cooking Time: 25 minutes; Serve: 8

Ingredients:

- 2 lbs ground beef
- 3 eggs
- ½ cup fresh parsley, minced
- 1 tsp cinnamon
- 1 ½ tsp dried oregano
- 2 tsp cumin
- 1 tsp garlic, minced
- 1 cup almond flour
- 1 medium onion, grated
- 1 tsp pepper
- 2 tsp salt

Directions:

1. Preheat the oven to 400 F.
2. Add all ingredients into the mixing bowl and mix until well combined.
3. Make small meatballs from mixture and place on greased baking tray and bake for 20-25 minutes.
4. Serve and enjoy.

Nutritional Value (Amount per Serving):

Calories 325; Fat 16 g; Carbohydrates 6 g; Sugar 2 g; Protein 40 g; Cholesterol 54 mg

Creamy Beef Stroganoff

Preparation Time: 10 minutes; Cooking Time: 20 minutes; Serve: 4

Ingredients:

- 1 lb beef strips
- 3/4 cup mushrooms, sliced
- 1 small onion, chopped
- 1 tbsp butter
- 2 tbsp olive oil
- 2 tbsp green onion, chopped
- 1/4 cup sour cream
- 1 cup chicken broth
- Pepper
- Salt

Directions:

1. Add meat in bowl and coat with 1 teaspoon oil, pepper and salt.
2. Heat remaining oil in a pan.
3. Add meat to pan and cook until golden brown on both sides.
4. Transfer meat in bowl and set aside.
5. Add butter in same pan.
6. Add onion and cook until onion softened.
7. Add mushrooms and sauté until the liquid is absorbed.
8. Add broth and cook until sauce thickened.

9. Add sour cream, green onion, and meat and stir well.

10. Cook over medium-high heat for 3-4 minutes.
11. Serve and enjoy.

Nutritional Value (Amount per Serving):
Calories 345; Fat 20 g; Carbohydrates 3 g; Sugar 2 g; Protein 35 g; Cholesterol 115 mg

Roasted Beef

Preparation Time: 10 minutes; Cooking Time: 30 minutes; Serve: 6
Ingredients:
- 2 lbs sirloin steak, cut into 1-inch cubes
- 1/4 cup water
- 1/4 cup olive oil
- 2 cups fresh parsley, chopped
- 3 garlic cloves, minced
- 2 tbsp fresh lemon juice
- 2 tsp dried oregano
- 1/2 tsp black pepper
- 1 tsp salt

Directions:
1. Add all ingredients except meat into the large bowl and coat well.
2. Cover bowl and place in fridge for 1 hour.
3. Preheat the oven 400 F.
4. Place marinated beef on a baking tray and bake for 30 minutes.
5. Serve and enjoy.

Nutritional Value (Amount per Serving):
Calories 366; Fat 18 g; Carbohydrates 2 g; Sugar 1 g; Protein 45 g; Cholesterol 132 mg

Braised Beef

Preparation Time: 10 minutes; Cooking Time: 8 Hours; Serve: 6
Ingredients:
- 2 lbs beef chuck roast
- ¼ cup balsamic vinegar
- 1 cup water
- 2 tbsp arrowroot
- 4 shallots, sliced
- 1 medium onion, sliced
- ¼ tsp pepper
- ½ tsp salt

Directions:
1. Place meat into the crock pot.
2. In a mixing bowl, mix together all remaining ingredients and pour over meat.
3. Cover and cook on low for 8 hours.
4. Serve and enjoy.

Nutritional Value (Amount per Serving):
Calories 560; Fat 42 g; Carbohydrates 2.2 g; Sugar 0.8 g; Protein 40 g; Cholesterol 156 mg

Delicious Barbacoa Beef

Preparation Time: 10 minutes; Cooking Time: 4 Hours; Serve: 6
Ingredients:
- 2 1/2 lbs chuck roast, boneless
- For sauce:

- 1 tsp Cloves
- 1/2 tbsp cumin
- 2 tbsp adobo sauce
- 2 tbsp olive oil
- 1/2 cup water
- 1 tsp oregano
- 2 tbsp fresh lime juice
- 3 garlic cloves
- 3 tbsp tomato paste
- 1/2 tsp pepper
- 1 tsp salt

Directions:

1. Add all sauce ingredients into the blender and blend well.
2. Place chuck roast into the crock pot.
3. Pour sauce over chuck roast.
4. Cover and cook on high for 4 hours.
5. Remove meat from crock pot and shred using fork.
6. Return shredded meat to the crock pot and stir well.
7. Serve and enjoy.

Nutritional Value (Amount per Serving):

Calories 465; Fat 21 g; Carbohydrates 4 g; Sugar 3 g; Protein 62 g; Cholesterol 190 mg

Italian Pot Roast

Preparation Time: 10 minutes; Cooking Time: 7 Hours 30 minutes; Serve: 6

Ingredients:

- 3 lbs beef chuck roast
- 1 tsp Italian seasoning
- 2 tbsp balsamic vinegar
- 1/4 cup sun-dried tomatoes, chopped
- 15 garlic cloves, peeled and sliced
- 6 green olives, sliced
- 1/2 cup dry red wine
- 1 tsp arrowroot
- 1/4 tsp black pepper

Directions:

1. Add sliced garlic and sun dried tomatoes into the crock pot.
2. Place meat on top of garlic and tomatoes.
3. Pour vinegar and red wine over meat.
4. Season with black pepper and Italian seasoning.
5. Cover and cook on low for 7 hours.
6. Transfer meat on a plate.
7. Set crock pot on high.
8. In a small bowl, whisk together 2 tsp water and arrowroot and pour into the crock pot. Stir well.
9. Cover and cook for 10 minutes more.
10. Stir in olives.
11. Serve and enjoy.

Nutritional Value (Amount per Serving):

Calories 871; Fat 65 g; Carbohydrates 5 g; Sugar 1 g; Protein 61 g; Cholesterol 235 mg

Meat Veggies Skillet

Preparation Time: 10 minutes; Cooking Time: 10 minutes; Serve: 4

Ingredients:

- 1 lb ground beef
- 1 medium zucchini, quartered
- 1 red bell pepper
- 1 onion
- 2 garlic clove, minced
- 1 tbsp feta cheese, crumbled
- 1/2 tsp oregano
- 1/4 cup tomato

- 1 tsp Dijon mustard
- 1/2 lb asparagus, cut into pieces
- 2 tbsp olive oil
- Black pepper
- Salt

Directions:
1. Heat oil into the pan over medium-high heat.
2. Add garlic and meat into the pan and cook for 6-7 minutes. Set aside.
3. Add pepper and onion to the same pan and cook for 4-5 minutes.
4. Add asparagus and zucchini and cook for 3-4 minutes.
5. Add ground beef to the pan again and mix everything well.
6. Add oregano, tomato, Dijon, pepper, and salt and cook for 2 minutes.
7. Garnish with crumbled cheese and serve.

Nutritional Value (Amount per Serving):
Calories 310; Fat 15 g; Carbohydrates 7 g; Sugar 8 g; Protein 35 g; Cholesterol 100 mg

Flavors Beef Carnitas

Preparation Time: 10 minutes; Cooking Time: 8 Hours; Serve: 4
Ingredients:
- 2 lbs flank steak
- 1 green bell pepper, chopped
- 1 onion, chopped
- 2 jalapeno, seeded and chopped
- 1 red bell pepper, chopped
- For rub:
- 1/4 tsp cayenne pepper
- 2 tsp chili powder
- 1/4 tsp garlic powder
- 1/4 tsp onion powder
- 1 tsp cumin
- 1/2 tsp black pepper
- 1 Tsp salt

Directions:
1. In a small bowl, mix together all spice ingredients and rub over meat.
2. Place meat into the crock pot.
3. Add jalapeno pepper, bell peppers, and onion over meat.
4. Cover and cook on low for 8 hours.
5. Remove meat from crock pot and shred using fork.
6. Return shredded meat to the crock pot.
7. Stir well and serve.

Nutritional Value (Amount per Serving):
Calories 475; Fat 20 g; Carbohydrates 8 g; Protein 65 g; Sugar 2.5 g; Cholesterol 124 mg

Artichoke Basil Pepper Beef

Preparation Time: 10 minutes; Cooking Time: 6 Hours; Serve: 6
Ingredients:
- 2 lbs stew beef, cut into 1-inch cubes
- 12 oz roasted red peppers, drained and sliced
- 12 oz artichoke hearts, drained
- 1 onion, diced
- 3/4 tsp dried basil
- 1/2 tsp dried oregano
- 2 cups marinara sauce

Directions:

1. Add all ingredients into the crock pot and stir well to combine.
2. Cover and cook on low for 6 hours.
3. Serve and enjoy.

Nutritional Value (Amount per Serving):

Calories 344; Fat 20 g; Carbohydrates 8 g; Sugar 11 g; Protein 65 g; Cholesterol 67 mg

Beef with Olives

Preparation Time: 10 minutes; Cooking Time: 6 Hours; Serve: 6

Ingredients:

- 2 lbs beef stew meat, cut into 1/2-inch pieces
- 3/4 cup olives, pitted and cut in half
- 28 oz can tomatoes, diced
- ½ cup feta cheese, crumbled
- ¼ tsp pepper
- ½ tsp salt

Directions:

1. Add all ingredients into the crock pot and stir well.
2. Cover and cook on high for 6 hours.
3. Season with pepper and salt.
4. Stir well and serve.

Nutritional Value (Amount per Serving):

Calories 369; Fat 15 g; Carbohydrates 9 g; Sugar 5 g; Protein 50 g; Cholesterol 85 mg

Herb Artichoke Beef

Preparation Time: 10 minutes; Cooking Time: 7 Hours 10 minutes; Serve: 6

Ingredients:

- 2 lbs stew beef, cut into 1-inch cubes
- 14.5 oz can artichoke hearts, drained and halved
- 3/4 cup olives, pitted and chopped
- 14 oz can tomatoes, diced
- 14.5 oz can tomato sauce
- 32 oz chicken stock
- 2 garlic cloves, chopped
- 1 onion, diced
- 1 bay leaf
- 1 tsp ground cumin
- 1/2 tsp dried basil
- 1/2 tsp dried parsley
- 1/2 tsp dried oregano
- 1 tbsp olive oil

Directions:

1. Heat oil in a large pot over medium-high heat.
2. Add meat and cook until brown, about 2 minutes on each side.
3. Transfer meat to the crock pot.
4. Add remaining ingredients and stir well.
5. Cover and cook on low for 7 hours.
6. Serve and enjoy.

Nutritional Value (Amount per Serving):

Calories 320; Fat 13 g; Carbohydrates 14 g; Sugar 6 g; Protein 35 g; Cholesterol 75 mg

Delicious Beef Skewers

Preparation Time: 10 minutes; Cooking Time: 8 minutes; Serve: 4

Ingredients:

- 2 lbs beef sirloin, cut into cubes
- 1 1/2 tsp fresh thyme, minced
- 2 tbsp fresh parsley, minced
- 1/2 tbsp lemon zest
- 2 garlic cloves, minced
- 2 tbsp fresh lemon juice
- ¼ cup olive oil
- 1 1/2 tsp dried oregano
- 2 tsp fresh rosemary, minced
- Pepper
- Salt

Directions:
1. Add all ingredients except meat in a large bowl and mix everything well.
2. Add meat to the bowl and coat well with marinade. Place in fridge for overnight.
3. Preheat the grill medium-high heat.
4. Slide meat onto soaked wooden skewers and grill for 6-8 minutes.
5. Serve and enjoy.

Nutritional Value (Amount per Serving):
Calories 540; Fat 26 g; Carbohydrates 3 g; Sugar 1 g; Protein 70 g; Cholesterol 64 mg

Beef Casserole

Preparation Time: 10 minutes; Cooking Time: 1 Hour 30 minutes; Serve: 6
Ingredients:
- 1 lb lean stew beef, cut into chunks
- 1/2 tsp garlic powder
- 1 1/2 tsp herb de Provence
- 2 tsp paprika
- 2 cups beef stock
- 3.5 oz black olives, sliced
- 8 oz can tomatoes, chopped
- 1 tbsp tomato puree
- 2 tbsp olive oil

Directions:
1. Preheat the oven to 350 F.
2. Heat oil in a pan over medium heat.
3. Add meat and cook until brown.
4. Add stock, olives, tomatoes, tomato puree, garlic powder, herb de Provence, and paprika. Stir well and bring to boil.
5. Pour meat mixture to the casserole dish.
6. Cover and cook in oven for 1 hour 30 minutes.
7. Serve and enjoy.

Nutritional Value (Amount per Serving):
Calories 320; Fat 13 g; Carbohydrates 14 g; Sugar 7 g; Protein 35 g; Cholesterol 65 mg

Herb Vegetable Beef

Preparation Time: 10 minutes; Cooking Time: 1 hour 20 minutes; Serve: 6
Ingredients:
- 2 lbs lean beef, cut into chunks
- 1/2 tsp dried thyme
- 3/4 lb eggplant, cubed
- 1 lb zucchini, sliced
- 1 large onion, chopped
- 5 tbsp olive oil
- 1 lb tomatoes, chopped
- 3 tbsp fresh mint, chopped
- 1/1 tsp dried sage
- Pepper
- Salt

Directions:

1. Heat half oil in a pot over medium heat.
2. Add meat to the pot and cook until brown.
3. Cover meat with water and simmer.
4. Heat remaining oil in other pot.
5. Add vegetables and onions to the pot and sauté until softened.
6. Add tomatoes and stir well with the meat.
7. Add mint, sage, thyme, pepper, and salt. Stir and bring to boil.
8. Reduce heat to low and simmer for 45 minutes.
9. Serve and enjoy.

Nutritional Value (Amount per Serving):

Calories 440; Fat 22 g; Carbohydrates 14 g; Sugar 7 g; Protein 49 g; Cholesterol 75 mg

Beef with Beans

Preparation Time: 10 minutes; Cooking Time: 25 minutes; Serve: 8
Ingredients:

- 1 lb ground beef
- 2 garlic cloves, minced
- 1 large onion, chopped
- 1 tbsp butter
- 1 tbsp olive oil
- 1/2 tbsp Worcestershire sauce
- 14.5 oz tomato sauce
- 1 lb green beans, trimmed and cut into pieces
- 1/2 tsp pepper
- 1 tsp kosher salt

Directions:

1. Heat oil and butter in a large pan over medium heat.
2. Add onion and sauté for 5 minutes.
3. Add garlic and sauté for a minute.
4. Add meat and cook. Stir in Worcestershire sauce, tomato sauce, pepper, and salt. Bring to boil.
5. Turn heat to low and simmer for 20 minutes.
6. Add green beans during last 10 minutes of cooking and stir well.
7. Serve and enjoy.

Nutritional Value (Amount per Serving):

Calories 174; Fat 7 g; Carbohydrates 10 g; Sugar 4 g; Protein 20 g; Cholesterol 54 mg

Sun-dried Meatloaf

Preparation Time: 10 minutes; Cooking Time: 55 minutes; Serve: 6
Ingredients:

- 1 1/2 lbs ground lamb
- 2 eggs
- 2 garlic cloves
- 2 tbsp balsamic vinegar
- 1/2 tbsp fresh rosemary
- 1/2 cup sun-dried tomatoes
- 2 large shallots, chopped
- Pepper
- Salt

Directions:

1. Preheat the oven 375 F.
2. In a bowl, whisk together eggs, salt, pepper, and vinegar.
3. Add rosemary, sun-dried tomatoes, shallots, and garlic and mix well.
4. Add meat and mix until combined.

5. Pour meatloaf mixture into the greased loaf pan and bake for 40-45 minutes.
6. Slice and serve.

Nutritional Value (Amount per Serving):
Calories 250; Fat 10 g; Carbohydrates 3 g; Sugar 2 g; Protein 35 g; Cholesterol 165 mg

Spicy Beef

Preparation Time: 10 minutes; Cooking Time: 4 Hours; Serve: 6
Ingredients:

- 2 lbs beef chuck, sliced
- 1 1/2 tsp garlic powder
- 1 cup beef broth
- 1/2 onion, sliced
- 3 bell pepper, chopped
- 1 tbsp sriracha sauce
- 1/2 cup parsley, chopped
- 1/2 tsp pepper
- 1 1/2 tsp salt

Directions:

1. Place meat into the crock pot.
2. Top with onion and bell pepper.
3. Season with garlic powder, pepper, and salt.
4. Mix together sriracha and broth and pour over meat.
5. Cover and cook on high for 4 hours.
6. Garnish with parsley and serve.

Nutritional Value (Amount per Serving):
Calories 326; Fat 12 g; Carbohydrates 6 g; Sugar 3 g; Protein 48 g; Cholesterol 66 mg

Herb Beef Roast

Preparation Time: 10 minutes; Cooking Time: 8 Hours; Serve: 8
Ingredients:

- 2 1/2 lbs beef round roast
- 1/2 cup red wine
- 1/2 cup water
- 1 onion, sliced
- 1/2 tsp marjoram
- 1 tsp thyme
- 1 tsp basil
- 1/4 tsp pepper
- 1 tsp kosher salt

Directions:

1. In a small bowl, combine together all spices. Set aside.
2. Place beef roast into the crock pot.
3. Sprinkle spice mixture over roast and top with onion.
4. Pour water and wine into the crock pot.
5. Cover and cook on low for 8 hours.
6. Shred the meat using fork
7. Serve and enjoy.

Nutritional Value (Amount per Serving):
Calories 280; Fat 10 g; Carbohydrates 2 g; Sugar 1 g; Protein 40 g; Cholesterol 120 mg

Tasty Shredded Beef

Preparation Time: 10 minutes; Cooking Time: 1 Hour 30 minutes; Serve: 6
Ingredients:

- 3 lbs chuck roast
- 1 1/2 tsp garlic powder
- 2 garlic cloves
- 1/4 cup apple cider vinegar
- 1 cup chicken stock
- 1/2 tsp oregano
- 1 tsp ground ginger
- 1/2 tsp onion powder
- 1/2 tsp marjoram
- 1/4 tsp basil
- 1 tsp sea salt

Directions:
1. Make slits on meat using knife and stuff garlic in each slit.
2. In a small bowl, mix together garlic powder, marjoram, basil, oregano, ginger, onion powder, and salt.
3. Rub garlic powder mixture over meat and place in the instant pot.
4. Pour vinegar and stock over meat.
5. Seal pot with lid and select manual and set timer for 90 minutes.
6. Allow to release pressure naturally then open the lid.
7. Remove meat from pot and shred using a fork.
8. Serve and enjoy.

Nutritional Value (Amount per Serving):
Calories 502; Fat 20 g; Carbohydrates 2 g; Sugar 1 g; Protein 75 g; Cholesterol 85 mg

Tasty Beef Brisket

Preparation Time: 10 minutes; Cooking Time: 6 Hours 20 minutes; Serve: 6
Ingredients:
- 3 1/2 lbs beef brisket
- 2 onion, sliced
- 1 tbsp olive oil
- 4 garlic cloves, minced
- 1 tbsp soy sauce
- 1 1/2 tbsp Worcestershire sauce
- 2 cups beef broth
- Pepper
- Salt

Directions:
1. Heat oil in the pan over medium heat.
2. Add onion and cook until caramelized, about 20 minutes.
3. Season meat with pepper and salt.
4. Heat another pan over medium heat.
5. Place meat in pan and cook until lightly brown.
6. Transfer meat into the crock pot.
7. Sprinkle garlic over meat then add onion.
8. Mix together soy sauce and Worcestershire sauce and pour over meat.
9. Cover crock pot with lid and cook on low for 6 hours.
10. Sliced and serve.

Nutritional Value (Amount per Serving):
Calories 554; Fat 20 g; Carbohydrates 7 g; Sugar 3 g; Protein 83 g; Cholesterol 235 mg

Simple Beef Tacos

Preparation Time: 10 minutes; Cooking Time: 60 minutes; Serve: 4
Ingredients:
- 1 1/2 lbs beef roast
- ¼ cup fresh lime juice
- 1 cup beef stock
- 1/2 tsp ground cumin

- ¼ tsp chili powder
- Pepper
- Salt

Directions:
1. Place meat into the instant pot.
2. Add remaining ingredients into the pot.
3. Seal pot with lid and select manual and cook for 60 minutes.
4. Release pressure using quick release method than open the lid.
5. Remove meat from pot and shred using a fork.
6. Serve and enjoy.

Nutritional Value (Amount per Serving):
Calories 325; Fat 11 g; Carbohydrates 2 g; Sugar 1 g; Protein 52 g; Cholesterol 57 mg

Beef Curry

Preparation Time: 10 minutes; Cooking Time: 6 Hours 10 minutes; Serve: 4
Ingredients:
- 2 lbs stewing beef, cut into cubes
- 1/2 tsp coriander
- 1 tsp cumin
- 1 tbsp garam masala
- 1 tsp turmeric
- 1 tbsp olive oil
- 1/2 tsp lemon zest
- 1tsp paprika
- 1/2 tsp cayenne pepper
- 2 garlic cloves, minced
- 1 onion, chopped
- 1/4 cup fresh cilantro, chopped
- 1/2 cup tomatoes, crushed
- 1/2 cup beef stock
- 1 tsp pepper
- 1 tsp salt

Directions:
1. Heat oil in a pan over medium heat.
2. Add garlic and onion and sauté for 5 minutes.
3. Add spices, pepper, and salt and stir for minute.
4. Stir in crushed tomatoes and transfer pan mixture into the blender and blend until smooth.
5. Place meat into the crock pot and pour sauce mixture, stock, and lemon zest over meat.
6. Cover and cook on low for 6 hours.
7. Garnish with cilantro and serve.

Nutritional Value (Amount per Serving):
Calories 480; Fat 19 g; Carbohydrates 6 g; Protein 71 g; Cholesterol 200 mg

Spicy Shredded Beef

Preparation Time: 10 minutes; Cooking Time: 8 Hours; Serve: 8
Ingredients:
- 3 lbs beef chuck roast
- 1/2 tbsp garlic powder
- 1/2 tbsp onion, minced
- 1/2 cup vinegar
- 4 tbsp butter
- 6 pepper rings
- 5 pepperoncini peppers, chopped
- 2 tsp red pepper flakes
- 1/2 tsp pepper
- 1 tsp kosher salt

Directions:

1. Season meat with pepper and salt.
2. Add all ingredients except meat into the crock pot and stir well.
3. Place meat into the crock pot.
4. Cover and cook on low for 8 hours.
5. Remove meat from crock pot and shred using fork.
6. Return shredded meat to the crock and stir well.
7. Serve and enjoy.

Nutritional Value (Amount per Serving):

Calories 685; Fat 54 g; Carbohydrates 4 g; Protein 46 g; Sugar 2 g; Cholesterol 189 mg

Lamb Patties

Preparation Time: 10 minutes; Cooking Time: 10 minutes; Serve: 4

Ingredients:

- 1 lb ground lamb
- 2 tsp fresh oregano, chopped
- 3 garlic cloves, minced
- 2 tbsp onion, diced
- ½ tsp pepper
- ½ tsp salt

Directions:

1. Preheat the grill over medium-high heat.
2. Add all ingredients into the mixing bowl and mix until well combined.
3. Make patties from meat mixture.
4. Place patties on hot grill and cook for 4 minutes on each side or until cooked through.
5. Serve and enjoy.

Nutritional Value (Amount per Serving):

Calories 219; Fat 8 g; Carbohydrates 1.9 g; Sugar 0.3 g; Protein 32g; Cholesterol 102 mg

Delicious Lamb Curry

Preparation Time: 10 minutes; Cooking Time: 35 minutes; Serve: 4

Ingredients:

- 1 lb lamb mince
- 3 tbsp water
- ½ tsp garam masala
- ½ tsp coriander powder
- ½ tsp turmeric
- ½ tsp cumin powder
- 1 ½ tbsp curry powder
- 2 tbsp olive oil
- ½ cup cheddar cheese, shredded
- 1 cup heavy cream
- ½ tbsp garlic, minced
- ½ tbsp ginger paste
- 1 onion, diced
- 2 tomatoes, diced
- Pepper
- Salt

Directions:

1. Heat oil in a pan over medium-high heat.
2. Add onion, ginger, garlic, and meat and sauté until meat is browned.
3. Add spices, tomatoes, and water and stir well.
4. Cover and simmer for 15-20 minutes.
5. Add cheese and stir for 3-4 minutes.
6. Serve and enjoy.

Nutritional Value (Amount per Serving):

Calories 510; Fat 43 g; Carbohydrates 8 g; Sugar 3 g; Protein 24 g; Cholesterol 56 mg

Lamb Meatballs

Preparation Time: 10 minutes; Cooking Time: 15 minutes; Serve: 6

Ingredients:
- 2 lbs ground lamb
- 2 tbsp olive oil
- 3 tbsp water
- 1 tbsp Italian seasoning
- 1 garlic clove, minced
- ¼ cup fresh parsley, chopped
- ½ cup almond flour
- 2 eggs, lightly beaten
- 1 tsp kosher salt

Directions:
1. Add all ingredients except oil into the mixing bowl and mix well.
2. Make meatballs from meat mixture.
3. Heat oil in a pan over medium heat.
4. Add meatballs in a pan and cook for 2-3 minutes on each side or until cooked through.
5. Serve and enjoy.

Nutritional Value (Amount per Serving):

Calories 404; Fat 22 g; Carbohydrates 2.7 g; Sugar 0.7 g; Protein 46 g; Cholesterol 192 mg

Gluten Free Lamb Curry

Preparation Time: 10 minutes; Cooking Time: 20 minutes; Serve: 4

Ingredients:
- 1 lb lamb stew meat
- 1 bell pepper, chopped
- 1 zucchini, chopped
- 2 cup kale, chopped
- 14 oz can tomatoes, diced
- 2 tsp cumin
- 1 tbsp garam masala
- 1 tsp turmeric
- 2 tsp coriander powder
- 2 whole cloves
- ½ tsp cardamom powder
- 1 ½ tbsp ginger, minced
- 2 garlic cloves, minced
- 1 onion, diced
- 1 tbsp butter
- 1 tsp salt

Directions:
1. Add butter in instant pot and set pot on sauté mode.
2. Add onion, ginger, garlic, and meat and stir for 1-2 minutes.
3. Add remaining ingredients except bell pepper, zucchini, and kale and mix well.
4. Seal pot with lid and cook on high for 20 minutes.
5. Release pressure using quick release method.
6. Set pot on sauté mode and add bell pepper, zucchini, and kale and cook for 5 minutes.
7. Serve and enjoy.

Nutritional Value (Amount per Serving):

Calories 276; Fat 11 g; Carbohydrates 14 g; Sugar 6 g; Protein 30 g; Cholesterol 46 mg

Lamb Cabbage Stir Fry

Preparation Time: 10 minutes; Cooking Time: 30 minutes; Serve: 4

Ingredients:
- 25 oz cabbage, shredded
- ½ cup fresh cilantro, chopped
- ½ onion, chopped
- 1 tbsp curry paste
- 1 tbsp vinegar
- 1 tsp onion powder
- 2 garlic cloves, minced
- 20 oz ground lamb
- 5.5 oz butter
- 1 tsp salt

Directions:
1. Melt half butter in a pan over medium-high heat.
2. Add cabbage to pan and sauté until soften, about 5 minutes.
3. Add vinegar and spices and sauté for minute. Transfer cabbage in a bowl.
4. Melt remaining butter in same pan.
5. Add curry paste, onion, and garlic and sauté for minute.
6. Add meat and cook until meat is completely cooked.
7. Turn heat to low and return cabbage to the pan stir everything well.
8. Garnish with cilantro and serve.

Nutritional Value (Amount per Serving):
Calories 624; Fat 44 g; Carbohydrates 13 g; Sugar 6.5 g; Protein 42 g; Cholesterol 210 mg

Flavors Lamb Curry

Preparation Time: 10 minutes; Cooking Time: 4 Hours; Serve: 6
Ingredients:
- 1 lb lamb cubed
- 1/2 tsp chili powder
- 1 tsp turmeric powder
- 2 tsp ground coriander
- 5 whole garlic cloves
- 2 tsp cardamom
- 2 tbsp ginger, minced
- 2 garlic cloves, minced
- 14.5 oz tomatoes, chopped
- 1 lb spinach, frozen
- 2 tsp ground cumin
- 2 tsp garam masala
- 1 onion, sliced

Directions:
1. Squeeze out excess liquid from spinach.
2. Add all ingredients into the crock pot and stir well.
3. Cover and cook on high for 4 hours.
4. Stir well and serve.

Nutritional Value (Amount per Serving):
Calories 158; Fat 6.3 g; Carbohydrates 7.7 g; Sugar 3.6 g; Protein 20.3 g; Cholesterol 68 mg

Grilled Kebabs

Preparation Time: 10 minutes; Cooking Time: 2 Hours 10 minutes; Serve: 6
Ingredients:
- 1 1/2 lbs lamb, cut into 2-inch pieces
- 5 garlic cloves, minced
- 2 tsp oregano, chopped
- 1 1/2 tbsp parsley, chopped
- 1 1/2 tbsp mint, chopped
- 1 1/2 tbsp rosemary, chopped
- 4 tbsp olive oil
- 1/8 tsp red pepper flakes
- 1 lemon zest
- 1/2 tsp black pepper

- 1 tsp kosher salt

Directions:

1. In a large bowl, mix together olive oil, red pepper flakes, lemon zest, pepper, salt, garlic, oregano, parsley, mint, and rosemary.
2. Meat into the bowl and mix well and place in fridge for 2 hours.
3. Preheat the grill over medium-high heat.
4. Slide the lamb chunks onto soaked skewers and grill for 10 minutes. Turn once.
5. Serve and enjoy.

Nutritional Value (Amount per Serving):

Calories 321; Fat 21 g; Carbohydrates 2 g; Sugar 0.1 g; Protein 31 g; Cholesterol 100 mg

Lemon Rosemary Lamb Leg

Preparation Time: 10 minutes; Cooking Time: 8 Hours; Serve: 12
Ingredients:

- 4 lbs lamb leg, boneless and slice of fat
- 1 1/2 tbsp rosemary, crushed
- ¼ tsp oregano
- 1/4 cup chicken stock
- 1/4 cup lemon juice
- 1 tsp pepper
- 1/4 tsp salt

Directions:

1. Place lamb into the crock pot.
2. Add remaining ingredients into the crock pot.
3. Cover and cook on low for 8 hours.
4. Remove lamb from crock pot and sliced.
5. Serve and enjoy.

Nutritional Value (Amount per Serving):

Calories 276; Fat 10 g; Carbohydrates 0.4 g; Sugar 0.1 g; Protein 43 g; Cholesterol 130 mg

Olive Thyme Lamb Stew

Preparation Time: 10 minutes; Cooking Time: 8 Hours; Serve: 2
Ingredients:

- 1/2 lb lamb, boneless and cubed
- 2 tbsp lemon juice
- 1 small onion, chopped
- 2 garlic cloves, minced
- 2 fresh thyme sprigs
- 1/4 tsp turmeric
- 1/4 cup green olives, sliced
- 1/2 tsp pepper
- 1/4 tsp salt

Directions:

1. Add all ingredients into the crock pot and stir well.
2. Cover and cook on low for 8 hours.
3. Stir well and serve.

Nutritional Value (Amount per Serving):

Calories 294; Fat 19 g; Carbohydrates 4 g; Sugar 1 g; Protein 21 g; Cholesterol 79 mg

Lamb Skewers

Preparation Time: 10 minutes; Cooking Time: 15 minutes; Serve: 4

Ingredients:

- 1 lb ground lamb
- 1/4 cup parsley, chopped
- 2 garlic cloves, minced
- 1 onion, minced
- 1/8 tsp ground cloves
- 1/2 tsp allspice
- 1/2 tsp cinnamon
- 1/4 tsp pepper
- 1/2 tsp salt

Directions:

1. Preheat the grill over medium-high heat.
2. In a bowl, add all ingredients and mix until well coated.
3. Divide meat mixture into 4 portions and shape each portion into sausage shape and thread onto a soaked wooden skewer.
4. Cook over hot grill for 10 minutes. Turn after every 2-3 minutes.
5. Serve and enjoy.

Nutritional Value (Amount per Serving):

Calories 225; Fat 7 g; Carbohydrates 3 g; Sugar 1 g; Protein 32 g; Cholesterol 101 mg

Buttery Lamb Chops

Preparation Time: 10 minutes; Cooking Time: 10 minutes; Serve: 4

Ingredients:

- 1 lb lamb chops
- 2 garlic cloves, minced
- 2 tbsp fresh basil, chopped
- 1/2 tsp garlic powder
- 2 tbsp butter
- 1 1/2 tsp Dijon mustard
- 1 tbsp olive oil

Directions:

1. Season pork chops with garlic powder and brush with oil.
2. Heat grill over medium-high heat.
3. Cook pork chops on hot grill for 4-5 minutes per side.
4. In a small bowl, mix together butter, mustard, and basil.
5. Spread butter mixture on each pork chops and serves.

Nutritional Value (Amount per Serving):

Calories 295; Fat 17.6 g; Carbohydrates 0.6 g; Sugar 0.1 g; Protein 32.1 g; Cholesterol 117 mg

Lemon Herb Lamb Chops

Preparation Time: 10 minutes; Cooking Time: 10 minutes; Serve: 4

Ingredients:

- 1 1/2 lbs lamb chops
- 1/4 cup olive oil
- 1/4 tsp pepper
- 1 1/2tsp oregano
- 1 tsp thyme
- 2 garlic cloves, chopped
- 2 tbsp lemon juice
- 1/4 tsp salt

Directions:

1. Marinate the lamb chops in the mixture of garlic, oregano, thyme, lemon juice, olive oil, pepper, and salt. Cover and place in the fridge overnight.

2. Cook pork chops over a hot grill for 3-5 minutes per side.

3. Serve and enjoy.

Nutritional Value (Amount per Serving):

Calories 435; Fat 24 g; Carbohydrates 2 g; Sugar 0.3 g; Protein 48 g; Cholesterol 152 mg

Fennel Grill Pork Chops

Preparation Time: 10 minutes; Cooking Time: 10 minutes; Serve: 4

Ingredients:

- 4 pork chops, bone-in
- 1 ¾ tsp dried sage, crumbled
- 1 tsp fennel seed, crushed
- 1/2 tsp dried thyme
- 1 ½ tsp dried rosemary, crumbled
- 1/3 cup olive oil
- 1 bay leaf, crushed
- 1 1/2 tsp salt

Directions:

1. In a bowl, mix together sage, bay leaf, fennel seed, thyme, rosemary, and salt.
2. Rub pork chops with herb sage mixture and brush with olive oil and place in fridge for overnight.
3. Preheat the grill over medium heat.
4. Place marinated pork chops on the hot grill and cook for 4 minutes on each side.
5. Serve and enjoy.

Nutritional Value (Amount per Serving):

Calories 404; Fat 37 g; Carbohydrates 1 g; Sugar 1 g; Protein 18 g; Cholesterol 35 mg

Herb Pork Roast

Preparation Time: 10 minutes; Cooking Time: 1 Hour; Serve: 6

Ingredients:

- 4 lbs pork loin roast, boneless
- 1/4 cup fresh sage leaves
- 1/3 cup fresh rosemary leaves
- 2 garlic cloves, peeled
- ¼ cup lemon juice
- ¼ tsp pepper
- 1/2 tbsp salt

Directions:

1. Add sage, rosemary, garlic, lemon juice, pepper, and salt into the blender and blend until smooth.
2. Rub herb paste over roast and place on hot grill.
3. Close grill hood and cook for 1 hour.
4. Sliced and serve.

Nutritional Value (Amount per Serving):

Calories 655; Fat 30 g; Carbohydrates 4 g; Sugar 0.4 g; Protein 87 g; Cholesterol 244 mg

Asian Pork Hock

Preparation Time: 10 minutes; Cooking Time: 4 Hours; Serve: 2

Ingredients:

- 1 lb pork hock
- 2 garlic cloves, crushed
- ½ tsp oregano
- ½ tsp Chinese five spice

- 1 tbsp butter
- 1 onion, sliced
- ¼ cup erythritol
- 1/3 cup white wine
- 1/3 cup soy sauce
- ¼ cup rice vinegar

Directions:
1. Spray pan with cooking spray and heat over medium heat.
2. Add onion and sauté until soften.
3. Transfer onion in crock pot.
4. Browned meat in same pan from all sides.
5. Transfer meat in crock pot along with remaining ingredients and cook for 2 hours.
6. Stir well and cook for 2 hours more.
7. Serve and enjoy.

Nutritional Value (Amount per Serving):
Calories 321; Fat 14.9 g; Carbohydrates 5.5 g; Sugar 1.7 g; Protein 33.8 g; Cholesterol 112 mg

Parmesan Meatballs

Preparation Time: 10 minutes; Cooking Time: 20 minutes; Serve: 12
Ingredients:
- 1 lb ground beef
- 1 egg
- ¼ cup parmesan cheese, shredded
- ¼ cup fresh parsley, chopped
- 1 tsp Italian seasoning
- ½ tsp garlic powder
- 2 tbsp onion, chopped
- 1/3 cup coconut milk
- ½ cup breadcrumbs
- 1 lb ground pork
- Pepper
- Salt

Directions:
1. Preheat the oven to 400 F.
2. Add all ingredients into the large bowl and mix until well combined.
3. Make balls from meat mixture and place on greased baking tray.
4. Bake for 20 minutes.
5. Serve and enjoy.

Nutritional Value (Amount per Serving):
Calories 193; Fat 7 g; Carbohydrates 4.3 g; Sugar 0.7 g; Protein 25 g; Cholesterol 80 mg

Beef Shawarma

Preparation Time: 10 minutes; Cooking Time: 15 minutes; Serve: 4
Ingredients:
- 1 lb ground beef
- ¼ cup parsley, chopped
- 3 cups cabbage, shredded
- 1 cup onion, sliced
- 2 tbsp olive oil
- 2 tbsp shawarma mix
- 1 tsp salt

Directions:
1. Heat oil in a pan over medium-high heat.
2. Add meat to the pan and cook until meat is not longer pink.
3. Add onion and sauté onion for 3-4 minutes.
4. Add shawarma mix and salt and stir well.
5. Add cabbage and stir to combine.
6. Add 2 tbsp water and cook for 1 minute.
7. Garnish with parsley and serve.

Nutritional Value (Amount per Serving):
Calories 252; Fat 12 g; Carbohydrates 7 g; Sugar 2 g; Protein 25 g; Cholesterol 68 mg

Spicy Pork Stir Fry

Preparation Time: 10 minutes; Cooking Time: 15 minutes; Serve: 4
Ingredients:

- 1 lb ground pork
- ½ cup cilantro, chopped
- ½ cup green onion, chopped
- 2 jalapeno pepper, chopped
- 1 tbsp lemon juice
- 2 tsp red chili sauce
- 1 tbsp soy sauce
- 1 tbsp garlic, minced
- 1 tbsp ginger, minced
- 2 tbsp sesame oil
- 1 tbsp olive oil

Directions:

1. Heat oil in a pan over medium heat.
2. Add ginger and garlic and sauté for 30 seconds.
3. Add meat and cook until meat is brown.
4. Once meat is completely cooked then add jalapeno, sesame oil, soy sauce, and red chili sauce and stir well.
5. Add cilantro, green onion, and lemon juice and stir well.
6. Serve and enjoy.

Nutritional Value (Amount per Serving):
Calories 414; Fat 32 g; Carbohydrates 3 g; Sugar 1 g; Protein 19 g; Cholesterol 120 mg

Delicious Taco Meatballs

Preparation Time: 10 minutes; Cooking Time: 10 minutes; Serve: 4
Ingredients:

- 1 lb ground beef
- 1 egg
- ½ cup cheddar cheese, shredded
- 2 tbsp taco seasoning
- 1 tbsp garlic, minced
- ¼ cup cilantro, chopped
- ¼ cup onion, minced
- Pepper
- Salt

Directions:

1. Add all ingredients into the large bowl and mix until well combined.
2. Make balls from meat mixture and place into the air fryer basket.
3. Spray meatballs with cooking spray.
4. Air fry at 400 F for 10 minutes.
5. Serve and enjoy.

Nutritional Value (Amount per Serving):
Calories 324; Fat 18 g; Carbohydrates 5 g; Sugar 2 g; Protein 33 g; Cholesterol 84 mg

Pork Goulash

Preparation Time: 10 minutes; Cooking Time: 55 minutes; Serve: 4
Ingredients:

- 1 cup chicken stock
- 14 oz tomatoes, chopped
- 2 tbsp tomato puree
- 2 tbsp vinegar
- 1 tsp oregano
- 3 bell peppers, sliced
- 1 tsp chili powder
- 2 tbsp paprika
- 1 lb pork fillet, cut into cubes
- 2 garlic cloves, minced
- 1 onion, chopped
- 1 tbsp olive oil

Directions:
1. Heat oil in a saucepan over medium heat.
2. Add garlic and onion and sauté for 3 minutes.
3. Add meat, chili powder, and paprika and cook for 5 minutes.
4. Add pepper, tomatoes, oregano, tomato puree, stock, and vinegar and stir well.
5. Turn heat to low. Cover and simmer for 15 minutes.
6. Remove lid and simmer for 30 minutes.
7. Serve and enjoy.

Nutritional Value (Amount per Serving):
Calories 375; Fat 19 g; Carbohydrates 14 g; Sugar 9 g; Protein 34 g; Cholesterol 85 mg

Smothered Pork Chops

Preparation Time: 10 minutes; Cooking Time: 8 Hours; Serve: 4
Ingredients:
- 4 pork chops, boneless
- ¼ cup water
- 2 tbsp arrowroot
- 1 packet onion soup seasoning
- 14.5 oz chicken broth

Directions:
1. Place pork chops in crock pot.
2. Pour remaining ingredients except arrowroot over pork chops.
3. Cover and cook on low for 8 hours.
4. In a small bowl, whisk together arrowroot and little water and add into the crock pot during last 30 minutes of cooking.
5. Serve and enjoy.

Nutritional Value (Amount per Serving):
Calories 275; Fat 20 g; Carbohydrates 1 g; Sugar 0.3 g; Protein 20 g; Cholesterol 69 mg

Ranch Pork Chops

Preparation Time: 10 minutes; Cooking Time: 20 minutes; Serve: 4
Ingredients:
- 4 pork chops, boneless
- 2 tbsp fresh parsley, chopped
- 1 tbsp ranch seasoning
- 1 tbsp olive oil
- Pepper
- Salt

Directions:
1. Preheat grill over medium-high heat.
2. Brush pork chops with oil and season with ranch seasoning, pepper, and salt.
3. Place pork chops on hot grill and cook for 8 minutes on each side.
4. Garnish with parsley and serve.

Nutritional Value (Amount per Serving):
Calories 287; Fat 23 g; Carbohydrates 0.1 g; Sugar 0 g; Protein 18 g; Cholesterol 69 mg

Flavorful Roasted Lamb Chops

Preparation Time: 10 minutes; Cooking Time: 15 minutes; Serve: 4

Ingredients:

- 8 lamb chops
- 2 tsp herb de provence
- 2 garlic cloves, minced
- 2 tbsp olive oil
- 2 tbsp Dijon mustard
- Pepper
- Salt

Directions:

1. Preheat the oven to 425 F.
2. Season pork chops with pepper and salt and place on a greased baking tray.
3. In a small bowl, mix together remaining ingredients and spoon over each pork chops and spread well.
4. Bake for 15 minutes.
5. Serve and enjoy.

Nutritional Value (Amount per Serving):

Calories 390; Fat 20 g; Carbohydrates 1 g; Sugar 0.6 g; Protein 47 g; Cholesterol 150 mg

Korean Beef

Preparation Time: 10 minutes; Cooking Time: 7 minutes; Serve: 5

Ingredients:

- 1 ¼ lbs ground beef
- 2 tbsp green onion, sliced
- 1 tsp red pepper flakes
- ½ tsp ginger, minced
- ¼ cup soy sauce
- ½ tsp liquid stevia
- 3 garlic cloves, minced
- 1 tbsp sesame oil

Directions:

1. Heat oil in a pan over medium heat.
2. Add meat and garlic to the pan and cook until meat is brown.
3. Add sweetener, soy sauce, red pepper flakes, and ginger and stir well.
4. Simmer and stir for minute.
5. Garnish with green onion and serve.

Nutritional Value (Amount per Serving):

Calories 261; Fat 11 g; Carbohydrates 2.1 g; Sugar 0.5 g; Protein 35 g; Cholesterol 83 mg

Herb Roasted Tenderloin

Preparation Time: 10 minutes; Cooking Time: 15 minutes; Serve: 4

Ingredients:

- 1 lb pork tenderloin
- 1 tsp oregano, dried
- 1 tsp thyme, dried
- ½ tsp dried parsley
- 1 tsp olive oil
- 1/2 tsp onion powder
- 1/2 tsp garlic powder
- ½ tsp dried basil
- 1/2 tsp pepper
- 1/2 tsp salt

Directions:

1. Preheat the oven at 400 F.

2. In small bowl, mix together onion powder, garlic powder, oregano, parsley, thyme, pepper and salt.

3. Brush pork with oil then rub herb mixture and place on baking tray.
4. Roast for 30 minutes.
5. Slice and serve.

Nutritional Value (Amount per Serving):
   Calories 177; Fat 5 g; Carbohydrates 1 g; Sugar 0.2 g; Protein 29 g; Cholesterol 83 mg

Steak Fajitas

Preparation Time: 10 minutes; Cooking Time: 4 Hours; Serve: 6
Ingredients:
- 2 lbs beef, sliced
- 2 bell pepper, sliced
- 1 ½ tbsp fajita seasoning
- 18.5 oz salsa
- 1 medium onion, sliced

Directions:
1. Add salsa into the slow cooker.
2. Add sliced beef, bell peppers, onion, and fajita seasoning. Stir well.
3. Cover and cook on high for 4 hours.
4. Serve and enjoy.

Nutritional Value (Amount per Serving):
   Calories 332; Fat 9 g; Carbohydrates 11 g; Sugar 5 g; Protein 47 g; Cholesterol 135 mg

Yummy Pork Carnitas

Preparation Time: 10 minutes; Cooking Time: 8 Hours; Serve: 8
Ingredients:
- 4 lbs pork shoulder, trimmed
- 1 tsp black pepper
- 2 tsp dried oregano
- 2 tsp ground cumin
- 1 tbsp chili powder
- 2 lime juice
- 2 orange juice
- 2 onions, quartered
- 2 garlic cloves, peeled
- 2 tsp salt

Directions:
1. In a small bowl, mix together chili powder, oregano, cumin, pepper, and salt.
2. Rub spice mixture over meat.
3. Add lime juice, orange juice, onions, and garlic into the slow cooker.
4. Place meat into the slow cooker.
5. Cover and cook on low for 8 hours.
6. Remove pork from slow cooker and shred using a fork.
7. Return shredded pork into the slow cooker and stir well with juices.
8. Serve and enjoy.

Nutritional Value (Amount per Serving):
   Calories 691; Fat 48 g; Carbohydrates 6 g; Sugar 3 g; Protein 53 g; Cholesterol 201 mg

Chipotle Tenderloin

Preparation Time: 10 minutes; Cooking Time: 6 Hours; Serve: 6
Ingredients:

- 2 lbs pork tenderloin
- 3 garlic cloves, minced
- 1/2 onion, chopped
- 2 tsp salt
- 1 orange juice
- 1 lime juice
- 1 jalapeno, chopped
- For rub:
- 1 tbsp olive oil
- 1 tbsp dried oregano
- 1 1/2 tsp ground cumin

Directions:

1. In a small bowl, mix together all rub ingredients and rub over meat and place into the slow cooker.
2. Add remaining ingredients on top of meat.
3. Cover and cook on low for 6 hours.
4. Remove meat from slow cooker and shred using fork.
5. Serve and enjoy.

Nutritional Value (Amount per Serving):

Calories 254; Fat 8 g; Carbohydrates 3 g; Sugar 2 g; Protein 40 g; Cholesterol 110 mg

Crispy Pork Carnitas

Preparation Time: 20 minutes; Cooking Time: 8 Hours 10 minutes; Serve: 10
Ingredients:

- 4 lbs pork shoulder
- 2 garlic cloves, minced
- 1 tsp black pepper
- 1/4 tsp cinnamon
- 2 tsp dried oregano
- 2 tsp ground cumin
- 1 bay leaf
- 12 oz chicken broth
- 2 lime juice
- 1/2 cup orange juice
- 1 tbsp chili powder
- 1 tbsp salt

Directions:

1. Place meat in the slow cooker.
2. In a small bowl, mix together chili powder, pepper, cinnamon, oregano, cumin, and salt.
3. Rub spice mixture over the meat.
4. Add garlic, bay leaf, broth, lime juice, and orange juice on top of meat.
5. Cover and cook on low for 8 hours.
6. Remove meat from slow cooker and shred using a fork.
7. Place shredded pork on a baking tray and broil for 10 minutes.
8. Serve and enjoy.

Nutritional Value (Amount per Serving):

Calories 547; Fat 39 g; Carbohydrates 2.6 g; Sugar 1.2 g; Protein 43 g; Cholesterol 163 mg

Easy Pork Chops

Preparation Time: 5 minutes; Cooking Time: 4 Hours; Serve: 6
Ingredients:

- 6 pork chops, boneless
- 1 can cream of chicken soup
- Pepper
- Salt
- Water

Directions:

1. Place pork chops in the slow cooker. Season with pepper and salt.
2. Pour cream of chicken soup over pork chops.
3. Fill soup can with water and pour over pork chops.
4. Cover and cook on low for 4 hours.
5. Serve and enjoy.

Nutritional Value (Amount per Serving):
Calories 302; Fat 22 g; Carbohydrates 3 g; Sugar 0.3 g; Protein 19 g; Cholesterol 73 mg

Pork Stroganoff

Preparation Time: 10 minutes; Cooking Time: 8 Hours; Serve: 4

Ingredients:
- 4 large pork chops
- 1 envelope pork gravy mix
- 1 can cream of mushroom soup
- 8 oz mushrooms, sliced
- 1/3 cup sour cream
- 1/2 cup water
- 1 tbsp butter

Directions:
1. In a small bowl, mix together gravy mix and mushroom soup. Pour into slow cooker.
2. Add mushrooms on top of soup mixture.
3. Melt butter in a pan over medium-high heat.
4. Brown pork chops in butter.
5. Transfer pork chops into the slow cooker.
6. Deglaze pan with water and pour over chops.
7. Cover and cook on low for 8 hours.
8. Remove pork chops from slow cooker and place on serving the dish.
9. Pour sour cream in slow cooker juice and stir until well mix.
10. Pour sauce over pork chops and serve.

Nutritional Value (Amount per Serving):
Calories 397; Fat 31 g; Carbohydrates 7 g; Sugar 2.1 g; Protein 21 g; Cholesterol 85 mg

Tasty Pork Tacos

Preparation Time: 10 minutes; Cooking Time: 8 Hours; Serve: 8

Ingredients:
- 2 lbs pork tenderloin
- 2 tbsp ground cumin
- 2 tbsp chili powder
- 24 oz salsa
- 3 tsp garlic powder
- 2 tsp cayenne pepper
- 1 1/2 tsp salt

Directions:
1. Place pork tenderloin in the slow cooker.
2. In a small bowl, mix together all remaining ingredients except salsa.
3. Rub spice mixture over pork tenderloin.
4. Pour salsa on top of pork tenderloin.
5. Cover and cook on low for 8 hours.
6. Remove meat from slow cooker and shred using a fork.
7. Return shredded pork into the slow cooker and stir well with salsa.
8. Serve and enjoy.

Nutritional Value (Amount per Serving):
Calories 202; Fat 4 g; Carbohydrates 8 g; Sugar 3.1 g; Protein 31 g; Cholesterol 83 mg

Flavors Tomatillo Pork

Preparation Time: 10 minutes; Cooking Time: 8 Hours; Serve: 8

Ingredients:

- 4 lbs pork butt, boneless and trimmed
- 3 garlic cloves, minced
- 1/2 cup onion, chopped
- 1/2 cup cilantro, chopped
- 2 cups can tomatillos
- 1 lime juice
- 1 tsp ground cumin
- 2 tsp dried oregano
- 1/2 tsp black pepper
- 1 tsp salt

Directions:

1. Place pork in the slow cooker.
2. Pour remaining ingredients over pork.
3. Cover and cook on low for 8 hours.
4. Remove pork from slow cooker and shred using a fork.
5. Return shredded pork into the slow cooker and stir well.
6. Serve and enjoy.

Nutritional Value (Amount per Serving):

Calories 455; Fat 15 g; Carbohydrates 3.5 g; Sugar 0.9 g; Protein 71 g; Cholesterol 209 mg

Smoky Hawaiian Pork

Preparation Time: 10 minutes; Cooking Time: 6 Hours; Serve: 6

Ingredients:

- 4 lbs pork roast
- 2 garlic cloves, minced
- 2 tbsp soy sauce
- 4 tbsp liquid smoke
- 1 onion, sliced
- 1 tbsp sea salt

Directions:

1. Place onion into the slow cooker.
2. In a small bowl, mix together garlic, soy sauce, liquid smoke, and sea salt.
3. Rub garlic mixture all over pork. Place pork in the slow cooker.
4. Cover and cook on low for 6 hours.
5. Shred the pork using a fork and stir well.
6. Serve and enjoy.

Nutritional Value (Amount per Serving):

Calories 640; Fat 28 g; Carbohydrates 2.8 g; Sugar 0.9 g; Protein 47 g; Cholesterol 260 mg

Chipotle Tacos

Preparation Time: 10 minutes; Cooking Time: 8 Hours 10 minutes; Serve: 10

Ingredients:

- 2 1/2 lbs beef chuck roast
- 1 tbsp olive oil
- 1 tbsp Italian seasoning
- 1/2 tsp smoked paprika
- 1 tsp ground cumin
- 1 cup chicken broth
- 2 tbsp tomato paste
- 1 tbsp chipotle in adobo sauce, minced
- 3 garlic cloves, minced
- 1 tsp chili powder
- 1 tsp salt

Directions:

1. In a small bowl, mix together chili powder, Italian seasoning, paprika, cumin, and salt.
2. Rub spices mixture all over chuck roast and place in the slow cooker.
3. Heat oil in a pan over medium heat. Add garlic and sauté for 2 minutes.
4. Add tomato paste, chipotle, and broth and stir well.
5. Remove pan from heat and pour broth mixture over meat.
6. Cover and cook on low for 8 hours.
7. Shred the meat using a fork and serve.

Nutritional Value (Amount per Serving):

Calories 438; Fat 33 g; Carbohydrates 1.5 g; Sugar 0.6 g; Protein 30g; Cholesterol 118 mg

Spicy Pepper Beef

Preparation Time: 10 minutes; Cooking Time: 4 Hours; Serve: 6

Ingredients:

- 2 lbs beef chuck, sliced
- 1 cup chicken broth
- 1 small onion, sliced
- 2 cups bell pepper, chopped
- 1 tsp sriracha sauce
- 1/3 cup parsley, chopped
- 2 garlic cloves, minced
- 1 tsp pepper
- 2 tsp salt

Directions:

1. Place meat into the slow cooker and top with onion and bell pepper.
2. Season with garlic, pepper, and salt.
3. Mix broth and sriracha together and pour into slow cooker.
4. Cover and cook on high for 4 hours.
5. Garnish with parsley and serve.

Nutritional Value (Amount per Serving):

Calories 308; Fat 9.8 g; Carbohydrates 5 g; Sugar 2.7 g; Protein 47 g; Cholesterol 135 mg

Italian Roast

Preparation Time: 10 minutes; Cooking Time: 8 Hours; Serve: 8

Ingredients:

- 2 1/2 lbs beef round roast
- 1/2 cup chicken broth
- 1 small onion, sliced
- 1/2 tsp marjoram
- 1/2 tsp thyme
- 1 ½ tsp basil
- 1/2 cup red wine
- 1/4 tsp pepper
- 1 tsp kosher salt

Directions:

1. In a small bowl, mix together all spices and rub all over beef roast.
2. Place roast in slow cooker and top with onion.
3. Pour broth and red wine into the slow cooker.
4. Cover and cook on low for 8 hours.
5. Shred meat using a fork and stir well.
6. Serve and enjoy.

Nutritional Value (Amount per Serving):

Calories 284; Fat 11 g; Carbohydrates 1.4 g; Sugar 0.5 g; Protein 39 g; Cholesterol 122 mg

Yummy Steak Bites

Preparation Time: 10 minutes; Cooking Time: 8 Hours; Serve: 4
Ingredients:

- 3 lbs round steak, cut into 1-inch cubes
- 1/2 cup chicken broth
- 4 tbsp butter, sliced
- 1 tsp garlic powder
- 1 tbsp onion, minced
- 1/2 tsp pepper
- 1/2 tsp salt

Directions:

1. Place meat cubes into the slow cooker and pour broth over the meat.
2. Sprinkle with garlic powder, onion, pepper, and salt.
3. Place butter slices on top of meat.
4. Cover and cook on low for 8 hours.
5. Serve and enjoy.

Nutritional Value (Amount per Serving):
Calories 845; Fat 44 g; Carbohydrates 1 g; Sugar 0.4 g; Protein 47 g; Cholesterol 320 mg

Flavors Curry Sausages

Preparation Time: 10 minutes; Cooking Time: 6 Hours 15 minutes; Serve: 6
Ingredients:

- 1 lb beef sausages
- 2 tsp garlic, crushed
- 1 onion, sliced
- 1 tbsp arrowroot
- 2 cups chicken stock
- 1 tbsp curry powder
- 2 carrots, cubed
- 1 tbsp water

Directions:

1. Cook sausages in a pan over medium heat.
2. Remove from heat and cut sausages into small chunks.
3. Add cooked sausages with remaining ingredients except water and arrowroot in the slow cooker and mix well.
4. Cover and cook on low for 6 hours.
5. Mix together arrowroot and water and pour into the slow cooker. Stir well and cook for 15 minutes.
6. Serve and enjoy.

Nutritional Value (Amount per Serving):
Calories 345; Fat 27 g; Carbohydrates 10 g; Sugar 3.2 g; Protein 13.2 g; Cholesterol 54 mg

Beef Barbacoa

Preparation Time: 10 minutes; Cooking Time: 8 Hours; Serve: 8
Ingredients:

- 3 lbs chuck roast, trimmed and cut into 2" cubes
- 2 bay leaves
- 3 tbsp apple cider vinegar
- 1/4 cup lime juice
- 4 oz can green chilies, diced

- 3 chipotles in adobo, chopped
- 3 garlic cloves, minced
- 1/2 cup chicken broth
- 1/2 tsp ground cloves
- 1 tbsp onion powder
- 1 tbsp dried oregano
- 1 tbsp ground cumin
- Pepper
- Salt

Directions:
1. Add all ingredients into the slow cooker and stir well to combine.
2. Cover and cook on low for 8 hours.
3. Discard bay leaves from the slow cooker.
4. Shred meat using fork and season with pepper and salt.
5. Serve and enjoy.

Nutritional Value (Amount per Serving):
Calories 384; Fat 14.5 g; Carbohydrates 2.6 g; Sugar 0.4 g; Protein 56g; Cholesterol 172 mg

Pepper Sirloin Steak

Preparation Time: 10 minutes; Cooking Time: 6 Hours; Serve: 4
Ingredients:
- 1 lb sirloin steak, sliced
- 1 tbsp sesame oil
- 3 tbsp soy sauce
- 1 onion, sliced
- 1 cup mushrooms, sliced
- 1 green bell pepper, sliced
- 1 tsp red pepper flakes
- 1 tsp fresh ginger, grated
- 1 garlic cloves, minced

Directions:
1. Add steak, onion, mushrooms, and green bell pepper into the slow cooker.
2. In a small bowl, mix together remaining ingredients and pour into the slow cooker.
3. Cover and cook on low for 6 hours.
4. Serve and enjoy.

Nutritional Value (Amount per Serving):
Calories 275; Fat 10.7 g; Carbohydrates 7 g; Sugar 3.2 g; Protein 36 g; Cholesterol 101 mg

Yummy Shredded Beef

Preparation Time: 10 minutes; Cooking Time: 8 Hours; Serve: 6
Ingredients:
- 2 1/2 lbs beef chuck roast, trimmed
- 4 oz can green chilies, diced
- 7 oz can chipotle sauce
- 14 oz can tomatoes, diced
- 2 tbsp chili powder
- 1 tsp cumin
- 1 onion, sliced

Directions:
1. Place beef roast in the slow cooker and top with remaining ingredients.
2. Cover and cook on low for 8 hours.
3. Shred the meat using a fork and serve.

Nutritional Value (Amount per Serving):
Calories 720; Fat 7.5 g; Carbohydrates 7.5 g; Sugar 3.2 g; Protein 50.8 g; Cholesterol 195 mg

Mexican Beef

Preparation Time: 10 minutes; Cooking Time: 6 Hours; Serve: 6
Ingredients:

- 3 lbs chuck roast, cut into 2-inch pieces
- 1 tsp oregano
- 1 tsp cumin
- 4 garlic cloves, diced
- 2 tbsp tomato paste
- 1 cup onion, diced
- 1 cup chicken broth
- 1/2 cup salsa
- 1 tbsp olive oil
- 1 tbsp chili powder
- 1 1/2 tsp sea salt

Directions:

1. Heat olive oil in a pan over medium heat.
2. Brown the in pan from all the sides and place in the slow cooker.
3. Add remaining ingredients into the slow cooker and mix well.
4. Cover and cook on low for 6 hours.
5. Serve and enjoy.

Nutritional Value (Amount per Serving):
Calories 544; Fat 21.8 g; Carbohydrates 6.1 g; Sugar 2.4g; Protein 76g; Cholesterol 229 g

Beef Ribs with Sauce

Preparation Time: 10 minutes; Cooking Time: 8 Hours; Serve: 8
Ingredients:

- 2 lbs beef short ribs
- 1/2 cup chicken broth
- 3 oz cream cheese, softened
- 1 tsp garlic powder
- 2 cups mushrooms, sliced
- 1 tsp black pepper
- 1 tsp salt

Directions:

1. Brown beef ribs in a pan over medium-high heat.
2. Add cream cheese, garlic powder, mushrooms, broth, pepper, and salt into the slow cooker and stir well.
3. Place beef ribs on the top of cream cheese mixture.
4. Cover and cook on low for 8 hours.
5. Serve and enjoy.

Nutritional Value (Amount per Serving):
Calories 378; Fat 14.1 g; Carbohydrates 1.3 g; Sugar 0.5 g; Protein 34.5 g; Cholesterol 115 mg

Spicy Goulash

Preparation Time: 10 minutes; Cooking Time: 2 Hours; Serve: 6
Ingredients:

- 3 lbs beef stew meat, cut into 1-inch chunks
- 8 garlic cloves, chopped
- 6 oz can tomato paste
- 2 cups chicken broth
- 3 onions, chopped
- 2 tbsp olive oil
- 2 tsp cayenne
- 1/4 cup paprika
- 1 tsp salt

Directions:
1. Heat olive oil in a large pan over medium heat.
2. Add meat, onion, and garlic and cook until meat is brown and onion is softened.
3. Transfer meat and onion mixture into the slow cooker.
4. Add remaining ingredients into the slow cooker and stir well.
5. Cover and cook on low for 6 hours.
6. Stir well and serve.

Nutritional Value (Amount per Serving):

Calories 518; Fat 20 g; Carbohydrates 9 g; Sugar 3 g; Protein 72 g; Cholesterol 203 mg

Chapter 5: Seafood & Fish Recipes

Delicious Seafood Dip

Preparation Time: 10 minutes; Cooking Time: 30 minutes; Serve: 16
Ingredients:

- 1/2 lb shrimp, cooked
- 4 oz can green chilies
- 2 cups pepper jack cheese
- 4 oz cream cheese
- 1/2 tsp old bay seasoning
- 2 garlic cloves, minced
- 1/2 cup spinach, minced
- 1/2 cup onion, minced
- 2 tbsp butter
- 4 oz crab meat

Directions:

1. Preheat the oven to 425 F.
2. Melt butter in a pan over medium heat.
3. Add garlic, old bay seasoning, spinach, crab meat, chilies, and shrimp and cook for 4-5 minutes.
4. Add 1 cup pepper jack cheese and cream cheese.
5. Top with remaining cheese and bake for 20 minutes.
6. Serve and enjoy.

Nutritional Value (Amount per Serving):
Calories 63; Fat 4 g; Carbohydrates 1 g; Sugar 0.2 g; Protein 5 g; Cholesterol 45 mg

Spinach Shrimp Alfredo

Preparation Time: 10 minutes; Cooking Time: 15 minutes; Serve: 2
Ingredients:

- 1/2 lb shrimp, deveined
- 2 garlic cloves, minced
- 2 tbsp onion, chopped
- 1 cup fresh spinach, chopped
- 1/2 cup heavy cream
- 1 tbsp butter
- Pepper
- Salt

Directions:

1. Melt butter in a pan over medium heat.
2. Add onion, garlic and shrimp in the pan and sauté for 3 minutes.
3. Add remaining ingredients and simmer for 7 minutes or until cooked.
4. Serve and enjoy.

Nutritional Value (Amount per Serving):
Calories 300; Fat 19 g; Carbohydrates 5 g; Sugar 0.5 g; Protein 27 g; Cholesterol 295 mg

Shrimp Scampi

Preparation Time: 10 minutes; Cooking Time: 10 minutes; Serve: 4
Ingredients:

- 1 lb shrimp
- 1/4 tsp red pepper flakes
- 1 tbsp fresh lemon juice
- 1/4 cup butter
- 1/2 cup chicken broth
- 2 garlic cloves, minced
- 1 shallot, sliced
- 3 tbsp olive oil

- 3 tbsp parsley, chopped
- Pepper
- Salt

Directions:
1. Heat oil in a pan over medium heat.
2. Add garlic and shallots and cook for 3 minutes.
3. Add broth, lemon juice, and butter and cook for 5 minutes.
4. Add red pepper flakes, parsley, pepper, and salt. Stir.
5. Add shrimp and cook for 3 minutes.
6. Serve and enjoy.

Nutritional Value (Amount per Serving):
Calories 336; Fat 24 g; Carbohydrates 3 g; Sugar 0.2 g; Protein 26 g; Cholesterol 269 mg

Crab Cakes

Preparation Time: 10 minutes; Cooking Time: 15 minutes; Serve: 4
Ingredients:
- 1 egg
- 2 tbsp butter
- 1 tbsp cilantro, chopped
- 1/2 cup almond flour
- 4 tbsp pork rinds
- 1 lb crab meat
- 3 tsp ginger garlic paste
- 2 tsp sriracha
- 2 tsp lemon juice
- 1 tsp Dijon mustard
- 1/4 cup mayonnaise

Directions:
1. Add all ingredients except butter in a large bowl and mix until well combined.
2. Preheat the oven to 350 F.
3. Heat butter in a pan over medium-high heat.
4. Make crab cake from mixture and place in the pan and cook for 5 minutes.
5. Transfer pan in preheated oven and bake for 10 minutes.
6. Serve and enjoy.

Nutritional Value (Amount per Serving):
Calories 251; Fat 16 g; Carbohydrates 7.4 g; Sugar 0.9 g; Protein 15 g; Cholesterol 97 mg

Shrimp & Broccoli

Preparation Time: 10 minutes; Cooking Time: 7 minutes; Serve: 2
Ingredients:
- 1/2 lb shrimp
- 1 tsp fresh lemon juice
- 2 tbsp butter
- 2 garlic cloves, minced
- 1 cup broccoli florets
- Salt

Directions:
1. Melt butter in a pan over medium heat.
2. Add garlic and broccoli to pan and cook for 3-4 minutes.
3. Add shrimp and cook for 3-4 minutes.
4. Add lemon juice and salt and stir well.
5. Serve and enjoy.

Nutritional Value (Amount per Serving):
Calories 257; Fat 13 g; Carbohydrates 6 g; Sugar 0.9 g; Protein 27 g; Cholesterol 269 mg

Baked Salmon

Preparation Time: 10 minutes; Cooking Time: 35 minutes; Serve: 4
Ingredients:

- 1 lb salmon fillet
- 4 tbsp parsley, chopped
- 1/4 cup mayonnaise
- 1/4 cup parmesan cheese, grated
- 2 garlic cloves, minced
- 2 tbsp butter

Directions:

1. Preheat the oven to 350 F.
2. Place salmon on greased baking tray.
3. Melt butter in a pan over medium heat.
4. Add garlic and sauté for minute.
5. Add remaining ingredient and stir to combined.
6. Spread pan mixture over salmon fillet.
7. Bake for 20-25 minutes.
8. Serve and enjoy.

Nutritional Value (Amount per Serving):
Calories 412; Fat 26 g; Carbohydrates 4.3 g; Sugar 1 g; Protein 34 g; Cholesterol 99 mg

Buttery Shrimp

Preparation Time: 5 minutes; Cooking Time: 15 minutes; Serve: 4
Ingredients:

- 1 1/2 lbs shrimp
- 1 tbsp Italian seasoning
- 1 lemon, sliced
- 1 stick butter, melted

Directions:

1. Add all ingredients into the large mixing bowl and toss well.
2. Transfer shrimp mixture on baking tray.
3. Bake at 350 F for 15 minutes.
4. Serve and enjoy.

Nutritional Value (Amount per Serving):
Calories 415; Fat 26 g; Carbohydrates 3 g; Sugar 0.3 g; Protein 39 g; Cholesterol 421 mg

Avocado Shrimp Salad

Preparation Time: 10 minutes; Cooking Time: 10 minutes; Serve: 6
Ingredients:

- 1 lb shrimp
- 3 bacon slices, cooked and crumbled
- 1/4 cup feta cheese, crumbled
- 1 tbsp lemon juice
- 1/2 cup tomatoes, chopped
- 2 avocados, chopped
- 2 garlic cloves, minced
- 1 tbsp olive oil
- Pepper
- Salt

Directions:

1. Heat oil in a pan over medium heat.
2. Add garlic and sauté for minute.
3. Add shrimp, pepper, and salt and cook for 5-7 minutes. Remove from heat and set aside.
4. Meanwhile, add remaining ingredients to the large mixing bowl.
5. Add shrimp and toss well.
6. Cover and place in fridge for 1 hour.
7. Serve and enjoy.

Nutritional Value (Amount per Serving):

Calories 268; Fat 18 g; Carbohydrates 8.1 g; Sugar 1.1 g; Protein 19.6 g; Cholesterol 165 mg

Garlic Shrimp

Preparation Time: 5 minutes; Cooking Time: 15 minutes; Serve: 4

Ingredients:

- 1 lb shrimp, peeled and deveined
- 1 tsp parsley, chopped
- 2 tbsp lemon juice
- 5 garlic cloves, minced
- 3 tbsp butter
- Salt

Directions:

1. Melt butter in a pan over high heat.
2. Add shrimp in pan and cook for 1 minutes. Season with salt.
3. Stir and cook shrimp until turn to pink.
4. Add lemon juice and garlic and cook for 2 minutes.
5. Turn heat to medium and cook for 4 minutes more.
6. Garnish with parsley and serve.

Nutritional Value (Amount per Serving):

Calories 219; Fat 10.6 g; Carbohydrates 3.2 g; Sugar 0.2 g; Protein 26 g; Cholesterol 262 mg

Salmon Patties

Preparation Time: 10 minutes; Cooking Time: 10 minutes; Serve: 3

Ingredients:

- 14.5 oz can salmon
- 4 tbsp butter
- 1 avocado, diced
- 2 eggs, lightly beaten
- 1/2 cup almond flour
- 1/2 onion, minced
- Pepper
- Salt

Directions:

1. Add all ingredients except butter in a large mixing bowl and mix until well combined.
2. Make six patties from mixture. Set aside.
3. Melt butter in a pan over medium heat.
4. Place patties on pan and cook for 4-5 minutes on each side.
5. Serve and enjoy.

Nutritional Value (Amount per Serving):

Calories 619; Fat 49 g; Carbohydrates 11 g; Sugar 2 g; Protein 36 g; Cholesterol 225 mg

Tuna Salad

Preparation Time: 5 minutes; Cooking Time: 5 minutes; Serve: 2

Ingredients:

- 5 oz can tuna, drained
- 1 tsp Dijon mustard
- 2 tbsp dill pickles, chopped
- 1 tbsp fresh chives, chopped
- 2 tbsp mayonnaise
- Pepper
- Salt

Directions:

1. Add all ingredients into the large bowl and mix well.
2. Serve and enjoy.

Nutritional Value (Amount per Serving):

Calories 143; Fat 5.6 g; Carbohydrates 4 g; Sugar 1 g; Protein 18 g; Cholesterol 25 mg

Flavors Shrimp Scampi

Preparation Time: 10 minutes; Cooking Time: 25 minutes; Serve: 4

Ingredients:

- 1 lb shrimp, peeled and deveined
- 4 tbsp parmesan cheese, grated
- 1 cup chicken broth
- 1 tbsp garlic, minced
- 1/2 cup butter

Directions:

1. Preheat the oven to 350 F.
2. Melt butter in a saucepan over medium heat.
3. Add garlic and sauté for minute. Add broth and stir well.
4. Add shrimp to glass dish and pour butter mixture over shrimp.
5. Top with grated cheese and bake for 10-12 minutes.
6. Serve and enjoy.

Nutritional Value (Amount per Serving):

Calories 388; Fat 27 g; Carbohydrates 2.7 g; Sugar 0.2 g; Protein 30.4 g; Cholesterol 307 mg

Grilled Salmon

Preparation Time: 10 minutes; Cooking Time: 25 minutes; Serve: 4

Ingredients:

- 4 salmon fillets
- 1 tsp dried rosemary
- 3 garlic cloves, minced
- 1/4 tsp pepper
- 1 tsp salt

Directions:

1. In a bowl, mix together rosemary, garlic, pepper, and salt.
2. Add salmon fillets in a bowl and coat well and let sit for 15 minutes.
3. Preheat the grill.
4. Place marinated salmon fillets on hot grill and cook for 10-12 minutes.
5. Serve and enjoy.

Nutritional Value (Amount per Serving):

Calories 240; Fat 11 g; Carbohydrates 1 g; Sugar 0 g; Protein 34 g; Cholesterol 78 mg

Salmon with Sauce

Preparation Time: 10 minutes; Cooking Time: 3 minutes; Serve: 4

Ingredients:

- 1 lb salmon
- 1/2 lemon juice
- 1 tbsp garlic, minced
- 1 tbsp Dijon mustard
- 1 tbsp dill, chopped
- 1 tbsp mayonnaise
- 1/3 cup sour cream
- Pepper

- Salt

Directions:

1. Preheat the oven to 425 F.
2. In a bowl, mix together sour cream, lemon juice, dill, Dijon, and mayonnaise.
3. Place salmon on baking tray and top with garlic, pepper, and salt.
4. Pour half sour cream mixture over salmon.
5. Cover and bake for 20 minutes. Uncover and bake for 10 minutes more.
6. Serve with remaining sauce.

Nutritional Value (Amount per Serving):

Calories 213; Fat 12 g; Carbohydrates 3.1 g; Sugar 0.3 g; Protein 23 g; Cholesterol 59 mg

Tasty Parmesan Salmon

Preparation Time: 10 minutes; Cooking Time: 15 minutes; Serve: 5

Ingredients:

- 1 1/2 lbs salmon fillets
- 1 tsp BBQ seasoning
- 1 tsp paprika
- 1 tbsp olive oil
- 4 tbsp parsley, chopped
- 3 garlic cloves, minced
- 1/2 cup parmesan cheese, shredded
- Pepper
- Salt

Directions:

1. Preheat the oven to 425 F.
2. Drizzle oil over salmon and sprinkle with seasonings.
3. In a small bowl, mix together parsley, cheese, and garlic and sprinkle on top of salmon.
4. Place salmon to a baking tray and cover with parchment paprt.
5. Bake for 10 minutes. Uncover and bake for 5 minutes more.
6. Serve and enjoy.

Nutritional Value (Amount per Serving):

Calories 209; Fat 11 g; Carbohydrates 1 g; Sugar 0.1 g; Protein 26 g; Cholesterol 60 mg

Shrimp Stir Fry

Preparation Time: 10 minutes; Cooking Time: 15 minutes; Serve: 4

Ingredients:

- 8 shrimp, peeled
- 1 tbsp parsley, chopped
- 2 tsp red pepper flakes
- 1 tsp garlic, minced
- 1 cup cabbage, shredded
- 1/4 cup water
- 2 1/2 tbsp butter

Directions:

1. Melt 1 tbsp butter in a pan over high heat.
2. Add cabbage and 1 tbsp water and stir for 1 minute.
3. Transfer cabbage on a plate.
4. Melt remaining butter in same pan.
5. Add shrimp and garlic and cook until shrimp turns to pink.
6. Add remaining ingredients and cook for 1 minute.
7. Pour pan mixture over cabbage and serve.

Nutritional Value (Amount per Serving):

Calories 125; Fat 8 g; Carbohydrates 2.5 g; Sugar 0.7 g; Protein 10 g; Cholesterol 112 mg

Parmesan Halibut

Preparation Time: 10 minutes; Cooking Time: 15 minutes; Serve: 6
Ingredients:

- 1 lb halibut fillets
- 1 tbsp dried parsley
- 2 tsp garlic powder
- 1 tbsp breadcrumbs
- 3 tbsp parmesan cheese, grated
- 1 stick butter
- Pepper
- Salt

Directions:
1. Preheat the oven to 400 F.
2. In a bowl, mix together all ingredients except fish fillets.
3. Place fish fillets on greased baking tray.
4. Spread bowl mixture on top of fish fillets.
5. Cook in preheated oven for 10-12 minutes.
6. Serve and enjoy.

Nutritional Value (Amount per Serving):
Calories 227; Fat 17 g; Carbohydrates 1.6 g; Sugar 0.3 g; Protein 16 g; Cholesterol 65 mg

Lime Garlic Fish Fillet

Preparation Time: 10 minutes; Cooking Time: 20 minutes; Serve: 2
Ingredients:

- 12 oz white fish fillets
- 1/4 tsp onion powder
- 2 garlic cloves, minced
- 2 tsp ginger, grated
- 1 lime zest
- 2 tbsp butter, cut into pieces
- Pepper
- Salt

Directions:
1. Place fish fillets in baking pan. Top with ginger, garlic and lime zest.
2. Season with onion powder, pepper, and salt.
3. Spread butter pieces on top of fish fillets.
4. Cook at 350 F for 20 minutes.
5. Serve and enjoy.

Nutritional Value (Amount per Serving):
Calories 271; Fat 16 g; Carbohydrates 1.7 g; Sugar 0.1 g; Protein 28 g; Cholesterol 108 mg

Shrimp Fajitas

Preparation Time: 10 minutes; Cooking Time: 6 hours 30 minutes; Serve: 4
Ingredients:

- 1 lb shrimp, deveined and peeled
- 1 onion, sliced
- 1 tomato, quartered
- 2 red peppers, sliced
- 2 green peppers, sliced
- 1 tsp paprika
- 1/2 tsp chili powder
- 1 taco seasoning packet
- 1/2 cup fish broth
- 1 tsp salt

Directions:

1. Add all ingredients except shrimp into the slow cooker.
2. Cover and cook on low for 6 hours.
3. Add shrimp and cook on high for 30 minutes more.
4. Serve and enjoy.

Nutritional Value (Amount per Serving):
Calories 175; Fat 2 g; Carbohydrates 10 g; Sugar 2 g; Protein 26 g; Cholesterol 240 mg

Simple Air Fried Salmon

Preparation Time: 5 minutes; Cooking Time: 7 minutes; Serve: 2
Ingredients:
- 2 salmon fillets, remove bones
- 2 tsp olive oil
- 1 1/2 tsp paprika
- Pepper
- Salt

Directions:
1. Rub each salmon fillet with oil, paprika, pepper, and salt.
2. Place salmon fillets in the air fryer basket and air fry at 390 F for 7 minutes.
3. Serve and enjoy.

Nutritional Value (Amount per Serving):
Calories 280; Fat 14 g; Carbohydrates 1 g; Sugar 0.2 g; Protein 35 g; Cholesterol 78 mg

Spicy Prawns

Preparation Time: 10 minutes; Cooking Time: 8 minutes; Serve: 2
Ingredients:
- 6 prawns
- 1/4 tsp pepper
- 1 tsp chili powder
- 1 tsp chili flakes
- 1/4 tsp salt

Directions:
1. Preheat the air fryer to 350 F.
2. In a bowl, add all ingredients and toss well.
3. Spray air fryer basket with cooking spray.
4. Transfer prawns to the air fryer basket and cook for 6-8 minutes.
5. Serve and enjoy.

Nutritional Value (Amount per Serving):
Calories 80; Fat 1 g; Carbohydrates 1.5 g; Sugar 0.1 g; Protein 14 g; Cholesterol 140 mg

Salmon Cheese Tomato Packets

Preparation Time: 10 minutes; Cooking Time: 20 minutes; Serve: 4
Ingredients:
- 4 salmon fillets
- 1 onion, chopped
- 1/2 cup pesto
- 3/4 cup feta cheese, crumbled
- 2 cups cherry tomatoes, halved

Directions:
1. Preheat the oven to 350 F.

2. Spray four aluminum foil pieces with cooking spray.
3. Place salmon fillet on top of each foil piece and top with remaining ingredients evenly.
4. Fold aluminum packets and close tightly and place on baking tray.
5. Bake for 20 minutes.
6. Serve and enjoy.

Nutritional Value (Amount per Serving):
Calories 445; Fat 27 g; Carbohydrates 9 g; Sugar 6 g; Protein 42 g; Cholesterol 102 mg

Fish in Sauce

Preparation Time: 10 minutes; Cooking Time: 30 minutes; Serve: 4
Ingredients:
- 4 white fish fillets
- 3 garlic cloves, sliced
- 1 tbsp olive oil
- 2 cups cherry tomatoes, halved
- 1/4 cup basil, chopped
- 1/4 cup dry white wine
- 1/4 cup chicken broth
- 1/2 tsp pepper
- 1/2 tsp salt

Directions:
1. Heat oil in a saucepan over medium heat.
2. Add garlic, tomatoes, pepper, and salt and sauté for 5 minutes.
3. Add broth, basil, fish fillets, and white wine.
4. Cover and simmer for 20-25 minutes.
5. Serve and enjoy.

Nutritional Value (Amount per Serving):
Calories 295; Fat 11.9 g; Carbohydrates 5 g; Sugar 2.6 g; Protein 37 g; Cholesterol 119 mg

Cheese Olives Salmon

Preparation Time: 10 minutes; Cooking Time: 15 minutes; Serve: 2
Ingredients:
- 2 salmon filets
- 1/2 cup olives, chopped
- 1 tbsp balsamic vinegar
- 1 tbsp olive oil
- 2 tbsp parsley, chopped
- 1/3 cup feta cheese, crumbled
- 1/2 cup tomato, diced
- Pepper
- Salt

Directions:
1. Preheat the oven to 350 F.
2. Season salmon with pepper and salt.
3. Place salmon on a baking tray and bake for 15 minutes.
4. Meanwhile, in a bowl mix together remaining ingredients.
5. Remove salmon from oven and top with tomato mixture.
6. Serve and enjoy.

Nutritional Value (Amount per Serving):
Calories 410; Fat 27 g; Carbohydrates 5 g; Sugar 2.3 g; Protein 39 g; Cholesterol 101 mg

Lemon Tilapia Fillets

Preparation Time: 10 minutes; Cooking Time: 18 minutes; Serve: 4

Ingredients:

- 1 lb tilapia fillets
- 3/4 tsp dried oregano
- 1 tsp fresh lemon juice
- 2 tsp olive oil
- 1 lemon, sliced
- 1/2 tsp garlic powder
- 1/2 tsp dried thyme
- 1/2 tsp pepper
- 1 tsp salt

Directions:

1. Preheat the oven to 400 F.
2. Place a fish fillet on a baking tray and brush with lemon juice and olive oil.
3. Mix together garlic powder, thyme, oregano, pepper, and salt and sprinkle over fish fillets.
4. Top with sliced lemon and bake for 15-18 minutes.
5. Serve and enjoy.

Nutritional Value (Amount per Serving):

Calories 120; Fat 3.4 g; Carbohydrates 1 g; Sugar 0.2 g; Protein 21 g; Cholesterol 55 mg

Chapter 6: Meatless Meals

Mexican Cauliflower Rice

Preparation Time: 10 minutes; Cooking Time: 10 minutes; Serve: 3
Ingredients:

- 1 large cauliflower head, cut into florets
- 2 garlic cloves, minced
- 1 onion, diced
- 1 tbsp olive oil
- 1/4 cup vegetable broth
- 3 tbsp tomato paste
- 1/2 tsp cumin
- 1 tsp salt

Directions:

1. Add cauliflower in food processor and process until it looks like rice.
2. Heat oil in a pan over medium heat.
3. Add onion and garlic and sauté for 3 minutes.
4. Add cauliflower rice, cumin, and salt and stir well.
5. Add broth and tomato paste and stir until well combined.
6. Serve and enjoy.

Nutritional Value (Amount per Serving):
Calories 90; Fat 5 g; Carbohydrates 10 g; Sugar 4 g; Protein 3 g; Cholesterol 0 mg

Balsamic Zucchini Noodles

Preparation Time: 10 minutes; Cooking Time: 15 minutes; Serve: 4
Ingredients:

- 4 zucchinis, spiralized using a slicer
- 1 1/2 tbsp balsamic vinegar
- 1/4 cup fresh basil leaves, chopped
- 4 mozzarella balls, quartered
- 1 1/2 cups cherry tomatoes, halved
- 2 tbsp olive oil
- Pepper
- Salt

Directions:

1. Add zucchini noodles in a bowl and season with pepper and salt. Set aside for 10 minutes.
2. Add mozzarella, tomatoes, and basil and toss well.
3. Drizzle with oil and balsamic vinegar.
4. Serve and enjoy.

Nutritional Value (Amount per Serving):
Calories 222; Fat 15 g; Carbohydrates 10 g; Sugar 5.8 g; Protein 9.5 g; Cholesterol 13 mg

Cauliflower Broccoli Rice

Preparation Time: 10 minutes; Cooking Time: 8 minutes; Serve: 4
Ingredients:

- 1 cup broccoli, process into rice
- 3 cups cauliflower rice
- 1/4 cup mascarpone cheese
- 1/2 cup parmesan cheese, shredded
- 1/8 tsp ground cinnamon
- ¼ tsp garlic powder
- ¼ tsp onion powder
- 1/4 tsp pepper

- 1 tbsp butter, melted

Directions:
1. In a heat-safe bowl, mix together cauliflower, nutmeg, garlic powder, onion powder, butter, broccoli, pepper, and salt and microwave for 4 minutes.
2. Stir well and microwave for 2 minutes more.

- 1/2 tsp salt

3. Add cheese and microwave for 2 minutes.
4. Add mascarpone cheese and stir until it looks creamy.
5. Serve and enjoy.

Nutritional Value (Amount per Serving):
Calories 135; Fat 10 g; Carbohydrates 6 g; Sugar 2 g; Protein 8 g; Cholesterol 30 mg

Cheesy Cauliflower Broccoli Risotto

Preparation Time: 10 minutes; Cooking Time: 15 minutes; Serve: 2
Ingredients:
- 2 cups broccoli florets
- 1 cauliflower head, cut into florets
- 2 green onion, chopped
- 1/2 cup parmesan cheese, grated
- 2 tbsp heavy cream

- 1/2 tbsp lemon zest
- 1/2 cup vegetable stock
- 2 tbsp butter
- 1/2 tsp pepper
- 1/2 tsp salt

Directions:
1. Add cauliflower and broccoli florets into the food processor and process until it looks like rice.
2. Melt butter in a saucepan over medium heat. Add onion and sauté for 2 minutes.
3. Add broccoli and cauliflower rice and sauté for 2-3 minutes.

4. Add stock and cover and cook for 10 minutes.
5. Add cheese and heavy cream, and lemon zest and stir until cheese is melted.
6. Serve and enjoy.

Nutritional Value (Amount per Serving):
Calories 315; Fat 22 g; Carbohydrates 12 g; Sugar 5 g; Protein 15 g; Cholesterol 60 mg

Tasty Creamy Spinach

Preparation Time: 10 minutes; Cooking Time: 20 minutes; Serve: 6
Ingredients:
- 1 lb fresh spinach
- 1 tbsp onion, minced
- 8 oz cream cheese
- 6 oz cheddar cheese, shredded

- 1/2 tsp garlic powder
- Pepper
- Salt

Directions:
1. Preheat the oven to 400 F.
2. Spray pan with cooking spray and heat over medium heat.

3. Add spinach to the pan and cook until wilted.
4. Add cream cheese, garlic powder, and onion and stir until cheese is melted.

5. Remove pan from heat and add cheddar cheese and season with pepper and salt.
6. Pour spinach mixture into the greased baking dish and bake for 20 minutes.
7. Serve and enjoy.

Nutritional Value (Amount per Serving):
Calories 250; Fat 20 g; Carbohydrates 5 g; Sugar 1.5 g; Protein 12 g; Cholesterol 75 mg

Cauliflower Mash

Preparation Time: 10 minutes; Cooking Time: 10 minutes; Serve: 4
Ingredients:
- 1 lb cauliflower, cut into florets
- 1 tbsp lemon juice
- 3 oz parmesan cheese, grated
- 4 oz butter
- ½ tsp garlic powder
- ¼ tsp onion powder
- Pepper
- Salt

Directions:
1. Boil cauliflower florets until tender. Drain well.
2. Add cooked cauliflower into the blender with remaining ingredients and blend until smooth.
3. Serve and enjoy.

Nutritional Value (Amount per Serving):
Calories 300; Fat 28 g; Carbohydrates 7 g; Sugar 3 g; Protein 10 g; Cholesterol 75 mg

Roasted Broccoli

Preparation Time: 10 minutes; Cooking Time: 15 minutes; Serve: 4
Ingredients:
- 2 lbs broccoli, cut into florets
- 3 tbsp olive oil
- 1 tbsp lemon juice
- 1/4 cup parmesan cheese, grated
- ¼ cup almonds, sliced and toasted
- 3 garlic cloves, sliced
- ½ tsp red pepper flakes
- 1/4 tsp pepper
- 1/4 tsp salt

Directions:
1. Preheat the oven to 425 F.
2. Add broccoli, pepper, salt, garlic, and oil in large bowl and toss well.
3. Spread broccoli on baking tray and roast in for 20 minutes.
4. Add lemon juice, grated cheese, red pepper flakes and almonds over broccoli and toss well.
5. Serve and enjoy.

Nutritional Value (Amount per Serving):
Calories 205; Fat 16 g; Carbohydrates 13 g; Sugar 3 g; Protein 7.5 g; Cholesterol 6 mg

Stir Fried Broccoli with Mushroom

Preparation Time: 10 minutes; Cooking Time: 20 minutes; Serve: 4
Ingredients:

- 2 cups broccoli, cut into florets
- 1 1/2 tsp fresh ginger, grated
- 1/4 tsp red pepper flakes
- 2 cups mushrooms, sliced
- 2 garlic cloves, minced
- 1 small onion, chopped
- 2 tbsp balsamic vinegar
- 1/2 tbsp sesame seeds
- 2 tbsp soy sauce, low-sodium
- 1/4 cup cashews
- 1 medium carrot, shredded
- 3 tbsp water

Directions:
1. Heat large pan over high heat.
2. Add broccoli, water, ginger, red pepper, mushrooms, garlic, and onion and cook until soft softened.
3. Add carrots, soy sauce, vinegar, and cashews. Stir well and simmer for 2 minutes.
4. Garnish with sesame seeds and serve

Nutritional Value (Amount per Serving):
Calories 105; Fat 5 g; Carbohydrates 12 g; Sugar 3 g; Protein 5 g; Cholesterol 0 mg

Flavors Zucchini Gratin

Preparation Time: 10 minutes; Cooking Time: 50 minutes; Serve: 9
Ingredients:
- 4 cups zucchini, sliced
- 2 tbsp butter
- 1 1/2 cups pepper jack cheese, shredded
- 1 onion, sliced
- 1/2 cup heavy cream
- 1/2 tsp garlic powder
- ¼ tsp onion powder
- Pepper
- Salt

Directions:
1. Preheat the oven to 375 F.
2. Add 1/3 sliced onion and zucchini in pan and season with pepper and salt.
3. Sprinkle 1/2 cup cheese on top of onion and zucchini.
4. In a baking dish, combine together heavy cream, butter, garlic powder, and onion powder and microwave for 1 minute.
5. Pour heavy cream mixture over sliced zucchini and onion.
6. Bake for 45 minutes.
7. Serve and enjoy.

Nutritional Value (Amount per Serving):
Calories 85; Fat 6 g; Carbohydrates 3 g; Sugar 1 g; Protein 1 g; Cholesterol 15 mg

Delicious Pumpkin Risotto

Preparation Time: 10 minutes; Cooking Time: 5 minutes; Serve: 1
Ingredients:
- 1/4 cup pumpkin, grated
- 1 tbsp butter
- 1/2 cup water
- 1 cup cauliflower, grated
- 2 garlic cloves, chopped
- 1/8 tsp cinnamon
- Pepper
- Salt

Directions:
1. Melt butter in a pan over medium heat.

2. Add garlic, cauliflower, cinnamon and pumpkin into the pan and season with pepper and salt.

3. Cook until lightly softened. Add water and cook until done.
4. Serve and enjoy.

Nutritional Value (Amount per Serving):
  Calories 155; Fat 11 g; Carbohydrates 11 g; Sugar 4.5 g; Protein 3.2 g; Cholesterol 30 mg

Easy Cauliflower Tabbouleh

Preparation Time: 10 minutes; Cooking Time: 5 minutes; Serve: 6
Ingredients:
- 2 cups cauliflower, grated
- 2 tomatoes, chopped
- ¼ cup fresh mint, chopped
- 1/2 cup fresh parsley, chopped
- 1/4 cup olive oil
- 2 tbsp fresh lemon juice
- 1 tbsp lemon zest
- 1/2 tsp pepper
- 1 tsp salt

Directions:
1. Add all ingredients into the large bowl and mix well.
2. Place in fridge for 1 hour.
3. Serve and enjoy.

Nutritional Value (Amount per Serving):
  Calories 90; Fat 8 g; Carbohydrates 4 g; Sugar 2 g; Protein 1 g; Cholesterol 0 mg

Creamy Cabbage

Preparation Time: 10 minutes; Cooking Time: 15 minutes; Serve: 4
Ingredients:
- 1/2 cabbage head, shredded
- 3 garlic cloves, chopped
- 1 onion, sliced
- 1 bell pepper, cut into strips
- 2 tbsp butter
- 3 oz cream cheese
- ¼ tsp onion powder
- ¼ tsp garlic powder
- 1/2 tsp pepper
- 1 tsp kosher salt

Directions:
1. Melt butter in a saucepan over medium heat.
2. Add garlic and onion and sauté for 5 minutes.
3. Add cabbage and bell pepper and cook for 5 minutes.
4. Add remaining ingredients and stir well.
5. Serve and enjoy.

Nutritional Value (Amount per Serving):
  Calories 170; Fat 13 g; Carbohydrates 12 g; Sugar 5 g; Protein 3 g; Cholesterol 40 mg

Rutabaga Noodles

Preparation Time: 10 minutes; Cooking Time: 10 minutes; Serve: 4
Ingredients:
- 25 oz rutabaga, peel, cut and spiralized using slicer
- 1/2 tbsp chili powder
- 1/3 cup olive oil

- 1/2 tsp garlic powder
- ¼ tsp onion powder
- 1 tsp salt

Directions:
1. Preheat the oven to 450 F.
2. Add all ingredients into the large bowl and toss well.
3. Spread rutabaga mixture on a baking tray and bake for 10 minutes.
4. Serve and enjoy.

Nutritional Value (Amount per Serving):
Calories 150; Fat 17 g; Carbohydrates 2 g; Sugar 0.6 g; Protein 0.4 g; Cholesterol 0 mg

Creamy Green Beans

Preparation Time: 10 minutes; Cooking Time: 15 minutes; Serve: 4
Ingredients:
- 1 lb fresh green beans, trim and rinse
- 1/2 lemon zest
- 1 cup heavy cream
- 3 oz butter
- 1/4 tsp pepper
- 1/2 tsp sea salt

Directions:
1. Melt butter in the pan over medium heat.
2. Add green beans to the pan and sauté for 4-5 minutes. Season with pepper and salt.
3. Add heavy cream and simmer for 2 minutes.
4. Sprinkle with lemon zest and serve.

Nutritional Value (Amount per Serving):
Calories 281; Fat 29 g; Carbohydrates 5 g; Sugar 1 g; Protein 2 g; Cholesterol 85 mg

Roasted Green Beans

Preparation Time: 10 minutes; Cooking Time: 25 minutes; Serve: 4
Ingredients:
- 1 lb frozen green beans
- ¼ tsp red pepper flakes
- 1/4 tsp garlic powder
- 2 tbsp olive oil
- 1/2 tsp onion powder
- 1/2 tsp pepper
- 1/2 tsp salt

Directions:
1. Preheat the oven to 425 F.
2. In a large bowl, add all ingredients and mix well.
3. Spread green beans baking tray and bake for 30 minutes.
4. Serve and enjoy.

Nutritional Value (Amount per Serving):
Calories 95; Fat 7 g; Carbohydrates 9 g; Sugar 2 g; Protein 2 g; Cholesterol 0 mg

Smooth Broccoli Cauliflower Mashed

Preparation Time: 10 minutes; Cooking Time: 10 minutes; Serve: 4
Ingredients:
- 2 cups cauliflower florets
- 2 cups broccoli florets
- 2 garlic cloves, peeled
- ¼ tsp onion powder

- 1 tbsp olive oil
- 1/2 tsp pepper
- 1/2 tsp salt

Directions:
1. Heat olive oil in a pan over medium heat.
2. Add cauliflower, broccoli, and salt in a pan and sauté until softened.
3. Transfer vegetables and garlic to the food processor and process until smooth.
4. Season with onion powder, pepper and salt.
5. Serve and enjoy.

Nutritional Value (Amount per Serving):
Calories 60; Fat 3 g; Carbohydrates 6 g; Sugar 2 g; Protein 2 g; Cholesterol 0 mg

Easy Roasted Radishes

Preparation Time: 10 minutes; Cooking Time: 35 minutes; Serve: 2
Ingredients:
- 3 cups radish, clean and cut in half
- 1 ½ tbsp fresh rosemary, chopped
- 8 black peppercorns, crushed
- 3 tbsp olive oil
- 2 tsp sea salt

Directions:
1. Preheat the oven to 425 F.
2. Add radish, 2 tbsp oil, rosemary, peppercorns, and salt into the bowl and toss well.
3. Transfer radishes mixture onto a baking tray and bake for 30 minutes.
4. Heat remaining olive oil in a pan over medium heat.
5. Add baked radishes to the pan and sauté for 2 minutes.
6. Serve and enjoy.

Nutritional Value (Amount per Serving):
Calories 220; Fat 20 g; Carbohydrates 7 g; Sugar 2 g; Protein 1 g; Cholesterol 0 mg

Avocado Zucchini Noodles

Preparation Time: 10 minutes; Cooking Time: 5 minutes; Serve: 1
Ingredients:
- 1 zucchini, spiralized using slicer
- 1/2 avocado
- 3 tbsp parmesan cheese, shredded
- 2 tbsp mascarpone
- Pepper
- Salt

Directions:
1. In a bowl, add avocado and mascarpone and mash until smooth.
2. Add avocado mixture to the small saucepan and heat until warm.
3. Add zucchini noodles into the saucepan and cook until heated through.
4. Season with pepper and salt. Stir in parmesan cheese and serve.

Nutritional Value (Amount per Serving):
Calories 325; Fat 29 g; Carbohydrates 12 g; Sugar 2 g; Protein 7 g; Cholesterol 25 mg

Sweet & Tangy Green Beans

Preparation Time: 10 minutes; Cooking Time: 10 minutes; Serve: 4

Ingredients:

- 1 lb green beans, washed and trimmed
- 1/2 tsp whole grain mustard
- 1 tbsp erythritol
- 2 tbsp apple cider vinegar
- 1 small onion, chopped
- 1 tbsp olive oil
- 1/4 tsp pepper
- 1/4 tsp salt

Directions:

1. Steam green beans in microwave until tender.
2. Meanwhile, in a pan heat olive oil over medium heat.
3. Add onion in a pan sauté until softened.
4. Add water, sweetener, apple cider vinegar, and mustard in the pan and stir well.
5. Add green beans and stir to coat well. Season with pepper and salt.
6. Serve and enjoy.

Nutritional Value (Amount per Serving):

Calories 70; Fat 4 g; Carbohydrates 9 g; Sugar 2 g; Protein 2 g; Cholesterol 0 mg

Tomato Cauliflower Rice

Preparation Time: 10 minutes; Cooking Time: 15 minutes; Serve: 3

Ingredients:

- 1 medium cauliflower head, cut into florets
- 2 tbsp olive oil
- 1 tomato, chopped
- 1 small onion, chopped
- 2 tbsp tomato paste
- 1 tsp white pepper
- 1 tsp black pepper
- 1/2 tbsp dried thyme
- 2 green chilies, chopped
- 3 garlic cloves, chopped
- 1/2 tsp salt

Directions:

1. Preheat the oven to 400 F.
2. Add cauliflower florets into the food processor and process until it looks like rice.
3. Stir in tomato paste, tomatoes, and spices and mix well.
4. Spread cauliflower mixture on a baking tray and drizzle with olive oil.
5. Bake for 15 minutes.
6. Serve and enjoy.

Nutritional Value (Amount per Serving):

Calories 135; Fat 10 g; Carbohydrates 13 g; Sugar 6 g; Protein 3 g; Cholesterol 0 mg

Spinach Pie

Preparation Time: 10 minutes; Cooking Time: 30 minutes; Serve: 8

Ingredients:

- 6 eggs, beaten
- 2 cup cheddar cheese, shredded
- 20 oz frozen spinach, chopped
- 15 oz cottage cheese
- 1 tsp black pepper
- 1 tsp salt

Directions:
1. Preheat the oven to 375 F.
2. Spray 8*8-inch baking dish with cooking spray and set aside.
3. In a large bowl, mix together spinach, eggs, cheddar cheese, cottage cheese, pepper, and salt.
4. Pour spinach mixture into the baking dish and bake for 10 minutes.
5. Serve and enjoy.

Nutritional Value (Amount per Serving):
Calories 225; Fat 14 g; Carbohydrates 5 g; Sugar 1 g; Protein 20 g; Cholesterol 155 mg

Zucchini Eggplant with Cheese

Preparation Time: 10 minutes; Cooking Time: 40 minutes; Serve: 6
Ingredients:
- 1 medium eggplant, sliced
- 4 tbsp parsley, chopped
- ½ cup fresh basil, chopped
- 3 zucchini, sliced
- 3 oz Parmesan cheese, grated
- 1 tbsp olive oil
- 1 cup cherry tomatoes, cut in half
- 2 garlic cloves, minced
- 1/4 tsp pepper
- 1/4 tsp salt

Directions:
1. Preheat the oven to 350 F.
2. In a bowl, add cherry tomatoes, eggplant, zucchini, olive oil, garlic, cheese, basil, pepper and salt toss well.
3. Transfer the eggplant mixture into the baking dish and bake for 35 minutes.
4. Garnish with chopped parsley and serve.

Nutritional Value (Amount per Serving):
Calories 111; Fat 6 g; Carbohydrates 11 g; Sugar 5 g; Protein 7 g; Cholesterol 10 mg

Turnips Mashed

Preparation Time: 10 minutes; Cooking Time: 10 minutes; Serve: 4
Ingredients:
- 3 cups turnip, diced
- 3 tbsp butter, melted
- 1/4 cup heavy cream
- 2 garlic cloves, minced
- ¼ tsp garlic powder
- ¼ tsp onion powder
- Pepper
- Salt

Directions:
1. Boil turnips in a saucepan until tender. Drain well and mashed turnips until smooth.
2. Add remaining ingredients and mix well.
3. Serve and enjoy.

Nutritional Value (Amount per Serving):
Calories 130; Fat 12 g; Carbohydrates 7 g; Sugar 9 g; Protein 2 g; Cholesterol 30 mg

Tasty Coconut Cauliflower Rice

Preparation Time: 10 minutes; Cooking Time: 7 minutes; Serve: 2
Ingredients:

- 2 cups cauliflower, chopped
- 2 tbsp water
- 2 tbsp unsweetened shredded coconut
- 2 tbsp coconut oil
- 1 tsp lime zest
- 1 tbsp fresh cilantro, chopped
- 3 tbsp coconut milk powder

Directions:

1. Add cauliflower, water, shredded coconut, coconut oil, and coconut milk powder in a microwave-safe dish and microwave on high for 7 minutes.
2. Add lime zest and cilantro and stir well.
3. Serve and enjoy.

Nutritional Value (Amount per Serving):
Calories 195; Fat 19 g; Carbohydrates 6 g; Sugar 3 g; Protein 2 g; Cholesterol 0 mg

Parmesan Zucchini Chips

Preparation Time: 10 minutes; Cooking Time: 15 minutes; Serve: 3
Ingredients:

- 2 medium zucchinis, sliced
- ½ tsp garlic powder
- ¼ tsp onion powder
- 1/2 cup parmesan cheese, grated
- Pepper
- Salt

Directions:

1. Arrange sliced zucchinis on a baking tray. Season with garlic powder, onion powder, pepper, and salt.
2. Sprinkle parmesan cheese on top of zucchini slices.
3. Bake at 425 F for 15 minutes.
4. Serve and enjoy.

Nutritional Value (Amount per Serving):
Calories 45; Fat 2 g; Carbohydrates 6 g; Sugar 2 g; Protein 4 g; Cholesterol 5 mg

Zucchini Carrot Patties

Preparation Time: 10 minutes; Cooking Time: 5 minutes; Serve: 4
Ingredients:

- 1 large egg, lightly beaten
- 1/2 cup mozzarella cheese, shredded
- 1 carrot, grated
- 1 cup zucchini, grated
- 1/3 cup parmesan cheese, grated
- 2 tsp olive oil
- 1/4 tsp pepper
- 1 tsp salt

Directions:

1. Add all ingredients except oil into the bowl and mix until well combined.
2. Heat oil in a pan over medium-high heat.
3. Drop tablespoon of zucchini mixture on a hot pan and cook for 2 minutes on each side.
4. Serve and enjoy.

Nutritional Value (Amount per Serving):
   Calories 102; Fat 7 g; Carbohydrates 2 g; Sugar 2 g; Protein 7 g; Cholesterol 55 mg

Cauliflower Mac n Cheese

Preparation Time: 10 minutes; Cooking Time: 20 minutes; Serve: 4
Ingredients:

- 1 medium cauliflower head, cut into florets
- 3/4 cup cheddar cheese, shredded
- 3 tbsp butter, melted
- 1/4 cup unsweetened coconut milk
- 1/4 cup heavy cream
- ¼ tsp garlic powder
- Pepper
- Salt

Directions:

1. Preheat the oven to 450 F.
2. Add cauliflower florets and 2 tbsp butter in a large bowl and toss well. Season with pepper and salt.
3. Spread cauliflower florets on a baking tray and roast in oven for 15 minutes.
4. Add roasted cauliflower into the large bowl and set aside.
5. In a saucepan, add remaining ingredients and heat over medium heat until cheese is melted.
6. Pour saucepan mixture over cauliflower and mix well.
7. Serve and enjoy.

Nutritional Value (Amount per Serving):
   Calories 265; Fat 25 g; Carbohydrates 5 g; Sugar 2 g; Protein 9 g; Cholesterol 60 mg

Stir Fried Zucchini

Preparation Time: 10 minutes; Cooking Time: 5 minutes; Serve: 4
Ingredients:

- 2 zucchini, cut into slices
- ¼ tsp garlic powder
- 1 tsp butter
- 1 tsp dried basil
- 2 medium tomatoes, chopped
- 1 medium onion, chopped
- 1/4 tsp pepper
- 1/2 tsp salt

Directions:

1. Melt butter in a pan over medium heat.
2. Add onion and cook until softened.
3. Add zucchini and cook for 3 minutes.
4. Add tomatoes, garlic powder, and basil and cook until zucchini is tender.
5. Season with pepper and salt.
6. Serve and enjoy.

Nutritional Value (Amount per Serving):
   Calories 40; Fat 1 g; Carbohydrates 8 g; Sugar 4 g; Protein 2 g; Cholesterol 3 mg

Stir Fry Cauliflower & Cabbage

Preparation Time: 10 minutes; Cooking Time: 15 minutes; Serve: 6
Ingredients:

- 2 cups cauliflower florets, chopped
- 3 cups cabbage, chopped
- 2/3 cup unsweetened coconut milk
- 1 tbsp olive oil
- ½ tsp garlic powder
- ¼ tsp onion powder
- 2 tbsp parsley, chopped
- Pepper
- Salt

Directions:
1. Heat olive oil in a pan over medium heat.
2. Add cauliflower, cabbage, onion powder, and garlic powder in a pan and sauté until softened.
3. Add coconut milk and stir well. Bring to boil.
4. Turn heat to low and simmer for 15 minutes or until sauce thickened.
5. Season with pepper and salt.
6. Garnish with parsley and serve.

Nutritional Value (Amount per Serving):
Calories 95; Fat 9 g; Carbohydrates 5 g; Sugar 3 g; Protein 2 g; Cholesterol 0 mg

Avocado Salsa

Preparation Time: 10 minutes; Cooking Time: 10 minutes; Serve: 8
Ingredients:
- 4 avocados, peeled and diced
- 1 onion, diced
- 1 chili, chopped
- 1 fresh lemon juice
- 2 tbsp fresh parsley, chopped
- 1 tbsp lemon juice
- 2 tomatoes, diced
- Pepper
- Salt

Directions:
1. Add all ingredients into the mixing bowl and mix well.
2. Serve and enjoy.

Nutritional Value (Amount per Serving):
Calories 215; Fat 20 g; Carbohydrates 10 g; Sugar 2 g; Protein 2 g; Cholesterol 0 mg

Cabbage Stir Fry

Preparation Time: 10 minutes; Cooking Time: 10 minutes; Serve: 4
Ingredients:
- 1 head cabbage, chopped
- 1 small onion, chopped
- 2 tbsp olive oil
- 1/8 tsp turmeric
- 2 tbsp shredded coconut
- 2 tbsp fresh parsley, chopped
- ¼ tsp cumin powder
- Pepper
- Salt

Directions:
1. Heat olive oil in a pan over medium heat.
2. Add onion to the pan and sauté until softened.
3. Add cabbage, shredded coconut, turmeric, and cumin powder and stir until cooked. Season with pepper and salt.
4. Serve and enjoy.

Nutritional Value (Amount per Serving):
Calories 110; Fat 7.2 g; Carbohydrates 12 g; Sugar 7 g; Protein 2.5 g; Cholesterol 0 mg

Cauliflower Fried Rice

Preparation Time: 10 minutes; Cooking Time: 5 minutes; Serve: 6
Ingredients:

- 3 cups cauliflower rice
- 3 eggs, lightly beaten
- 2 garlic cloves, minced
- 3 tbsp olive oil
- ¼ cup carrots, peeled and chopped
- 1 small onion, chopped
- 1/2 tbsp coconut aminos
- 2 tbsp unsweetened coconut milk
- Pepper
- Salt

Directions:

1. Heat olive oil in a pan over medium-high heat.
2. Add onion and garlic and sauté until softened.
3. Add cauliflower rice and carrots and stir well and set cauliflower rice to one side of pan.
4. Whisk together coconut milk and eggs and pour into the pan and stir until eggs are scrambled.
5. Stir scrambled eggs into the cauliflower rice.
6. Add coconut aminos and stir well and cook for 2 minutes more.
7. Serve and enjoy.

Nutritional Value (Amount per Serving):
Calories 115; Fat 9 g; Carbohydrates 5 g; Sugar 2 g; Protein 5 g; Cholesterol 80 mg

Basil Eggplant Casserole

Preparation Time: 10 minutes; Cooking Time: 40 minutes; Serve: 6
Ingredients:

- 3 zucchini, sliced
- ¼ cup fresh basil, chopped
- 1 cup cherry tomatoes, halved
- 1 medium eggplant, sliced
- 1 tbsp olive oil
- 2 garlic cloves, minced
- 3 oz parmesan cheese, grated
- 1/4 cup parsley, chopped
- 1/4 tsp pepper
- 1/4 tsp salt

Directions:

1. Preheat the oven to 350 F.
2. Add all ingredients into the large bowl and toss well to combine.
3. Pour eggplant mixture into baking dish and bake for 35 minutes.
4. Serve and enjoy.

Nutritional Value (Amount per Serving):
Calories 105; Fat 6 g; Carbohydrates 10 g; Sugar 4 g; Protein 7 g; Cholesterol 10 mg

Broccoli Fritters

Preparation Time: 10 minutes; Cooking Time: 10 minutes; Serve: 4
Ingredients:

- 8 oz broccoli, chopped
- 1 cup cheddar cheese, shredded
- ¼ tsp garlic powder
- ¼ tsp onion powder
- ¼ tsp dried thyme
- 1 tbsp olive oil
- 2 tbsp almond flour
- 2 eggs, beaten
- ¼ tsp paprika
- Pepper
- Salt

Directions:
1. Steam chopped broccoli in the microwave and drain excess water.
2. Add broccoli, almond flour, spices, cheese, eggs, and salt in a bowl and stir until combined.
3. Heat olive oil in a pan over medium heat.
4. Pour tablespoon of batter onto hot pan and cook until lightly brown and crusty about 2-3 minutes.
5. Turn to another side and cook until lightly brown.
6. Serve and enjoy.

Nutritional Value (Amount per Serving):
Calories 212; Fat 16 g; Carbohydrates 5.5 g; Sugar 1 g; Protein 13 g; Cholesterol 110 mg

Simple Stir Fry Brussels sprouts

Preparation Time: 10 minutes; Cooking Time: 15 minutes; Serve: 4
Ingredients:
- 1 lb Brussels sprouts, trimmed and halved
- 1 onion, chopped
- 1 tbsp olive oil
- 2 jalapeno pepper, seeded and chopped
- 2 tbsp parsley, chopped
- Pepper
- Salt

Directions:
1. Heat olive oil in a pan over medium heat.
2. Add onion and jalapeno and sauté until softened.
3. Add Brussels sprouts and stir fry for 10 minutes.
4. Season with pepper and salt.
5. Garnish with parsley and serve.

Nutritional Value (Amount per Serving):
Calories 90; Fat 4 g; Carbohydrates 13 g; Sugar 4 g; Protein 4 g; Cholesterol 0 mg

Sautéed Mushrooms & Zucchini

Preparation Time: 10 minutes; Cooking Time: 7 minutes; Serve: 4
Ingredients:
- 1/2 cup mushrooms, sliced
- 1 squash, diced
- 1 zucchini, diced
- 3 tbsp olive oil
- ¼ tsp coriander powder
- ¼ tsp garlic powder
- ¼ tsp cumin powder
- ¼ tsp paprika
- ¼ tsp chili powder
- 2 tsp pepper
- Salt

Directions:

1. In a medium bowl, whisk together spices, pepper, olive oil, and salt.
2. Add vegetables to a bowl and toss well to coat.
3. Heat pan over medium-high heat.
4. Add vegetables in pan and sauté for 5-7 minutes or until vegetables are tender.
5. Serve and enjoy.

Nutritional Value (Amount per Serving):
Calories 105; Fat 10 g; Carbohydrates 3.6 g; Sugar 1.5 g; Protein 1 g; Cholesterol 0 mg

Healthy Spinach Stir Fry

Preparation Time: 10 minutes; Cooking Time: 15 minutes; Serve: 2
Ingredients:
- 4 cups spinach
- 1/2 onion, sliced
- 2 tsp olive oil
- 5 mushrooms, sliced
- 1 garlic clove, diced
- 1/2 tsp lemon zest
- 1/2 cup cherry tomatoes, halved
- 1 tsp butter
- Pepper
- Salt

Directions:
1. Heat butter in a pan over medium heat.
2. Add mushrooms and sauté for 3-4 minutes or until lightly browned.
3. Remove mushrooms to a dish and set aside.
4. Heat oil in same pan over medium heat.
5. Add onion and sauté for 2-3 minutes.
6. Add tomatoes, garlic, lemon zest, pepper, and salt and cook for 2-3 minutes.
7. Add mushrooms and spinach and cook until spinach is wilted.
8. Drizzle with lemon juice and serve.

Nutritional Value (Amount per Serving):
Calories 102; Fat 7 g; Carbohydrates 9 g; Sugar 3 g; Protein 4 g; Cholesterol 5 mg

Roasted Carrots

Preparation Time: 10 minutes; Cooking Time: 35 minutes; Serve: 6
Ingredients:
- 15 baby carrots
- 2 tbsp fresh parsley, chopped
- 5 garlic cloves, minced
- 1/2 tbsp dried basil
- 4 tbsp olive oil
- 1 1/2 tsp salt

Directions:
1. Preheat the oven to 375 F.
2. In a bowl, combine together oil, carrots, basil, garlic, and salt.
3. Spread the carrots onto a baking tray and bake for 35 minutes.
4. Garnish with parsley and serve.

Nutritional Value (Amount per Serving):
Calories 140; Fat 9 g; Carbohydrates 13 g; Sugar 6 g; Protein 2 g; Cholesterol 0 mg

Creamy Garlic Basil Mushrooms

Preparation Time: 10 minutes; Cooking Time: 35 minutes; Serve: 4
Ingredients:

- 1 1/2 lbs mushrooms, rinsed and quartered
- 3 garlic cloves, minced
- 1 onion, sliced
- 2 tbsp butter
- 1/2 cup heavy cream
- 1/2 cup dry red wine
- 1 tbsp dried basil
- 1/2 tsp pepper
- 1 1/2 tsp salt

Directions:

1. Melt butter in a large pan over medium-high heat.
2. Add onion and sauté for 15 minutes.
3. Add mushrooms and season with pepper and salt and cook for 15 minutes.
4. Add basil and garlic and stir well.
5. Add wine and stir well.
6. Turn heat to low and cook until wine reduced.
7. Add cream and stir for a minute.
8. Serve and enjoy.

Nutritional Value (Amount per Serving):

Calories 175; Fat 12 g; Carbohydrates 10.1 g; Sugar 5 g; Protein 6.2 g; Cholesterol 35 mg

Zucchini Noodles with Spinach

Preparation Time: 10 minutes; Cooking Time: 15 minutes; Serve: 4

Ingredients:

- 2 medium zucchini, spiralized using slicer
- 1 cup baby spinach
- 1/4 cup basil leaves
- 2 garlic cloves, chopped
- 1 tbsp olive oil
- 1/3 cup parmesan cheese, grated
- 4 oz cream cheese
- 1/2 tsp pepper
- 1/2 tsp salt

Directions:

1. Heat oil in a saucepan over medium heat.
2. Add garlic and sauté for 3-5 minutes.
3. Add zucchini noodles and cook for 10 minutes.
4. Add cream cheese, basil, and spinach and stir until cream cheese is melted.
5. Add parmesan cheese and season with pepper and salt.
6. Serve and enjoy.

Nutritional Value (Amount per Serving):

Calories 175; Fat 15 g; Carbohydrates 6 g; Sugar 2 g; Protein 6 g; Cholesterol 35 mg

Parmesan Pepper Eggs

Preparation Time: 5 minutes; Cooking Time: 5 minutes; Serve: 4

Ingredients:

- 4 eggs
- 1/4 cup parmesan cheese, grated
- 1 bell pepper, cut into rings
- ¼ tsp garlic powder
- 1 tbsp olive oil
- Pepper
- Salt

Directions:

1. Heat olive oil in a pan over medium heat.
2. Add bell pepper rings to the pan and sauté for minute.

3. Add 1 egg into the center of each pepper slice.
4. Season with garlic powder, pepper and salt and cook for 3 minutes, then turn it carefully.

5. Sprinkle with parmesan cheese and cook for a minute.
6. Serve and enjoy.

Nutritional Value (Amount per Serving):
Calories 141; Fat 11 g; Carbohydrates 3 g; Sugar 2 g; Protein 9 g; Cholesterol 170 mg

Vegetable Egg Scramble

Preparation Time: 10 minutes; Cooking Time: 10 minutes; Serve: 1
Ingredients:
- 3 eggs, beaten
- 1/2 cup baby spinach, chopped
- 1 bell pepper, chopped
- 5 mushrooms, sliced
- 1 tbsp olive oil
- Pepper
- Salt

Directions:
1. Heat half tbsp oil in a pan over medium heat.
2. Add vegetables and sauté for 5 minutes.
3. Heat remaining oil in another pan and add beaten eggs into the pan and cook over medium heat, stirring constantly.
4. Season with pepper and salt.
5. Add sautéed vegetables to egg mixture and mix well.
6. Serve and enjoy.

Nutritional Value (Amount per Serving):
Calories 320; Fat 27 g; Carbohydrates 4.5 g; Sugar 3 g; Protein 18 g; Cholesterol 490 mg

Spinach Broccoli Curry

Preparation Time: 10 minutes; Cooking Time: 30 minutes; Serve: 4
Ingredients:
- 1 cup broccoli florets
- 1/2 cup spinach, chopped
- 1 tbsp curry paste
- 1 1/2 tsp soy sauce
- 1 tsp ginger, minced
- 2 garlic cloves, minced
- 1/2 cup coconut cream
- 1 small onion, sliced
- 4 tbsp olive oil

Directions:
1. Heat 2 tbsp oil to a pan over medium-high heat.
2. Add onion and sauté until softened.
3. Add garlic and sauté for minute.
4. Turn heat to medium-low and add broccoli and stir well.
5. Once broccoli is cooked then set vegetables to the one side of pan.
6. Add curry paste and cook for a minute.
7. Add spinach and cook until wilted.
8. Add coconut cream, remaining oil, ginger, and soy sauce.
9. Stir everything well and simmer for 5 minutes.
10. Serve and enjoy.

Nutritional Value (Amount per Serving):
Calories 225; Fat 23 g; Carbohydrates 6 g; Sugar 2 g; Protein 2 g; Cholesterol 0 mg

Eggplant Stir Fry

Preparation Time: 10 minutes; Cooking Time: 25 minutes; Serve: 4
Ingredients:

- 4 cups eggplant, sliced
- 1/2 tsp ground ginger
- 1/2 tsp red pepper flakes
- 5 tbsp tamari sauce
- 1 tbsp olive oil
- 1 bell pepper, sliced
- 3 garlic cloves, minced
- 1 onion, chopped

Directions:

1. Heat oil in a pan over medium-high heat.
2. Add onion and garlic and sauté for 6-8 minutes.
3. Turn heat to medium and add eggplant and bell pepper.
4. Stir well and cook for few minutes.
5. Add red pepper flakes, ginger, and tamari and stir well.
6. Cook for 12 minutes. Stir occasionally.
7. Serve and enjoy.

Nutritional Value (Amount per Serving):
Calories 85; Fat 3 g; Carbohydrates 10 g; Sugar 4 g; Protein 4 g; Cholesterol 0 mg

Easy Grilled Veggies

Preparation Time: 10 minutes; Cooking Time: 15 minutes; Serve: 4
Ingredients:

- 4 bell peppers, diced
- 2 eggplants, diced
- 2 tbsp olive oil
- 2 cups mushrooms, sliced
- 1 tsp Cajun seasoning
- 1/4 tsp pepper
- 1 tsp salt

Directions:

1. Add all vegetables in a baking dish and drizzle with olive oil and season with seasoning, pepper and salt.
2. Cook at 392 F for 15-20 minutes
3. Serve and enjoy.

Nutritional Value (Amount per Serving):
Calories 55; Fat 3 g; Carbohydrates 5 g; Sugar 3 g; Protein 2 g; Cholesterol 0 mg

Avocado Green Beans

Preparation Time: 10 minutes; Cooking Time: 5 minutes; Serve: 6
Ingredients:

- 1 lb fresh green beans, trimmed
- ¼ cup green onion, chopped
- 3 avocado, peel and mashed
- 4 tbsp olive oil
- 1/4 tsp pepper
- 1/4 tsp salt

Directions:

1. Heat olive oil in pan over medium high heat.
2. Add green beans in pan and sauté for 4 minutes.
3. Season beans with pepper and salt and set aside.
4. In a mixing bowl, add green beans, avocado, and green onion and mix well.
5. Serve and enjoy.

Nutritional Value (Amount per Serving):
Calories 315; Fat 30 g; Carbohydrates 14 g; Sugar 2 g; Protein 3.6 g; Cholesterol 0 mg

Caper Broccoli Stir Fry

Preparation Time: 10 minutes; Cooking Time: 5 minutes; Serve: 4
Ingredients:
- 1 lb broccoli, cut into florets
- ¼ cup green onion, chopped
- 3 oz butter
- 2 tbsp capers, chopped
- Pepper
- Salt

Directions:
1. Melt butter in pan over medium heat.
2. Add broccoli florets and stir fry for 5 minutes over high heat.
3. Season broccoli with pepper and salt.
4. Add chopped capers and green onion and fry for 2 minutes.
5. Serve and enjoy.

Nutritional Value (Amount per Serving):
Calories 195; Fat 18 g; Carbohydrates 9 g; Sugar 2 g; Protein 4 g; Cholesterol 45 mg

Simple Carrot Mash

Preparation Time: 10 minutes; Cooking Time: 15 minutes; Serve: 6
Ingredients:
- 2 lbs carrots, peeled and chopped
- 1/2 cup vegetable stock
- 1 1/2 tsp garlic powder
- 4 tbsp butter
- Pepper
- Salt

Directions:
1. In a large pot add water and bring to boil.
2. Add carrot in pot and boil for 15 minutes. Drain well and place return in pot.
3. Add stock, butter, pepper, garlic powder, and salt.
4. Using masher mash the carrots until smooth.
5. Serve and enjoy.

Nutritional Value (Amount per Serving):
Calories 133; Fat 8 g; Carbohydrates 14 g; Sugar 7 g; Protein 2 g; Cholesterol 20 mg

Spicy Eggplant

Preparation Time: 10 minutes; Cooking Time: 2 hours 30 minutes; Serve: 8
Ingredients:

- 2 medium eggplants remove stem and cut into ½-inch pieces
- 1 tbsp garam masala
- 1 tbsp chili powder
- 1 tbsp ground cumin
- 2 jalapeno pepper, seeded and minced
- 5 garlic cloves, chopped

- 1 tsp ginger paste
- 1 tbsp fresh parsley, chopped
- 1/4 cup olive oil
- 1 tsp turmeric powder
- 1 onion, chopped
- 1/2 tbsp salt

Directions:

1. Add all ingredients except salt and parsley into the crock pot and stir well.
2. Cover and cook on high for 2 hours. Stir after 1 hour.
3. Stir well and cook on low for 30 minutes more.
4. Add parsley and salt and stir well.
5. Serve and enjoy.

Nutritional Value (Amount per Serving):
Calories 100; Fat 7 g; Carbohydrates 10 g; Sugar 4 g; Protein 2 g; Cholesterol 0 mg

Healthy Rutabaga Fritters

Preparation Time: 10 minutes; Cooking Time: 20 minutes; Serve: 4
Ingredients:

- 1 lb rutabaga, peel and grated
- 4 eggs
- 1/2 lb mozzarella cheese, shredded
- 4 oz butter

- 3 tbsp coconut flour
- 1/4 tsp pepper
- 1 tsp salt

Directions:

1. Add all ingredients except butter in bowl and mix well and set aside for few minutes.
2. Make round shape patties from mixture.
3. Melt butter in pan over medium heat.
4. Once butter is melted then place patties on hot pan and cook until golden brown.
5. Turn patties and cook for few minutes more.
6. Serve and enjoy.

Nutritional Value (Amount per Serving):
Calories 515; Fat 44 g; Carbohydrates 11 g; Sugar 8 g; Protein 20 g; Cholesterol 270 mg

Cheesy Turnip Gratin

Preparation Time: 10 minutes; Cooking Time: 35 minutes; Serve: 4
Ingredients:

- 1 1/2 lbs turnip, peel and sliced
- 5 tbsp fresh chives, chopped
- 2 garlic cloves, minced
- 1/2 onion, sliced
- 6.5 oz parmesan cheese, shredded

- 1 1/4 cup unsweetened coconut milk
- 1 3/4 oz butter
- 1/4 tsp pepper
- 1/2 tsp salt

Directions:

1. Preheat the oven to 400 F.
2. Arrange turnip and onion slices in greased baking dish. Season with pepper and salt.

3. Add garlic and butter on top.
4. Pour coconut milk and sprinkle shredded cheese on top.
5. Bake in oven for 30 minutes.
6. Garnish with chives and serve.

Nutritional Value (Amount per Serving):
Calories 515; Fat 45 g; Carbohydrates 14 g; Sugar 10 g; Protein 16 g; Cholesterol 80 mg

Tasty Salsa

Preparation Time: 10 minutes; Cooking Time: 2 hours; Serve: 6
Ingredients:
- 3 large tomatoes, chopped
- 1/4 cup fresh cilantro, chopped
- 1 tbsp white vinegar
- 2 garlic cloves, minced
- 1 bell pepper, chopped
- 1 small onion, chopped
- 1/4 tsp pepper
- 1/2 tsp cumin
- 1 tsp salt

Directions:
1. Add all ingredients into the crock pot and mix well.
2. Cover and cook on low for 2 hours.
3. Stir well and serve.

Nutritional Value (Amount per Serving):
Calories 30; Fat 1 g; Carbohydrates 6 g; Sugar 4 g; Protein 1 g; Cholesterol 0 mg

Eggplant Pie

Preparation Time: 10 minutes; Cooking Time: 35 minutes; Serve: 4
Ingredients:
- 1 eggplant, peel and diced
- 1 small onion, chopped
- 2 tomatoes, sliced
- 1/4 cup parmesan cheese, shredded
- 1 tbsp fresh basil, chopped
- 1 tbsp olive oil
- 2 tbsp pesto
- 1 tbsp butter, melted
- 1 egg, beaten
- 3 garlic cloves, minced

Directions:
1. Heat oil in a pan over medium heat.
2. Add onion and garlic and sauté until onion softened.
3. Remove pan from heat and set aside.
4. Add eggplant in boiling water and boil until soften.
5. Drain eggplant well and mash.
6. Add sautéed garlic and onion into the eggplant mash and mix well.
7. Now add egg, garlic, pesto, and butter and mix well to combined.
8. Arrange one tomato slices on the bottom of the greased pie pan.
9. Add eggplant mixture over the tomato slices then layer with remaining tomato slices.
10. Sprinkle parmesan cheese and basil on top.
11. Bake in oven for 30 minutes.
12. Serve and enjoy.

Nutritional Value (Amount per Serving):
Calories 175; Fat 12 g; Carbohydrates 11 g; Sugar 6 g; Protein 7 g; Cholesterol 55 mg

Tofu Skewers

Preparation Time: 10 minutes; Cooking Time: 15 minutes; Serve: 6

Ingredients:

- 14 oz tofu, drained, pressed and cut into 1-inch pieces
- 1 red bell pepper, cut into chunks
- 1/4 tsp pepper
- 1/4 tsp cayenne pepper
- 1/2 tsp turmeric
- 2 tsp ground cumin
- 2 tsp paprika
- 1 small zucchini, cut into chunks
- 2 garlic cloves, minced
- 2 tbsp tomato paste
- 2 tbsp lemon juice
- 1 cup unsweetened coconut milk
- 3/4 tsp salt

Directions:

1. Preheat the grill over medium-high heat.
2. Add all ingredients into the mixing bowl and mix well.
3. Cover bowl and place in fridge for 1 hour.
4. Arrange marinated tofu, bell pepper, and zucchini pieces on soaked wooden skewers.
5. Place tofu skewers on hot grill and cook for 10 minutes or until lightly golden brown.
6. Serve and enjoy.

Nutritional Value (Amount per Serving):

Calories 160; Fat 12 g; Carbohydrates 8 g; Sugar 4 g; Protein 8 g; Cholesterol 0 mg

Healthy Vegetables Roast

Preparation Time: 10 minutes; Cooking Time: 25 minutes; Serve: 4

Ingredients:

- 1 cup eggplant, diced
- 4 mushroom, sliced
- 2 garlic cloves, minced
- 2 tbsp parsley, chopped
- 3 tbsp vinegar
- 8 small asparagus spears, ends removed
- 2 bell pepper, cut into strips
- 1 cup zucchini, sliced
- 1/4 cup olive oil
- 1/2 tsp pepper
- 1 tsp salt

Directions:

1. Preheat the oven to 375 F.
2. In a large bowl, whisk together oil, garlic, parsley, pepper, salt, and vinegar.
3. Add vegetables in a bowl and toss well.
4. Place vegetables in an aluminum foil container and pour remaining marinade over vegetables. Seal container.
5. Bake in oven for 25 minutes. Season with pepper and salt.
6. Serve and enjoy.

Nutritional Value (Amount per Serving):

Calories 150; Fat 13 g; Carbohydrates 8 g; Sugar 4 g; Protein 2 g; Cholesterol 0 mg

Spaghetti Squash

Preparation Time: 10 minutes; Cooking Time: 15 minutes; Serve: 4
Ingredients:

- 4 cups spaghetti squash, cooked
- 2 tbsp fresh parsley, chopped
- 1/2 tsp dried thyme
- 1/2 tsp dried rosemary
- 1/2 tsp garlic powder
- 2 tbsp olive oil
- ½ tsp pepper
- ½ tsp sage
- 1 tsp salt

Directions:

1. Preheat the oven to 350 F.
2. Add all ingredients into the large bowl and mix well to combine.
3. Transfer bowl mixture to the baking dish and cook in oven for 15 minutes.
4. Stir well and serve.

Nutritional Value (Amount per Serving):
   Calories 95; Fat 7 g; Carbohydrates 8 g; Sugar 0.2 g; Protein 0.9 g; Cholesterol 0 mg

Creamy Asparagus Mash

Preparation Time: 10 minutes; Cooking Time: 10 minutes; Serve: 2
Ingredients:

- 10 asparagus spears, trimmed and chopped
- 1 tsp lemon juice
- 2 tbsp coconut cream
- 1 small onion, diced
- 2 tbsp fresh parsley, chopped
- 1 tbsp olive oil
- Pepper
- Salt

Directions:

1. Sauté onion in pan over medium heat until onion is softened.
2. Blanch chopped asparagus in boiling water for 2 minutes and drain well.
3. Add sautéed onion, lemon juice, parsley, coconut cream, asparagus, pepper, and salt into the blender and blend until smooth.
4. Serve and enjoy.

Nutritional Value (Amount per Serving):
   Calories 124; Fat 10 g; Carbohydrates 7 g; Sugar 3 g; Protein 3 g; Cholesterol 0 mg

Roasted Summer Squash

Preparation Time: 10 minutes; Cooking Time: 60 minutes; Serve: 3
Ingredients:

- 2 lbs summer squash, cut into 1-inch pieces
- 1/4 tsp garlic powder
- 3 tbsp olive oil
- 1 tbsp lemon juice
- 1/4 tsp paprika
- Pepper
- Salt

Directions:

1. Preheat the oven to 400 F.

2. Place squash pieces onto a baking tray and drizzle with olive oil.
3. Season with garlic powder, paprika, pepper, and salt.
4. Drizzle with lemon juice and bake in oven for 50-60 minutes.
5. Serve and enjoy.

Nutritional Value (Amount per Serving):
Calories 180; Fat 15 g; Carbohydrates 12 g; Sugar 10 g; Protein 3 g; Cholesterol 0 mg

Carrots with Green Beans

Preparation Time: 10 minutes; Cooking Time: 10 minutes; Serve: 2

Ingredients:
- 2 cups green beans, trimmed
- 1 cup baby carrots, halved lengthwise
- 1 tbsp fresh lemon juice
- ¼ tsp garlic powder
- ¼ tsp paprika
- 2 tbsp butter
- 1 tbsp olive oil
- Pepper
- Salt

Directions:
1. Heat olive oil in a pan over medium-high heat.
2. Add carrots sauté for a minute.
3. Add green beans and sauté until tender. Season with pepper and salt.
4. Transfer vegetables on a plate.
5. Melt butter in same pan. Once butter is melted then add lemon juice, garlic powder, and paprika and stir well.
6. Return vegetables to pan and toss well to coat.
7. Serve and enjoy.

Nutritional Value (Amount per Serving):
Calories 230; Fat 18 g; Carbohydrates 14 g; Sugar 6 g; Protein 2 g; Cholesterol 0 mg

Simple Spinach Omelet

Preparation Time: 10 minutes; Cooking Time: 5 minutes; Serve: 1

Ingredients:
- 2 eggs
- 1/2 cup baby spinach
- 1 tsp olive oil
- Pepper
- Salt

Directions:
1. Add eggs, spinach, pepper, and salt in the blender and blend until well combined.
2. Heat olive oil in a pan over medium heat.
3. Pour egg mixture into a hot pan and cook for 2-3 minutes then flip to other side and cook for 2 minutes more.
4. Serve and enjoy.

Nutritional Value (Amount per Serving):
Calories 375; Fat 30 g; Carbohydrates 8 g; Sugar 1 g; Protein 12 g; Cholesterol 320 mg

Zucchini Hummus

Preparation Time: 10 minutes; Cooking Time: 10 minutes; Serve: 4

Ingredients:

- 4 zucchini, cut in half
- 1/4 cup parsley, chopped
- 1 tbsp lemon juice
- 1 tbsp olive oil
- 2 garlic cloves
- 1 tsp cumin
- 2 1/2 tbsp tahini
- Pepper
- Salt

Directions:

1. Place zucchini on hot grill and season with pepper and salt.
2. Grilled zucchini for 10 minutes.
3. Add grilled zucchini, parsley, cumin, tahini, lemon juice, olive oil, garlic, pepper and salt in a blender and blend until smooth.
4. Pour zucchini mixture in a bowl and sprinkle with paprika.
5. Serve and enjoy.

Nutritional Value (Amount per Serving):

Calories 135; Fat 10 g; Carbohydrates 10 g; Sugar 4 g; Protein 5 g; Cholesterol 0 mg

Veggie Medley

Preparation Time: 10 minutes; Cooking Time: 6 hours; Serve: 8
Ingredients:

- 2 cups mushrooms, sliced
- 1 bell pepper, chopped
- 1 onion, chopped
- 1/2 tsp oregano
- ¼ tsp dried thyme
- 14.5 oz can tomatoes, diced
- 1 zucchini, chopped
- 1/4 tsp garlic powder
- 1/8 tsp pepper

Directions:

1. Add all ingredients into the crock pot and stir well.
2. Cover and cook on low for 6 hours.
3. Stir well and serve.

Nutritional Value (Amount per Serving):

Calories 30; Fat 0.2 g; Carbohydrates 6 g; Sugar 3 g; Protein 2 g; Cholesterol 0 mg

Asian Vegetable Medley

Preparation Time: 10 minutes; Cooking Time: 3 hours; Serve: 8
Ingredients:

- 12 oz zucchini, halved and cut into 1-inch slices
- 1/2 tbsp fresh ginger, grated
- 1/3 cup unsweetened coconut milk
- 2 tbsp curry paste
- 2 tbsp vegetable stock
- 2 cups mushrooms, quartered
- 8 oz squash, halved and sliced
- 3 garlic cloves, minced
- 1/2 cup leeks, sliced
- 1/4 cup fresh basil leaves
- 1 sweet pepper, seeded and cut into pieces

Directions:

1. Add all ingredients except ginger, coconut milk, and basil into the crock pot and stir well.
2. Cover and cook on low for 3 hours.
3. Add ginger and coconut milk and stir well.

4. Garnish with basil and serve.

Nutritional Value (Amount per Serving):

Calories 65; Fat 4 g; Carbohydrates 7 g; Sugar 2 g; Protein 2 g; Cholesterol 0 mg

Baba Ganoush

Preparation Time: 10 minutes; Cooking Time: 60 minutes; Serve: 6

Ingredients:

- 1 medium eggplant, peel and diced
- 1/4 tsp liquid smoke
- 2 garlic cloves, minced
- 2 tbsp lemon juice
- 1 tbsp tahini
- 1/2 tsp olive oil
- 1/4 cup fresh parsley, chopped
- Pepper
- Salt

Directions:

1. Add all ingredients into the crock pot and stir well.
2. Cover and cook on high for 1 hour.
3. Mash eggplant mixture using masher until smooth.
4. Serve and enjoy.

Nutritional Value (Amount per Serving):

Calories 40; Fat 2 g; Carbohydrates 5 g; Sugar 2 g; Protein 1 g; Cholesterol 0 mg

Cheesy Spinach Artichoke Dip

Preparation Time: 10 minutes; Cooking Time: 4 hours; Serve: 10

Ingredients:

- 14.5 oz can artichoke hearts, drained and chopped
- 3 garlic cloves, minced
- 8 oz cheddar cheese, shredded
- 2 cups mozzarella cheese, shredded
- 10 oz fresh spinach, chopped
- 1/2 cup parmesan cheese, shredded
- 3/4 cup Greek yogurt
- 1/2 tsp pepper
- 1 tsp salt

Directions:

1. Spray crock pot with cooking spray.
2. Add all ingredients into the large bowl and mix well.
3. Pour artichoke mixture into the crock pot.
4. Cover and cook on low for 4 hours.
5. Serve and enjoy.

Nutritional Value (Amount per Serving):

Calories 175; Fat 11 g; Carbohydrates 5 g; Sugar 1 g; Protein 13 g; Cholesterol 35 mg

Skillet Zucchini

Preparation Time: 10 minutes; Cooking Time: 20 minutes; Serve: 4

Ingredients:

- 1 lb zucchini, diced
- ½ cup feta cheese, crumbled
- ½ tsp pickled jalapeno, minced
- 1 green onion, sliced
- 2 medium tomatoes, diced
- 1 tbsp olive oil
- 2 garlic cloves, chopped
- Pepper

- Salt

Directions:
1. Heat oil in a skillet over medium heat.
2. Add garlic and sauté for minutes.
3. Add zucchini and sauté for 3 minutes.
4. Add green onion and tomato and sauté for 3 minutes.
5. Remove pan from heat and add jalapeno and stir well.
6. Top with crumbled cheese and season with pepper and salt.
7. Serve and enjoy.

Nutritional Value (Amount per Serving):
Calories 100; Fat 5 g; Carbohydrates 7 g; Sugar 3 g; Protein 5 g; Cholesterol 16 mg

Quick Guacamole

Preparation Time: 5 minutes; Cooking Time: 5 minutes; Serve: 8

Ingredients:
- 3 avocados, pitted and halved
- 2 tbsp fresh parsley, chopped
- 2 garlic cloves, minced
- 1 small onion, minced
- 2 tbsp fresh lime juice
- Pepper
- Salt

Directions:
1. Remove avocado pulp using a spoon and place in bowl.
2. Mash avocado pulp using a fork.
3. Add remaining ingredients and stir well.
4. Serve and enjoy.

Nutritional Value (Amount per Serving):
Calories 92; Fat 8 g; Carbohydrates 6 g; Sugar 0 g; Protein 1 g; Cholesterol 0 mg

Parmesan Zucchini Bake

Preparation Time: 10 minutes; Cooking Time: 25 minutes; Serve: 6

Ingredients:
- 2 large zucchini, diced
- ¼ cup basil, chopped
- ¼ cup fresh parsley, chopped
- 1 tsp Italian seasoning
- ½ cup parmesan cheese, grated
- 4 garlic cloves, minced
- 2 tomatoes, diced
- Pepper
- Salt

Directions:
1. Preheat the oven to 350 F.
2. In a large bowl, add all ingredients except basil and parsley and stir well to combine.
3. Transfer bowl mixture to a baking dish and bake for 25 minutes.
4. Garnish with basil and parsley and serve.

Nutritional Value (Amount per Serving):
Calories 81; Fat 3.5 g; Carbohydrates 6 g; Sugar 3 g; Protein 6 g; Cholesterol 11 mg

Asian Bok Choy

Preparation Time: 10 minutes; Cooking Time: 5 minutes; Serve: 2

Ingredients:
- 4 baby bok choy heads, chopped
- ½ tbsp soy sauce
- 1 tsp chili paste
- ½ tbsp ginger, grated
- 2 garlic cloves, minced
- 1 tbsp sesame oil

Directions:
1. Heat oil in a pan over medium-high heat.
2. Add ginger and garlic and sauté for minute.
3. Add bok choy, soy sauce, and chili paste and cook for 4-5 minutes.
4. Serve and enjoy.

Nutritional Value (Amount per Serving):
Calories 130; Fat 8 g; Carbohydrates 12 g; Sugar 2.8 g; Protein 6 g; Cholesterol 1 mg

Flavorful Baked Okra

Preparation Time: 10 minutes; Cooking Time: 15 minutes; Serve: 4
Ingredients:
- 1 lb okra, cut into ½ inch pieces
- 1/8 tsp cayenne pepper
- ½ tsp paprika
- 2 tbsp olive oil
- Salt

Directions:
1. Preheat the oven to 450 F.
2. Spread okra on baking tray and drizzle with olive oil.
3. Season with cayenne pepper, paprika, and salt. Stir well.
4. Bake in preheated oven for 15 minutes.
5. Serve and enjoy.

Nutritional Value (Amount per Serving):
Calories 105; Fat 7 g; Carbohydrates 8 g; Sugar 1.7 g; Protein 2.2 g; Cholesterol 0 mg

Broccoli with Cheese

Preparation Time: 5 minutes; Cooking Time: 10 minutes; Serve: 6
Ingredients:
- 1 ½ lbs broccoli florets
- ¼ cup feta cheese, crumbled
- 2 tbsp olive oil
- 2 green onion, sliced
- ½ tsp pepper
- ½ tsp kosher salt

Directions:
1. Heat oil in a pan over medium heat.
2. Add broccoli to pan and sauté for 5 minutes.
3. Add green onion and stir well. Season with pepper and salt and cook for 2-3 minutes.
4. Add crumbled cheese and stir well.
5. Serve and enjoy.

Nutritional Value (Amount per Serving):
Calories 97; Fat 6 g; Carbohydrates 8 g; Sugar 2 g; Protein 4 g; Cholesterol 6 mg

Curried Cauliflower Rice

Preparation Time: 10 minutes; Cooking Time: 10 minutes; Serve: 4
Ingredients:

- 4 cups cauliflower rice
- ½ cup vegetable stock
- 1 tsp turmeric powder
- 1 tbsp olive oil
- ½ tbsp curry powder
- Salt

Directions:

1. Heat oil in a saucepan over medium heat.
2. Add turmeric and curry powder and sauté for 30 seconds.
3. Add remaining ingredients and stir well and cook until stock is completely absorbed.
4. Stir well and serve.

Nutritional Value (Amount per Serving):
Calories 92; Fat 8 g; Carbohydrates 6 g; Sugar 0 g; Protein 1 g; Cholesterol 0 mg

Grilled Eggplant

Preparation Time: 10 minutes; Cooking Time: 10 minutes; Serve: 6
Ingredients:

- 2 medium eggplant, cut ¾-inch thick slices
- 1 tsp Italian seasoning
- 2 garlic clove, minced
- 4 tbsp olive oil
- Pepper
- Salt

Directions:

1. Preheat the grill to medium-high heat.
2. In a small bowl, mix together Italian seasoning, garlic, and olive oil.
3. Brush eggplant slices with olive oil mixture and place on hot grill.
4. Grill for 3-5 minutes on each side.
5. Serve and enjoy.

Nutritional Value (Amount per Serving):
Calories 120; Fat 9 g; Carbohydrates 8 g; Sugar 5 g; Protein 2 g; Cholesterol 0 mg

Roasted Eggplant

Preparation Time: 10 minutes; Cooking Time: 25 minutes; Serve: 4
Ingredients:

- 1 lb eggplant, peeled and cut into 2-inch cubes
- 2 tbsp olive oil
- ½ tsp pepper
- 1 tsp kosher salt

Directions:

1. Preheat the oven to 425 F.
2. Place eggplant cubes on baking tray and drizzle with olive oil. Season with pepper and salt.
3. Roast in preheated oven for 25 minutes.
4. Serve and enjoy.

Nutritional Value (Amount per Serving):

Calories 90; Fat 7 g; Carbohydrates 7 g; Sugar 4 g; Protein 1 g; Cholesterol 0 mg

Sauteed Bell Peppers

Preparation Time: 10 minutes; Cooking Time: 10 minutes; Serve: 3

Ingredients:

- 3 bell peppers, sliced
- 1 tbsp olive oil
- 1 onion, sliced
- ½ tsp chipotle powder
- Pepper
- Salt

Directions:

1. Heat oil in a pan over medium-high heat.
2. Add onion and bell peppers to the pan and sauté for 10 minutes.
3. Season with chipotle powder, pepper, and salt.
4. Stir well and serve.

Nutritional Value (Amount per Serving):

Calories 90; Fat 5 g; Carbohydrates 12 g; Sugar 7 g; Protein 1.6 g; Cholesterol 0 mg

Chapter 7: Soups, Stews & Salads

Broccoli Cheese Soup

Preparation Time: 10 minutes; Cooking Time: 2 hours 30 minutes; Serve: 4
Ingredients:

- 5 cups broccoli florets
- 2 cups cheddar cheese, shredded
- 1/2 cup mozzarella cheese, shredded
- 4 tbsp cream cheese
- 3 tbsp butter
- ½ cup heavy cream
- 2 cups chicken stock
- Pepper
- Salt

Directions:

1. Add broccoli, stock, heavy cream, cream cheese, and butter to the slow cooker and stir well.
2. Cover and cook on high for 1 hour 30 minutes.
3. Stir well and add remaining ingredients and cook for 1 hour more.
4. Serve and enjoy.

Nutritional Value (Amount per Serving):
Calories 444; Fat 37 g; Carbohydrates 10 g; Sugar 2.5 g; Protein 20 g; Cholesterol 116mg

Hearty Cabbage Beef Soup

Preparation Time: 10 minutes; Cooking Time: 45 minutes; Serve: 10
Ingredients:

- 2 lbs ground beef
- 4 cups chicken stock
- 10 oz Rotel tomatoes, diced
- 3 cube bouillon
- 1 large cabbage head, chopped
- ½ tsp cumin powder
- 2 garlic cloves, minced
- ¼ onion, diced
- Pepper
- Salt

Directions:

1. Brown the meat in pan over medium heat.
2. Add onion and cook until soften.
3. Transfer meat mixture to the stock pot.
4. Add remaining ingredients to the stock pot stir well and bring to boil over high heat.
5. Turn heat to medium-low and simmer for 45 minutes.

Nutritional Value (Amount per Serving):
Calories 260; Fat 18 g; Carbohydrates 5 g; Sugar 2 g; Protein 15 g; Cholesterol 64 mg

Tasty Taco Soup

Preparation Time: 10 minutes; Cooking Time: 4 hours; Serve: 8
Ingredients:

- 2 lbs ground beef
- 2 tbsp fresh cilantro, chopped

- 4 cups chicken stock
- 2 tbsp taco seasoning
- 20 oz Rotel
- 16 oz cream cheese

Directions:
1. Brown meat until fully cooked.
2. Transfer cooked meat in slow cooker.
3. Add remaining ingredients and stir well.
4. Cover and cook on low for 4 hours.
5. Stir well and serve.

Nutritional Value (Amount per Serving):

Calories 547; Fat 43 g; Carbohydrates 5 g; Sugar 4 g; Protein 33 g; Cholesterol 42 mg

Delicious Chicken Taco Soup

Preparation Time: 10 minutes; Cooking Time: 6 hours; Serve: 8

Ingredients:
- 2 lbs chicken breasts, skinless and boneless
- 4 cups chicken stock
- 20 oz Rotel tomatoes, diced
- 2 tbsp Mrs. Dash seasoning
- 1 oz ranch seasoning
- 16 oz cream cheese

Directions:
1. Add all ingredients into the slow cooker and stir well.
2. Cover and cook on low for 6 hours.
3. Remove chicken from slow cooker and shred using fork.
4. Return shredded chicken to the slow cooker and stir well.
5. Serve and enjoy.

Nutritional Value (Amount per Serving):

Calories 418; Fat 28 g; Carbohydrates 2 g; Sugar 0.5 g; Protein 37 g; Cholesterol 163 mg

Mushroom Chicken Soup

Preparation Time: 10 minutes; Cooking Time: 20 minutes; Serve: 4

Ingredients:
- 1 tsp Italian seasoning
- 2 ½ cups chicken broth
- 1 lb chicken breast, boneless and skinless
- 1 squash, chopped
- 1 ½ cups mushrooms, chopped
- 2 garlic cloves, minced
- 1 onion, chopped
- Pepper
- Salt

Directions:
1. Add all ingredients into the instant pot and stir well.
2. Cover slow cooker and cook on high for 15 minutes.
3. Allow to release pressure naturally then open the lid.
4. Remove chicken from pot and shred using fork.
5. Puree the soup using immersion blender.
6. Return shredded chicken to the instant pot and stir well.
7. Serve and enjoy.

Nutritional Value (Amount per Serving):

Calories 290; Fat 14 g; Carbohydrates 8 g; Sugar 3 g; Protein 30 g; Cholesterol 110 mg

Easy Mexican Chicken Soup

Preparation Time: 10 minutes; Cooking Time: 4 hours; Serve: 6
Ingredients:

- 8 oz pepper jack cheese, shredded
- 14.5 oz chicken stock
- 14 oz salsa
- 2 lbs chicken, boneless and skinless
- Pepper
- Salt

Directions:

1. Add all ingredients into the slow cooker and stir well.
2. Cover and cook on high for 4 hours.
3. Remove chicken from slow cooker and shred using fork.
4. Return shredded chicken to the slow cooker and stir well.
5. Serve and enjoy.

Nutritional Value (Amount per Serving):
   Calories 330; Fat 23 g; Carbohydrates 4 g; Sugar 3 g; Protein 24 g; Cholesterol 90 mg

Creamy Crab Dip Soup

Preparation Time: 10 minutes; Cooking Time: 5 minutes; Serve: 8
Ingredients:

- 1 lb crabmeat
- 1 cup parmesan cheese, grated
- 2 ¾ cup half and half
- 8 oz cream cheese
- 1 tbsp bae seasoning
- 1 tbsp butter
- Pepper
- Salt

Directions:

1. Melt butter in a saucepan over medium heat.
2. Add half and half and cream cheese and stir until creamy.
3. Add cheese and stir until cheese is melted.
4. Add crabmeat and turn heat to low and cook until crabmeat heated trough.
5. Serve and enjoy.

Nutritional Value (Amount per Serving):
   Calories 350; Fat 27 g; Carbohydrates 5 g; Sugar 2 g; Protein 20 g; Cholesterol 130 mg

Veggie Shrimp Soup

Preparation Time: 10 minutes; Cooking Time: 5 hours; Serve: 6
Ingredients:

- 8.5 oz shrimp
- 4 cups chicken broth
- 2 cups heavy cream
- 4 oz turnip, diced
- 5 oz broccoli florets
- 6 oz cauliflower florets
- 4 cups water
- 2 bouillon cubes

Directions:

1. Add all ingredients except shrimp into the slow cooker and stir well.
2. Cover and cook on low for 4 hours 30 minutes.

3. Add shrimp and stir well. Cover and cook for 30 minutes more.

4. Season with salt and serve.

Nutritional Value (Amount per Serving):
Calories 345; Fat 31 g; Carbohydrates 6 g; Sugar 1 g; Protein 10 g; Cholesterol 205 mg

Avocado Soup

Preparation Time: 10 minutes; Cooking Time: 10 minutes; Serve: 6
Ingredients:
- 2 avocados, peel and pitted
- 1 cup heavy cream
- 2 tbsp dry sherry
- 2 cups vegetable broth
- ½ tsp fresh lemon juice
- Pepper
- Salt

Directions:
1. Add avocado, lemon juice, sherry, and broth to the blender and blend until smooth.
2. Pour blended mixture into a bowl and stir in cream.
3. Season with pepper and salt.
4. Serve and enjoy.

Nutritional Value (Amount per Serving):
Calories 102; Fat 9.5 g; Carbohydrates 1.9 g; Sugar 0.3 g; Protein 2.4 g; Cholesterol 27 mg

Almond Celery Soup

Preparation Time: 10 minutes; Cooking Time: 8 minutes; Serve: 2
Ingredients:
- ¼ cup almonds, chopped
- 6 celery stalks, chopped
- 3 cups vegetable stock
- Pepper
- Salt

Directions:
1. Pour stock in a saucepan and boil over high heat for 2 minutes.
2. Add celery in stock and cook for 8 minutes.
3. Remove from heat and pour in blender and blend until smooth.
4. Add almonds and stir well.
5. Season with pepper and salt.
6. Serve and enjoy.

Nutritional Value (Amount per Serving):
Calories 82; Fat 7 g; Carbohydrates 5 g; Sugar 2.2 g; Protein 2.9 g; Cholesterol 0 mg

Yogurt Cucumber Soup

Preparation Time: 10 minutes; Cooking Time: 10 minutes; Serve: 4
Ingredients:
- 1 cucumber, peel and grate
- 1 tbsp olive oil
- ¾ cup milk
- 1 tbsp fresh dill, chopped
- 1 garlic clove, chopped
- 2 cups yogurt

- ½ tsp salt

Directions:

1. In a bowl, mix together yogurt, grated cucumber, dill, garlic, and salt.
2. Stir in oil and milk. Place in refrigerator for 1 hour.
3. Serve and enjoy.

Nutritional Value (Amount per Serving):

Calories 155; Fat 6 g; Carbohydrates 13 g; Sugar 12 g; Protein 9 g; Cholesterol 11 mg

Creamy Cauliflower Soup

Preparation Time: 10 minutes; Cooking Time: 25 minutes; Serve: 4

Ingredients:

- 1/2 head cauliflower, chopped
- ½ tsp garlic powder
- ¼ cup onion, diced
- 1/4 tbsp olive oil
- 2 garlic cloves, minced
- 15 oz vegetable stock
- ¼ tsp pepper
- 1/2 tsp salt

Directions:

1. Heat olive oil in a saucepan over medium heat.
2. Add onion and garlic and sauté for 4 minutes.
3. Add cauliflower and stock and stir well. Bring to boil.
4. Cover pan with lid and simmer for 15 minutes.
5. Season with garlic powder, pepper, and salt.
6. Puree the soup using blender until smooth.
7. Serve and enjoy.

Nutritional Value (Amount per Serving):

Calories 41; Fat 2 g; Carbohydrates 4 g; Sugar 2 g; Protein 3 g; Cholesterol 0 mg

Ginger Carrot Soup

Preparation Time: 10 minutes; Cooking Time: 10 minutes; Serve: 4

Ingredients:

- 4 carrots, peeled and chopped
- 1 tsp turmeric powder
- 3 cups vegetable stock
- 2 tsp coconut oil
- 3 garlic cloves, minced
- 1 onion, chopped
- 1 parsnip, peeled and chopped
- 1 tbsp fresh lemon juice
- 1/4 tsp cayenne pepper
- 1/2 tbsp ginger, grated

Directions:

1. Preheat the oven to 350 F.
2. Add carrots, garlic, onion, parsnip, coconut oil, and cayenne pepper in a bowl and toss well.
3. Spread bowl mixture on baking tray and roast in oven for 15 minutes.
4. Transfer roasted veggie in blender along with ginger, lemon juice, and stock into the blender and blend until smooth.
5. Serve and enjoy.

Nutritional Value (Amount per Serving):

Calories 72; Fat 4 g; Carbohydrates 11 g; Sugar 5 g; Protein 1 g; Cholesterol 0 mg

Coconut Squash Soup

Preparation Time: 10 minutes; Cooking Time: 25 minutes; Serve: 8
Ingredients:

- 3 cups butternut squash, chopped
- 2 garlic cloves, chopped
- 1 tbsp coconut oil
- 1 tsp dried onion flakes
- 1 ½ cups unsweetened coconut milk
- 1 tbsp curry powder
- 4 cups vegetable stock
- 1 tsp kosher salt

Directions:

1. Add squash, coconut oil, onion flakes, curry powder, stock, garlic, and salt into a large saucepan. Bring to boil.
2. Turn heat to medium and simmer for 20 minutes.
3. Puree the soup using a blender until smooth.
4. Return soup to the saucepan and stir in coconut milk and cook for 2 minutes.
5. Serve and enjoy.

Nutritional Value (Amount per Serving):
Calories 145; Fat 12 g; Carbohydrates 10 g; Sugar 3 g; Protein 2 g; Cholesterol 0 mg

Cheese Mushroom Shrimp Soup

Preparation Time: 10 minutes; Cooking Time: 15 minutes; Serve: 8
Ingredients:

- 24 oz shrimp, cooked
- 8 oz cheddar cheese, shredded
- ½ cup butter
- 1 cup heavy cream
- 32 oz vegetable stock
- 2 cups mushrooms, sliced
- Pepper
- Salt

Directions:

1. Add stock and mushrooms to a large pot. Bring to boil.
2. Turn heat to medium and add cheese, heavy cream, and butter and stir until cheese is melted.
3. Add shrimp. Stir well and cook for 2 minutes more.
4. Serve and enjoy.

Nutritional Value (Amount per Serving):
Calories 390; Fat 28 g; Carbohydrates 3 g; Sugar 0.8 g; Protein 30 g; Cholesterol 17 mg

Beef Veggie Soup

Preparation Time: 10 minutes; Cooking Time: 55 minutes; Serve: 8
Ingredients:

- 1 ½ lbs ground beef
- 15 oz can tomatoes, diced
- ¼ cup tomato paste
- 2 celery stalk, chopped
- 10 oz carrots, cut into julienne
- 3 garlic cloves, minced
- 1 medium onion, chopped
- 4 cans chicken stock

- ½ cup green beans, chopped
- 1 medium zucchini, chopped
- ½ tsp dried oregano
- 1 tsp dried basil

- 1 ½ cups cabbage, shredded
- ¼ tsp pepper
- ¼ tsp salt

Directions:

1. Add garlic, onion, and meat in stockpot and cook over medium heat for 8 minutes.
2. Add celery and carrots and cook for 6-8 minutes.
3. Add tomato paste and cook for a minute.
4. Add tomatoes, stock, seasonings, green beans, zucchini, and cabbage. Bring to boil.
5. Reduce heat and simmer for 40-45 minutes.
6. Serve and enjoy.

Nutritional Value (Amount per Serving):

Calories 208; Fat 5 g; Carbohydrates 11 g; Sugar 6 g; Protein 6 g; Cholesterol 76 mg

Zucchini Soup

Preparation Time: 10 minutes; Cooking Time: 28 minutes; Serve: 4

Ingredients:

- 1 zucchini, chopped
- 1 cup unsweetened coconut milk
- 1 cup vegetable stock
- 1 bell pepper, chopped

- 2 carrots, chopped
- 1 tbsp olive oil
- Pepper
- Salt

Directions:

1. Heat olive oil in a pan over medium heat.
2. Add vegetables to the pan and cook for 7-8 minutes.
3. Add coconut milk and stir well and cook for 5 minutes.
4. Add stock and cook for 15 minutes.
5. Puree soup using blender until smooth. Season with pepper and salt.
6. Serve and enjoy.

Nutritional Value (Amount per Serving):

Calories 200; Fat 18 g; Carbohydrates 10 g; Sugar 5 g; Protein 2 g; Cholesterol 13 mg

Basil Broccoli Soup

Preparation Time: 10 minutes; Cooking Time: 10 minutes; Serve: 4

Ingredients:

- 2/3 lb broccoli florets
- 3 1/4 vegetable stock
- 1/2 lb cream cheese
- 1 leek, chopped
- 2 garlic cloves, chopped

- ½ cup fresh basil
- 3 oz olive oil
- Pepper
- Salt

Directions:

1. Add broccoli, leek, salt, and stock in saucepan. Bring to boil.
2. Transfer broccoli mixture in blender with olive oil, cream cheese, pepper and basil and blend until smooth.

3. Serve and enjoy.

Nutritional Value (Amount per Serving):

Calories 410; Fat 39 g; Carbohydrates 10 g; Sugar 2 g; Protein 7 g; Cholesterol 60 mg

Basil Tomato Soup

Preparation Time: 10 minutes; Cooking Time: 15 minutes; Serve: 2

Ingredients:

- 5 oz grape tomatoes, halved
- 14 oz tomatoes, diced
- 2 tsp turmeric
- 3 garlic cloves, minced
- 1 small onion, diced
- 1/2 cup vegetable stock
- 1 tbsp vinegar
- 1 tsp basil, dried
- 1 tsp coconut oil
- 1/4 tsp pepper
- 1/2 tsp salt

Directions:

1. Heat olive oil in a saucepan over medium heat.
2. Add garlic and onion and sauté for a minute.
3. Add grape tomatoes and turmeric and cook until tomatoes soften.
4. Add basil, vinegar, vinegar, stock and tomatoes. Bring to boil.
5. Cover saucepan with lid and simmer for 5 minutes.
6. Puree the soup using blender until smooth. Season with pepper and salt.
7. Serve and enjoy.

Nutritional Value (Amount per Serving):

Calories 102; Fat 4 g; Carbohydrates 15 g; Sugar 8 g; Protein 2 g; Cholesterol 0 mg

Garlic Leek Onion Soup

Preparation Time: 10 minutes; Cooking Time: 35 minutes; Serve: 4

Ingredients:

- 1 onion, sliced
- 1 leek, sliced
- 1 1/2 tbsp olive oil
- 1 shallot, sliced
- 4 cups vegetable stock
- 2 garlic cloves, chopped
- Pepper
- Salt

Directions:

1. Add stock and olive oil in a saucepan and bring to boil.
2. Add remaining ingredients and stir well.
3. Cover and simmer for 25 minutes.
4. Puree the soup using blender until smooth.
5. Serve and enjoy.

Nutritional Value (Amount per Serving):

Calories 105; Fat 7 g; Carbohydrates 7 g; Sugar 3 g; Protein 5 g; Cholesterol 0 mg

Zucchini Basil Soup

Preparation Time: 10 minutes; Cooking Time: 10 minutes; Serve: 8

Ingredients:

- 2.5 lbs zucchini, peeled and sliced
- 4 cups vegetable stock
- 3 garlic cloves, chopped
- 2 tbsp olive oil
- 1/3 cup fresh basil leaves
- 1 medium onion, diced
- Pepper
- Salt

Directions:

1. Heat olive oil in a pan over medium-low heat.
2. Add zucchini and onion and sauté until softened.
3. Add garlic and sauté for a minute.
4. Add stock and simmer for 15 minutes. Turn off the heat.
5. Stir in basil and puree the soup using a blender until smooth.
6. Season with pepper and salt.
7. Serve and enjoy.

Nutritional Value (Amount per Serving):
Calories 60; Fat 4 g; Carbohydrates 7 g; Sugar 3 g; Protein 2 g; Cholesterol 0 mg

Cilantro Avocado Soup

Preparation Time: 10 minutes; Cooking Time: 10 minutes; Serve: 4
Ingredients:

- 2 avocados, pitted
- 3/4 tsp garlic powder
- ½ lb bacon, cooked and crumbled
- 2 tbsp fresh lime juice
- 1/3 cup fresh cilantro, chopped
- 4 cups vegetable stock
- Pepper
- Salt

Directions:

1. Add stock into the saucepan and bring to boil.
2. Add avocados, lime juice, garlic powder, and cilantro into the blender.
3. Add 1 cup warm stock into the blender and blend until smooth.
4. Remove saucepan from heat.
5. Add avocado mixture and bacon into the saucepan and stir well.
6. Season with pepper and salt.
7. Serve and enjoy.

Nutritional Value (Amount per Serving):
Calories 350; Fat 25 g; Carbohydrates 4 g; Sugar 1 g; Protein 22 g; Cholesterol 8 mg

Healthy Spinach Soup

Preparation Time: 10 minutes; Cooking Time: 7 minutes; Serve: 4
Ingredients:

- 3 cups baby spinach, wash and chopped
- 1 1/2 cups vegetable stock
- 1 cup unsweetened coconut milk
- ¼ tsp garlic powder
- ¼ tsp onion powder
- 1 tsp olive oil
- Pepper
- Salt

Directions:

1. Heat olive oil in a saucepan over medium heat.
2. Add spinach and sauté for 2 minutes.
3. Add stock and stir well. Bring to boil.

4. Remove from heat let it cool for 5 minutes.
5. Blend spinach mixture using blender until smooth.
6. Return spinach mixture into the saucepan.
7. Add coconut milk, garlic powder, onion powder, pepper, and salt. Stir well and cook over medium heat for 2 minutes.
8. Serve and enjoy.

Nutritional Value (Amount per Serving):
Calories 150; Fat 15 g; Carbohydrates 4 g; Sugar 2 g; Protein 2 g; Cholesterol 12 mg

Zucchini Asparagus Soup

Preparation Time: 10 minutes; Cooking Time: 30 minutes; Serve: 4
Ingredients:
- 1 lb asparagus, trimmed and chopped
- 1 lb zucchini, chopped
- 4 cups vegetable stock
- ½ tsp garlic powder
- Pepper
- Salt

Directions:
1. Add zucchini, asparagus, and stock in saucepan and bring to boil over medium heat for 20 minutes.
2. Remove from heat and puree the soup until smooth. Season with garlic powder, pepper and salt.
3. Serve and enjoy.

Nutritional Value (Amount per Serving):
Calories 80; Fat 2 g; Carbohydrates 9 g; Sugar 4 g; Protein 9 g; Cholesterol 0 mg

Kale Spinach Soup

Preparation Time: 10 minutes; Cooking Time: 10 minutes; Serve: 4
Ingredients:
- 1/2 lb fresh spinach
- 1/2 lb kale
- 2 avocados
- 2 tbsp fresh lime juice
- 1 cup vegetable stock
- 3 1/3 cup unsweetened coconut milk
- 3 oz olive oil
- 1/4 tsp pepper
- 1 tsp salt

Directions:
1. Heat oil in pan over medium heat.
2. Add kale and spinach and sauté until spinach wilted.
3. Add stock, avocado, coconut milk, pepper, and salt and puree the soup using blender until smooth.
4. Add lime juice and stir well.
5. Serve and enjoy.

Nutritional Value (Amount per Serving):
Calories 280; Fat 26 g; Carbohydrates 11 g; Sugar 0.7 g; Protein 4 g; Cholesterol 0 mg

Anti-inflammatory Broccoli Soup

Preparation Time: 10 minutes; Cooking Time: 3 hours; Serve: 6
Ingredients:
- 8 cups broccoli florets
- 1 tbsp sesame oil
- 4 cups leeks, chopped
- 6 cups vegetable stock
- 2 tbsp olive oil
- 1 tsp turmeric
- 1 1/2 tbsp ginger, chopped
- 1 tsp salt

Directions:
1. Heat olive oil in a pan over medium heat.
2. Add leek and sauté for 8 minutes.
3. Add sesame oil, turmeric, broccoli, ginger, stock, and salt in slow cooker and stir well.
4. Cover and cook on low for 3 hours.
5. Puree the soup using blender until smooth.
6. Serve and enjoy.

Nutritional Value (Amount per Serving):
Calories 180; Fat 10 g; Carbohydrates 14 g; Sugar 5 g; Protein 9 g; Cholesterol 0 mg

Coconut Spicy Cabbage Soup

Preparation Time: 10 minutes; Cooking Time: 25 minutes; Serve: 4
Ingredients:
- 1 cabbage head, chopped
- 1/4 cup unsweetened coconut milk
- 1/2 tsp ground cumin
- 1 1/2 tsp ground turmeric
- 3 garlic cloves, chopped
- 2 tbsp olive oil
- 3 cups vegetable stock
- 1/2 tsp pepper
- 1/2 tsp salt

Directions:
1. Heat oil in a saucepan over medium heat.
2. Add cabbage and garlic in a pan and sauté for 10 minutes.
3. Add stock and stir well.
4. Cover and simmer for 20 minutes.
5. Remove saucepan from heat and add coconut milk and spices.
6. Puree the soup using blender until smooth.
7. Season with pepper and salt.
8. Serve and enjoy.

Nutritional Value (Amount per Serving):
Calories 150; Fat 12 g; Carbohydrates 13 g; Sugar 6 g; Protein 3 g; Cholesterol 0 mg

Celery Dill Soup

Preparation Time: 10 minutes; Cooking Time: 30 minutes; Serve: 4
Ingredients:
- 6 cups celery, diced
- 1 onion, diced
- 2 cups vegetable stock
- 1 cup unsweetened coconut milk
- 1 tsp dill
- 1/4 tsp pepper
- 1/2 tsp sea salt

Directions:

1. Add all ingredients into the saucepan and bring to boil.
2. Turn heat to low and simmer for 30 minutes.
3. Puree the soup using blender until smooth.
4. Serve and enjoy.

Nutritional Value (Amount per Serving):

Calories 175; Fat 15 g; Carbohydrates 10 g; Sugar 4 g; Protein 2.5 g; Cholesterol 0 mg

Asparagus Cauliflower Soup

Preparation Time: 10 minutes; Cooking Time: 20 minutes; Serve: 4

Ingredients:

- 20 asparagus spears, chopped
- ½ cauliflower head, chopped
- 3 garlic cloves, chopped
- 1 tbsp coconut oil
- 4 cups vegetable stock
- ¼ tsp onion powder
- ¼ tsp cayenne pepper
- Pepper
- Salt

Directions:

1. Heat oil in a saucepan over medium heat.
2. Add garlic and sauté for minute.
3. Add cauliflower, stock, onion powder, cayenne, pepper, and salt. Stir well and bring to boil.
4. Turn heat to low and simmer for 20 minutes.
5. Add chopped asparagus and cook until softened.
6. Puree the soup using a blender until smooth
7. Serve and enjoy.

Nutritional Value (Amount per Serving):

Calories 75; Fat 5 g; Carbohydrates 9 g; Sugar 5 g; Protein 3 g; Cholesterol 4 mg

Chilled Cucumber Avocado Soup

Preparation Time: 10 minutes; Cooking Time: 30 minutes; Serve: 3

Ingredients:

- 2 avocados, pitted
- 1 cucumber, peeled and sliced
- 1 cup vegetable stock
- 3 garlic cloves
- ¼ cup green onion, sliced
- ¼ cup fresh lemon juice
- ½ tsp pepper
- ½ tsp pink salt

Directions:

1. Add all ingredients into the blender and blend until smooth.
2. Place in refrigerator for 30 minutes.
3. Serve chilled and enjoy.

Nutritional Value (Amount per Serving):

Calories 72; Fat 4 g; Carbohydrates 10 g; Sugar 3 g; Protein 3 g; Cholesterol 0 mg

Quick Avocado Broccoli Soup

Preparation Time: 10 minutes; Cooking Time: 15 minutes; Serve: 4

Ingredients:

- 2 cups broccoli florets, chopped
- 2 avocados, chopped
- 5 cups vegetable stock
- ¼ tsp garlic powder
- ¼ tsp cayenne
- Pepper
- Salt

Directions:

1. Cook broccoli in boiling water for 5 minutes. Drain well.
2. Add broccoli, vegetable broth, avocados, garlic powder, cayenne, pepper, and salt to the blender and blend until smooth.
3. Serve and enjoy.

Nutritional Value (Amount per Serving):

Calories 270; Fat 20 g; Carbohydrates 12 g; Sugar 2 g; Protein 9 g; Cholesterol 0 mg

Curried Pumpkin Soup

Preparation Time: 10 minutes; Cooking Time: 15 minutes; Serve: 4

Ingredients:

- 2 cups pumpkin, diced
- 1/2 tsp paprika
- 2 cups vegetable stock
- 1 tsp olive oil
- 2 garlic cloves, minced
- 1 tomato, chopped
- 1 onion, chopped
- 2 tsp curry powder
- Salt

Directions:

1. In a saucepan, add oil, garlic, and onion and sauté for 3 minutes over medium heat.
2. Add remaining ingredients and bring to boil.
3. Reduce heat and cover and simmer for 10 minutes.
4. Puree the soup using a blender until smooth.
5. Serve and enjoy.

Nutritional Value (Amount per Serving):

Calories 71; Fat 3 g; Carbohydrates 13 g; Sugar 6 g; Protein 2 g; Cholesterol 0 mg

Creamy Cinnamon Pumpkin Soup

Preparation Time: 10 minutes; Cooking Time: 45 minutes; Serve: 4

Ingredients:

- 1 cup pumpkin puree
- 1 bay leaf
- 1/8 tsp nutmeg
- 1/4 tsp coriander
- 1/2 tsp ginger, minced
- 3 garlic cloves, minced
- 1 small onion, chopped
- 1/4 tsp cinnamon
- 4 tbsp butter
- 1 1/2 cups vegetable stock
- 1/2 cup heavy cream
- 1/2 tsp pepper

- 1/2 tsp salt

Directions:
1. Melt butter in a saucepan over medium-low heat.
2. Add ginger, garlic, and onion to the pan and sauté for 2-3 minutes.
3. Add spices and sauté for 2 minutes.
4. Add stock and pumpkin puree and stir well. Bring to boil.
5. Reduce heat to low and simmer for 20 minutes.
6. Puree the soup using blender until smooth then simmer for 20 minutes.
7. Turn off from heat and add heavy cream and stir well.
8. Serve and enjoy.

Nutritional Value (Amount per Serving):
Calories 195; Fat 17 g; Carbohydrates 7 g; Sugar 3 g; Protein 3 g; Cholesterol 11 mg

Lime Mint Avocado Soup

Preparation Time: 5 minutes; Cooking Time: 5 minutes; Serve: 2
Ingredients:
- 1 avocado, peeled, pitted, and cut into pieces
- 2 romaine lettuce leaves
- 25 fresh mint leaves
- 1 tbsp fresh lime juice
- 1 cup unsweetened coconut milk
- ¼ tsp pepper
- 1/8 tsp salt

Directions:
1. Add all ingredients into the blender and blend until smooth.
2. Pour into the serving bowls and place in the refrigerator for 15 minutes.
3. Serve chilled and enjoy.

Nutritional Value (Amount per Serving):
Calories 270; Fat 25 g; Carbohydrates 10 g; Sugar 0.5 g; Protein 3 g; Cholesterol 0 mg

Creamy Squash Soup

Preparation Time: 10 minutes; Cooking Time: 35 minutes; Serve: 8
Ingredients:
- 1 lb butternut squash, peeled and diced
- 1/2 cup heavy cream
- 1 bay leaf
- 4 cups vegetable stock
- 2 garlic cloves, minced
- 5 tbsp olive oil, divided
- ¼ tsp pepper
- 1 tsp sea salt

Directions:
1. Heat 1 tbsp oil in a saucepan over medium heat.
2. Add butternut squash, salt, and garlic and sauté until lightly golden brown.
3. Add stock, remaining oil, and bay leaf. Bring to boil.
4. Simmer for 30 minute.
5. Remove bay leaves and puree the soup using blender until smooth.
6. Add heavy cream and stir well.
7. Serve and enjoy.

Nutritional Value (Amount per Serving):
Calories 170; Fat 14 g; Carbohydrates 7 g; Sugar 1.5 g; Protein 3 g; Cholesterol 5 mg

Cauliflower Coconut Mushroom Soup

Preparation Time: 10 minutes; Cooking Time: 20 minutes; Serve: 2

Ingredients:

- 1 cup baby spinach
- 1 cup cauliflower rice
- 1/4 cup coconut milk
- 1 tsp thyme
- 4 garlic cloves, sliced
- 2 cups mushrooms, sliced
- 1 cup vegetable stock
- 2 tbsp vinegar
- 1/8 tsp nutmeg
- 1 tsp black pepper
- 1 tbsp coconut oil
- 1 tsp salt

Directions:

1. Heat oil in a pot over medium heat.
2. Add mushrooms, garlic, pepper, salt, and thyme and sauté for 6-8 minutes.
3. Add vinegar and stir well.
4. Add coconut milk and stock and bring to simmer.
5. Add spinach and cauliflower rice. Stir well and cook for 5 minutes.
6. Serve and enjoy.

Nutritional Value (Amount per Serving):

Calories 182; Fat 15 g; Carbohydrates 10 g; Sugar 4 g; Protein 5 g; Cholesterol 0 mg

Cheese Tomato Soup

Preparation Time: 10 minutes; Cooking Time: 20 minutes; Serve: 6

Ingredients:

- 14 oz can tomatoes, peeled
- 3 garlic cloves, minced
- 2/3 cup feta cheese, crumbled
- 3 cups water
- 1/2 tsp erythritol
- 1 tsp dried basil
- 1/2 tsp dried oregano
- 1/8 tsp black pepper
- 1/3 cup heavy cream
- 1/4 cup onion, chopped
- 2 tbsp olive oil
- 1/2 tsp salt

Directions:

1. Heat oil in a pot over medium heat.
2. Add onion and sauté for 2 minutes.
3. Add garlic and sauté for a minute.
4. Add tomatoes, water, tomato paste, basil, oregano, pepper, and salt. Stir well and bring to boil.
5. Reduce heat and simmer.
6. Add erythritol and stir well and cook for 20 minutes.
7. Puree the soup using blender until smooth.
8. Add cream and cheese and stir for a minute.
9. Serve and enjoy.

Nutritional Value (Amount per Serving):

Calories 172; Fat 14 g; Carbohydrates 11 g; Sugar 5 g; Protein 5 g; Cholesterol 42 mg

Fennel Zucchini Soup

Preparation Time: 10 minutes; Cooking Time: 15 minutes; Serve: 4

Ingredients:

- 2 zucchinis, chopped
- 1 tsp olive oil
- 2 cups vegetable stock
- 1 onion, chopped
- 2 fennel bulbs, chopped
- Pepper
- Salt

Directions:
1. Heat oil in a saucepan over medium heat.
2. Add onion and sauté for 3 minutes.
3. Add zucchini and fennel and cook for 5 minutes.
4. Add stock and stir well. Bring to boil.
5. Cover and simmer for 15 minutes.
6. Puree the soup using blender until smooth. Season with pepper and salt.
7. Serve and enjoy.

Nutritional Value (Amount per Serving):
Calories 80; Fat 2.5 g; Carbohydrates 13 g; Sugar 3 g; Protein 3 g; Cholesterol 0 mg

Spicy Cauliflower Soup

Preparation Time: 10 minutes; Cooking Time: 20 minutes; Serve: 4
Ingredients:
- 1 cauliflower head, cut into florets
- 2 cups vegetable stock
- 5 jalapeno peppers, chopped
- 3 garlic cloves, chopped
- 2 tbsp olive oil
- 2 cups cheddar cheese, grated
- 1/2 tsp garlic powder
- 1 onion, chopped
- Pepper
- Salt

Directions:
1. Heat oil in a saucepan over medium heat.
2. Add onions, garlic, and jalapeno and sauté for 5 minutes.
3. Add cauliflower and sauté for 2 minutes.
4. Add garlic powder and stock, bring to boil and simmer for 20 minutes.
5. Add cheddar cheese and season with pepper and salt and cook for 5 minutes.
6. Serve and enjoy.

Nutritional Value (Amount per Serving):
Calories 330; Fat 25 g; Carbohydrates 10 g; Sugar 4 g; Protein 15 g; Cholesterol 60 mg

Easy Chicken Soup

Preparation Time: 10 minutes; Cooking Time: 4 hours; Serve: 6
Ingredients:
- 1 1/2 lbs chicken, skinless, boneless, and cut into pieces
- 14.5 oz chicken stock
- 14 oz salsa
- 8 oz cheddar cheese, shredded
- Pepper
- Salt

Directions:
1. Add chicken into the slow cooker.
2. Pour remaining ingredients over the chicken.
3. Cover and cook on high for 4 hours.
4. Shred the chicken using fork and stir well.
5. Serve and enjoy.

Nutritional Value (Amount per Serving):

Calories 402; Fat 23 g; Carbohydrates 7 g; Sugar 5 g; Protein 39 g; Cholesterol 140 mg

Beef Stew

Preparation Time: 10 minutes; Cooking Time: 6 hours; Serve: 4
Ingredients:

- 1 lb beef, cut into cubes
- 6 cups chicken broth
- 1 ½ tsp Italian seasoning
- 2 garlic cloves, minced
- 2 celery stalks, chopped
- 1 tsp onion powder
- 2 parsnips, sliced
- 1 large carrots, sliced
- Pepper
- Salt

Directions:

1. Add all ingredients into the slow cooker and stir well to combine.
2. Cover and cook on low for 6 hours.
3. Serve and enjoy.

Nutritional Value (Amount per Serving):
Calories 312; Fat 9.8 g; Carbohydrates 10 g; Sugar 4 g; Protein 42 g; Cholesterol 100 mg

Beef Vegetable Stew

Preparation Time: 10 minutes; Cooking Time: 2 hours; Serve: 10
Ingredients:

- 3 lbs beef stew meat
- ¼ tsp thyme
- ¼ tsp dried basil
- 1 tsp onion powder
- 1 tsp garlic powder
- 7 cups water
- 4 cups chicken broth
- 14 oz can tomatoes
- 1 cauliflower head, cut into florets
- 2 celery stalks, chopped
- 8 oz mushrooms, sliced
- 2 garlic cloves, chopped
- ½ onion, chopped
- 4 tbsp olive oil
- Pepper
- Salt

Directions:

1. Heat oil in large stock pot over high heat.
2. Add garlic and onion and sauté until soften.
3. Add meat and cook for 10 minutes.
4. Add remaining ingredients and stir well and cook over medium-high heat for 30 minutes.
5. Turn heat to low and simmer for 1 hour.
6. Serve and enjoy.

Nutritional Value (Amount per Serving):
Calories 340; Fat 14 g; Carbohydrates 6 g; Sugar 3 g; Protein 45 g; Cholesterol 120 mg

Fish Stew

Preparation Time: 10 minutes; Cooking Time: 18 minutes; Serve: 4
Ingredients:

- 1 ½ lbs cod , cut into pieces
- 1 tbsp fresh cilantro
- ½ tsp red pepper flakes
- 2 bell pepper, sliced

- 2 tbsp tomato paste
- ½ cup sour cream
- ½ cup unsweetened coconut milk
- 14 oz can tomatoes, diced
- 3 garlic cloves, minced
- ½ onion, diced
- 2 tbsp olive oil
- Pepper
- Salt

Directions:
1. Heat oil in a saucepan.
2. Add garlic and onion and sauté for 3 minutes.
3. Add tomatoes, tomato paste, sour cream, and coconut milk. Stir and cook for 2-3 minutes.
4. Add bell pepper, red pepper flakes, cod, pepper, and salt.
5. Cover and simmer for 10-12 minutes.
6. Garnish with cilantro and serve.

Nutritional Value (Amount per Serving):
Calories 362; Fat 15 g; Carbohydrates 14 g; Sugar 8 g; Protein 40 g; Cholesterol 105 mg

Spicy Spinach Pork Stew

Preparation Time: 10 minutes; Cooking Time: 30 minutes; Serve: 4
Ingredients:
- 1 lb pork butt, cut into chunks
- 1 ½ tsp Cajun seasoning
- 1 tsp dried thyme
- 10 oz Rotel tomatoes, diced
- 3 garlic cloves, minced
- 1 onion, chopped
- 4 cups baby spinach, chopped
- ½ cup heavy cream

Directions:
1. Add all ingredients except spinach and cream into the instant pot and stir well.
2. Seal and cook on meat mode for 20 minutes.
3. Allow to release pressure naturally then open the lid.
4. Set pot on sauté mode and add spinach and cream and cook until spinach wilted.
5. Serve and enjoy.

Nutritional Value (Amount per Serving):
Calories 303; Fat 13 g; Carbohydrates 7 g; Sugar 1.3 g; Protein 37 g; Cholesterol 125 mg

Cinnamon Beef Okra Stew

Preparation Time: 10 minutes; Cooking Time: 4 hours; Serve: 2
Ingredients:
- 1 cup fresh okra, chopped
- 2 cups vegetable stock
- 1 onion, chopped
- 1 lb beef, diced
- 1/4 tsp cinnamon
- 1/2 tsp pepper
- 1/2 tsp cumin
- 3 garlic cloves, crushed
- 1 tbsp olive oil
- Salt

Directions:
1. Heat oil in a pan over medium heat.
2. Add meat and cook until brown then transfer in crock pot.

3. Add remaining ingredients into the crock pot and stir well.
4. Cover and cook on low for 4 hours.
5. Serve and enjoy.

Nutritional Value (Amount per Serving):
Calories 535; Fat 30 g; Carbohydrates 14 g; Sugar 7 g; Protein 49 g; Cholesterol 150 mg

Salmon Stew

Preparation Time: 10 minutes; Cooking Time: 2 Hours; Serve: 4
Ingredients:
- 8 oz salmon
- 1 tbsp curry powder
- 1/2 onion, diced
- 1/2 cup vegetable stock
- 14 oz unsweetened coconut milk
- 1 tsp coriander powder
- 1 tsp ginger, chopped
- 1/4 tsp pepper
- 1 1/2 tsp salt

Directions:
1. Add all ingredients into the crock pot and stir well.
2. Cover and cook on high for 2 hours.
3. Serve and enjoy.

Nutritional Value (Amount per Serving):
Calories 320; Fat 27 g; Carbohydrates 8 g; Sugar 4 g; Protein 16 g; Cholesterol 30 mg

Beet Carrot Stew

Preparation Time: 10 minutes; Cooking Time: 15 minutes; Serve: 4
Ingredients:
- 1 cup beets, shredded
- 2 cups green cabbage, shredded
- 1/2 cup carrots, shredded
- 1 1/2 tbsp fresh lemon juice
- 2 tbsp olive oil
- 3 cups vegetable stock
- 1/2 tsp garlic powder
- 1/2 tsp onion powder
- Pepper
- Salt

Directions:
1. Heat oil in a stock pot over medium-low heat.
2. Add cabbage, carrots, and beets and sauté for minutes.
3. Add stock and seasoning and simmer until vegetable are soften.
4. Serve and enjoy.

Nutritional Value (Amount per Serving):
Calories 95; Fat 9 g; Carbohydrates 10 g; Sugar 6 g; Protein 2 g; Cholesterol 0 mg

Flavorful Pork Stew

Preparation Time: 10 minutes; Cooking Time: 8 Hours; Serve: 8
Ingredients:
- 2 1/2 lbs pork chops, boneless
- 1/2 cup onion, chopped
- 1 1/2 cups rutabaga, peeled and cubed
- 14.5 oz can tomatoes, diced
- 4 cups chicken stock
- 2 tbsp olive oil

- 1/2 tsp cumin
- 1 1/2 tsp oregano
- 1 tbsp chili powder
- 3 garlic cloves, minced
- 1/2 tsp black pepper
- 1 tsp kosher salt

Directions:
1. Add all ingredients into the crock pot and stir well to mix.
2. Cover and cook on low for 8 hours.
3. Remove meat from crock pot and shred using fork.
4. Return shredded pork to the crock pot and stir well.
5. Season with pepper and salt.
6. Serve and enjoy.

Nutritional Value (Amount per Serving):

Calories 530; Fat 40 g; Carbohydrates 7 g; Sugar 4 g; Protein 35 g; Cholesterol 120 mg

Bacon Beef Stew

Preparation Time: 10 minutes; Cooking Time: 6 Hours; Serve: 10
Ingredients:
- 2 lbs stew beef
- 12 oz bacon, cooked and crumbled
- 3 garlic cloves, minced
- 1/2 small onion, chopped
- 1 small carrot, chopped
- 1 celery rib, chopped
- 3 oz mushrooms, sliced
- 3 oz bell peppers, chopped
- 14.5 oz can tomatoes, diced
- 2 cups chicken stock
- 1/2 tsp oregano
- 1/2 tsp onion powder
- 1 tsp garlic powder
- 1 1/2 tsp black pepper
- 1 tbsp tomato paste
- 2 tbsp olive oil
- 1 tsp salt

Directions:
1. Heat oil in a pan over medium heat.
2. Add meat and cook until brown.
3. Transfer meat to the crock pot.
4. Add all remaining ingredients into the crock pot and stir well to combine.
5. Cover and cook on low for 6 hours.
6. Stir well and serve.

Nutritional Value (Amount per Serving):

Calories 375; Fat 23 g; Carbohydrates 8 g; Sugar 4 g; Protein 35 g; Cholesterol 35 mg

Delicious Chicken Stew

Preparation Time: 10 minutes; Cooking Time: 4 Hours; Serve: 4
Ingredients:
- 28 oz chicken thighs, skinless
- 1/2 tsp dried thyme
- 3 garlic cloves, minced
- 1/2 tsp dried rosemary
- 1 onion, diced
- 1 cup celery, diced
- 2 carrots, peeled and diced
- 1/2 cup heavy cream
- 1 cup fresh spinach
- 1/2 tsp oregano
- 2 cups chicken stock
- Pepper
- Salt

Directions:

1. Add all ingredients except cream and spinach into the crock pot and stir well.
2. Cover and cook on low for 4 hours.
3. Remove chicken from crock pot and shred using fork.
4. Return shredded chicken to the crock pot and stir well.
5. Stir in heavy cream and spinach.
6. Serve and enjoy.

Nutritional Value (Amount per Serving):

Calories 460; Fat 20 g; Carbohydrates 7 g; Sugar 3 g; Protein 60 g; Cholesterol 200 mg

Feta Zucchini Arugula Salad

Preparation Time: 10 minutes; Cooking Time: 5 minutes; Serve: 2

Ingredients:

- 1 zucchini, spiralized into ribbons
- 1 cup arugula
- ¾ cup feta cheese, crumbled
- For dressing:
- 2 tbsp lemon juice
- 1 tbsp olive oil
- Pepper
- Salt

Directions:

1. Add all ingredients into the large mixing bowl and toss well.
2. Serve and enjoy.

Nutritional Value (Amount per Serving):

Calories 230; Fat 19 g; Carbohydrates 6 g; Sugar 4.5 g; Protein 10 g; Cholesterol 50 mg

Cucumber Yogurt Egg Salad

Preparation Time: 10 minutes; Cooking Time: 10 minutes; Serve: 2

Ingredients:

- 3 eggs, hard-boiled and quartered
- 2 tbsp dill, chopped
- ½ cup yogurt
- 1 cup cucumber, sliced
- 1 cup radish, sliced
- 1 cup lettuce
- For dressing:
- 1 tbsp lemon juice
- 1 tbsp olive oil
- Pepper
- Salt

Directions:

1. Add all ingredients into the large mixing bowl and toss well.
2. Serve and enjoy.

Nutritional Value (Amount per Serving):

Calories 229; Fat 14 g; Carbohydrates 11 g; Sugar 7 g; Protein 13 g; Cholesterol 249 mg

Pumpkin Cranberry Salad

Preparation Time: 10 minutes; Cooking Time: 10 minutes; Serve: 2

Ingredients:

- 1 cup pumpkin, cubed and baked
- 1 cup lettuce

- ¼ cup walnuts, chopped
- ¼ cup dried cranberries
- For dressing:
- 1 tbsp lemon juice
- 1 tbsp olive oil
- Pepper
- Salt

Directions:

1. Add all ingredients into the large mixing bowl and toss well.
2. Serve and enjoy.

Nutritional Value (Amount per Serving):

Calories 211; Fat 16 g; Carbohydrates 13 g; Sugar 5.2 g; Protein 5.3 g; Cholesterol 0 mg

Avocado Watermelon Salad

Preparation Time: 10 minutes; Cooking Time: 5 minutes; Serve: 2

Ingredients:

- 1 avocado, diced
- 2 cups arugula
- 1 ½ cups watermelon, cubed
- For dressing:
- 1 tbsp lemon juice
- 1 tbsp olive oil
- Pepper
- Salt

Directions:

1. Add all ingredients into the large mixing bowl and toss well.
2. Serve and enjoy.

Nutritional Value (Amount per Serving):

Calories 131; Fat 10 g; Carbohydrates 11 g; Sugar 7.5 g; Protein 1.8 g; Cholesterol 0 mg

Mushroom Pepper Tomato Salad

Preparation Time: 10 minutes; Cooking Time: 5 minutes; Serve: 2

Ingredients:

- 1 cup lettuce
- 1 large tomato, chopped
- 1 bell pepper, chopped
- 1 cup mushrooms, grilled and sliced
- For dressing:
- 1 tbsp lemon juice
- 1 tbsp olive oil
- Pepper
- Salt

Directions:

1. Add all ingredients into the large mixing bowl and toss well.
2. Serve and enjoy.

Nutritional Value (Amount per Serving):

Calories 109; Fat 7 g; Carbohydrates 10 g; Sugar 6 g; Protein 2.7 g; Cholesterol 0 mg

Chicken Broccoli Cranberry Salad

Preparation Time: 10 minutes; Cooking Time: 5 minutes; Serve: 2

Ingredients:

- ½ cup fresh spinach
- ¼ cup dried cranberries

- ½ cup lettuce
- 1 cup chicken, gilled
- 1 cup broccoli florets
- For dressing:
- 1 tbsp lemon juice
- 1 tbsp olive oil
- Pepper
- Salt

Directions:

1. Add all ingredients into the large mixing bowl and toss well.
2. Serve and enjoy.

Nutritional Value (Amount per Serving):

Calories 194; Fat 9.4 g; Carbohydrates 5 g; Sugar 1.6 g; Protein 21 g; Cholesterol 54 mg

Egg Apple Spinach Salad

Preparation Time: 10 minutes; Cooking Time: 5 minutes; Serve: 2
Ingredients:

- 2 cups baby spinach
- 1 apple, chopped
- 4 eggs, hard-boiled and chopped
- For dressing:
- 1 tbsp lemon juice
- 1 tbsp olive oil
- Pepper
- Salt

Directions:

1. Add all ingredients into the large mixing bowl and toss well.
2. Serve and enjoy.

Nutritional Value (Amount per Serving):

Calories 235; Fat 15 g; Carbohydrates 12 g; Sugar 9 g; Protein 12 g; Cholesterol 327 mg

Shrimp Watermelon Spinach Salad

Preparation Time: 10 minutes; Cooking Time: 5 minutes; Serve: 3
Ingredients:

- ½ cup feta cheese, crumbled
- 1 cup baby spinach
- 1 cup watermelon, chopped
- 1 cup shrimp, grilled
- For dressing:
- 1 tbsp fresh basil
- 1 tbsp lemon juice
- 1 tbsp olive oil
- Pepper
- Salt

Directions:

1. Add all ingredients into the large mixing bowl and toss well.
2. Serve and enjoy.

Nutritional Value (Amount per Serving):

Calories 231; Fat 12 g; Carbohydrates 14 g; Sugar 4 g; Protein 13 g; Cholesterol 87 mg

Bacon Chicken Salad

Preparation Time: 10 minutes; Cooking Time: 5 minutes; Serve: 2
Ingredients:

- 2 cups chicken breast, cooked and shredded
- 1 cup cheddar cheese, shredded
- 1 cup celery, chopped
- 1/2 cup sour cream
- 1/4 cup mayonnaise
- 1/2 cup bacon, cooked and crumbles
- 2 green onions, sliced
- 1 small onion, chopped
- Pepper
- Salt

Directions:

1. Add all ingredients into the mixing bowl and toss well to combine.
2. Serve and enjoy.

Nutritional Value (Amount per Serving):

Calories 770; Fat 55 g; Carbohydrates 14 g; Sugar 4 g; Protein 53 g; Cholesterol 185 mg

Dill Cucumber Salad

Preparation Time: 10 minutes; Cooking Time: 5 minutes; Serve: 6

Ingredients:

- 2 lbs cucumbers, thinly sliced
- 2 small onion, sliced
- 1/2 cup fresh dill, chopped
- For dressing:
- 1 tsp erythritol
- 3 tbsp olive oil
- 4 tbsp vinegar
- Salt

Directions:

1. Add cucumbers, dill, and onion into the large bowl.
2. In a small bowl, whisk together all dressing ingredients.
3. Pour dressing over salad and toss well.
4. Serve and enjoy.

Nutritional Value (Amount per Serving):

Calories 100; Fat 0 g; Carbohydrates 9 g; Sugar 3 g; Protein 2 g; Cholesterol 0 mg

Basil Cucumber Tomato Salad

Preparation Time: 15 minutes; Cooking Time: 5 minutes; Serve: 6

Ingredients:

- 3 cups cucumbers, sliced
- 3 tomatoes, sliced
- 1/4 cup fresh basil, chopped
- 1 medium onion, chopped
- For dressing:
- 1 tsp erythritol
- 1/2 tbsp red wine vinegar
- 3/4 cup apple cider vinegar
- 1/2 tsp dill
- 1/4 cup olive oil
- 1/4 tsp pepper
- 1/4 tsp salt

Directions:

1. In a small bowl, mix together all dressing ingredients.
2. Add all salad ingredients into the mixing bowl and mix well.
3. Pour dressing over salad and toss well.
4. Serve and enjoy.

Nutritional Value (Amount per Serving):

Calories 95; Fat 8 g; Carbohydrates 5 g; Sugar 3 g; Protein 1 g; Cholesterol 0 mg

Tasty Chicken Ranch Salad

Preparation Time: 10 minutes; Cooking Time: 5 minutes; Serve: 4
Ingredients:

- 3 cups chicken breast, cooked and shredded
- 1 tbsp ranch seasoning
- 3 tbsp hot sauce
- ¾ cup mayonnaise
- 1/2 cup green onion, chopped
- 2 carrots, chopped
- 1 1/4 cups celery, chopped
- 1 small onion, diced

Directions:

1. In small bowl, combine together ranch seasoning, hot sauce, and mayonnaise.
2. In a large bowl, add remaining ingredients and toss well.
3. Ranch seasoning mixture over salad and mix well.
4. Serve and enjoy.

Nutritional Value (Amount per Serving):
Calories 270; Fat 15 g; Carbohydrates 13 g; Sugar 4 g; Protein 20 g; Cholesterol 65 mg

Dijon Chicken Salad

Preparation Time: 10 minutes; Cooking Time: 30 minutes; Serve: 6
Ingredients:

- 2 lbs chicken breasts, skinless, boneless, cooked and shredded
- 1/2 cup mayonnaise
- 1/2 cup yogurt
- 1/4 cup green onions, diced
- 1/2 cup pecans, chopped
- 1 tbsp fresh lemon juice
- 1/4 tsp garlic powder
- 1/2 tsp paprika
- 1/2 tsp sage
- 1/4 cup Dijon mustard
- 1 1/2 cups cherry tomatoes, halved
- Pepper
- Salt

Directions:

1. In a large bowl, combine together green onions, pecans, cherry tomatoes, and shredded chicken.
2. In a small bowl, combine together mayonnaise, yogurt, lemon juice, garlic
   powder, paprika, sage, mustard, pepper, and salt.
3. Pour mayonnaise mixture over the chicken and toss well.
4. Serve and enjoy.

Nutritional Value (Amount per Serving):
Calories 482; Fat 24 g; Carbohydrates 14 g; Sugar 8 g; Protein 45 g; Cholesterol 140 mg

Chicken Cranberry Salad

Preparation Time: 15 minutes; Cooking Time: 5 minutes; Serve: 4
Ingredients:

- 1 lb chicken breast, skinless, boneless, cooked and shredded
- 1/4 tsp garlic powder
- 1/2 cup celery, chopped
- 1/4 cup almonds, sliced
- 3 tbsp dried cranberries
- 1/4 cup mayonnaise
- 1/4 cup yogurt
- 1/4 tsp onion powder
- 1/4 tsp pepper
- 1/2 tsp sea salt

Directions:
1. Add all ingredients into the mixing bowl and toss well.
2. Place bowl into the refrigerator for few hours.
3. Serve chilled and enjoy.

Nutritional Value (Amount per Serving):
Calories 240; Fat 9 g; Carbohydrates 8 g; Sugar 2 g; Protein 25 g; Cholesterol 75 mg

Creamy Chicken Salad

Preparation Time: 5 minutes; Cooking Time: 5 minutes; Serve: 6
Ingredients:
- 1 1/2 lbs chicken breasts, boneless, skinless, cooked and shredded
- 2 celery stalks, chopped
- 3/4 cup mayonnaise
- ¼ tsp garlic powder
- 1/4 tsp pepper
- 1/4 tsp salt

Directions:
1. Add all ingredients into the mixing bowl and stir well to combine.
2. Serve and enjoy.

Nutritional Value (Amount per Serving):
Calories 440; Fat 24 g; Carbohydrates 9 g; Sugar 2 g; Protein 45 g; Cholesterol 144 mg

Egg Arugula Salad

Preparation Time: 10 minutes; Cooking Time: 10 minutes; Serve: 2
Ingredients:
- 4 large eggs, hard-boiled, peel and chopped
- 1/2 cup sour cream
- 4 cups arugula
- 1 avocado, peel and sliced
- 1 1/2 tsp Dijon mustard
- 3 garlic cloves, minced
- Pepper
- Salt

Directions:
1. In a small bowl, mix together Dijon mustard, garlic, sour cream, pepper, and salt.
2. Add eggs, arugula, and avocado in a mixing bowl and toss well.
3. Pour dressing over salad and mix well.
4. Serve and enjoy.

Nutritional Value (Amount per Serving):
Calories 485; Fat 40 g; Carbohydrates 12 g; Sugar 1 g; Protein 16 g; Cholesterol 395 mg

Tomato Lettuce Salad

Preparation Time: 5 minutes; Cooking Time: 5 minutes; Serve: 2

Ingredients:

- 2 cups romaine lettuce, chopped
- 1 tomato, chopped
- For dressing:
- 5 drops liquid stevia
- 2 tsp lemon juice
- 1/4 cup mayonnaise
- 2 tsp apple cider vinegar
- Pepper
- Salt

Directions:

1. In a small bowl, whisk together all dressing ingredients.
2. In a large bowl, add chopped romaine lettuce and tomato and toss well.
3. Pour dressing over salad and toss well.
4. Serve and enjoy.

Nutritional Value (Amount per Serving):

Calories 134; Fat 11 g; Carbohydrates 10 g; Sugar 4 g; Protein 2 g; Cholesterol 6 mg

Cucumber Feta Salad

Preparation Time: 10 minutes; Cooking Time: 5 minutes; Serve: 4

Ingredients:

For salad:

- 1/2 cup olives, pitted
- 8 oz feta cheese, cubed
- 1 small onion, sliced
- 1 avocado, diced
- 1 bell pepper, deseeded and sliced
- 3 tomatoes, cut into wedges
- 1 cucumber, chopped

For dressing:

- 2 tbsp vinegar
- 1/4 cup olive oil
- 1 1/2 tsp dried oregano
- 2 garlic cloves, minced
- 1/4 tsp salt

Directions:

1. Add all salad ingredients into the mixing bowl and mix well.
2. In a small bowl, mix together all dressing ingredients and pour over salad.
3. Serve and enjoy.

Nutritional Value (Amount per Serving):

Calories 302; Fat 26 g; Carbohydrates 11 g; Sugar 6 g; Protein 10 g; Cholesterol 45 mg

Flavorful Greek Salad

Preparation Time: 10 minutes; Cooking Time: 5 minutes; Serve: 4

Ingredients:

- 1 cup strawberries, quartered
- 4 cups fresh spinach
- 1/2 cup cherry tomatoes, halved
- 1 avocado, chopped
- 1 cup mozzarella cheese, crumbled
- 1/4 cup basil, chopped

- Pepper
- Salt

For dressing:
- 1/2 tsp dried oregano
- 4 tbsp mayonnaise
- 1 garlic clove, minced
- 1 1/2 tbsp balsamic vinegar
- 2 tbsp red wine vinegar
- 3 tbsp olive oil
- Pepper
- Salt

Directions:
1. In a large mixing bowl, toss together avocado, basil, mozzarella, strawberries, and tomatoes.
2. Divide spinach between four serving dishes and top with salad mixture.
3. In a small bowl, combine together all dressing ingredients.
4. Drizzle dressing over salad and serve.

Nutritional Value (Amount per Serving):
Calories 280; Fat 25 g; Carbohydrates 11 g; Sugar 3 g; Protein 4 g; Cholesterol 6 mg

Broccoli Salad

Preparation Time: 10 minutes; Cooking Time: 5 minutes; Serve: 6
Ingredients:
- 5 1/2 cups broccoli florets
- 3/4 cup bacon, cooked and crumbled
- ½ tsp parsley
- 1 ¼ tsp garlic powder
- ½ cup sour cream
- 1/2 cup mayonnaise
- 1 ¼ tsp onion powder
- ½ cup cheddar cheese, shredded
- 2 tsp dill
- ¼ tsp salt

Directions:
1. In a small bowl, mix together sour cream, mayonnaise, and seasonings.
2. Add broccoli, cheese, and bacon into the mixing bowl mix well.
3. Pour cream mixture over the broccoli and toss well.
4. Serve and enjoy.

Nutritional Value (Amount per Serving):
Calories 280; Fat 23 g; Carbohydrates 11 g; Sugar 3 g; Protein 7 g; Cholesterol 30 mg

Almond Cabbage Zucchini Salad

Preparation Time: 10 minutes; Cooking Time: 5 minutes; Serve: 10
Ingredients:
- 1 zucchini, spiralized using slicer
- 3/4 cup olive oil
- 1 cup almonds, sliced
- 3/4 cup sunflower seeds shelled
- 1 lb cabbage, shredded
- 1 tsp erythritol
- 1/3 cup rice vinegar

Directions:
1. In mixing bowl, mix together cabbage, almonds, sunflower seeds, and zucchini.
2. In a small bowl, mix together oil, sweetener, and vinegar and pour over vegetables.

3. Toss salad well and place in fridge for 2-3 hours.

4. Serve and enjoy.

Nutritional Value (Amount per Serving):

Calories 224; Fat 22 g; Carbohydrates 7 g; Sugar 2 g; Protein 4 g; Cholesterol 0 mg

Egg Cucumber Salad

Preparation Time: 10 minutes; Cooking Time: 5 minutes; Serve: 4

Ingredients:

- 6 eggs, hard boiled, peeled and diced
- 1/4 cup mayonnaise
- 1 avocado, peel and cubed
- 1 cucumber, peel and chopped
- 1 tsp paprika
- Pepper
- Salt

Directions:

1. Add all ingredients into the mixing bowl and mix well.

2. Serve and enjoy.

Nutritional Value (Amount per Serving):

Calories 175; Fat 13 g; Carbohydrates 7 g; Sugar 2 g; Protein 10 g; Cholesterol 250 mg

Celery Egg Salad

Preparation Time: 10 minutes; Cooking Time: 5 minutes; Serve: 4

Ingredients:

- 12 eggs, hard-boiled and peeled
- 1 tbsp Dijon mustard
- 1 cup mayonnaise
- ¼ cup green onion, sliced
- 1/2 cup celery, diced
- Pepper
- Salt

Directions:

1. Separate egg white part and egg yolk. Chop egg whites.
2. In a bowl, mix together mayonnaise, mustard, egg yolk, and salt until well combined.
3. Add chopped egg whites, green onion, and celery in a large bowl then add mayonnaise mixture and mix well. Season with pepper and salt.
4. Serve and enjoy.

Nutritional Value (Amount per Serving):

Calories 365; Fat 27 g; Carbohydrates 11 g; Sugar 4 g; Protein 16 g; Cholesterol 500 mg

Cucumber Tomato Salad

Preparation Time: 5 minutes; Cooking Time: 5 minutes; Serve: 2

Ingredients:

- 1/4 cup olives, sliced
- 1/2 cup cherry tomatoes, cut in half
- 1 large cucumber, chopped
- 1/4 cup olive oil vinaigrette
- 1/2 small onion, chopped
- Pepper
- Salt

Directions:
1. Add all ingredients into the mixing bowl and toss well.
2. Serve and enjoy.

Nutritional Value (Amount per Serving):
    Calories 64; Fat 3 g; Carbohydrates 11 g; Sugar 4 g; Protein 2 g; Cholesterol 0 mg

Egg Carrot Cabbage Salad

Preparation Time: 5 minutes; Cooking Time: 5 minutes; Serve: 1
Ingredients:
- 2 eggs, hard-boiled, peeled and sliced
- 1/3 cup red cabbage, shredded
- 1/4 cup carrots, shredded
- 1/2 cup spinach leaves
- 2 tbsp sunflower seeds
- 1 1/2 cups lettuce

Directions:
1. Add all ingredients into the mixing bowl and mix well.
2. Serve and enjoy.

Nutritional Value (Amount per Serving):
    Calories 235; Fat 13 g; Carbohydrates 13 g; Sugar 4 g; Protein 17 g; Cholesterol 325 mg

Delicious Mexican Salad

Preparation Time: 10 minutes; Cooking Time: 5 minutes; Serve: 4
Ingredients:
- 1/2 cup salsa
- 1 bag frozen cauliflower
- 1 tbsp cilantro, chopped
- 1/2 tsp onion powder
- 1 tsp chili powder
- 1 tomato, diced
- 1 avocado, diced
- 1/4 cup cheddar cheese, shredded
- 1 tbsp lemon juice
- 1/4 cup mayonnaise
- 1/2 tsp paprika
- 1/2 tsp cumin
- Pepper
- Salt

Directions:
1. Add cauliflower in a baking dish and microwave on high for 4 minutes.
2. In a large bowl, mix together salsa, seasonings, lemon juice, and mayonnaise.
3. Stir in cauliflower, cheese, tomato, herbs, and avocado.
4. Place in fridge for 2 hours.
5. Serve and enjoy.

Nutritional Value (Amount per Serving):
    Calories 150; Fat 10 g; Carbohydrates 13 g; Sugar 5 g; Protein 6 g; Cholesterol 11 mg

Brussels Sprout Salad

Preparation Time: 10 minutes; Cooking Time: 5 minutes; Serve: 1
Ingredients:
- 8 Brussels sprouts, wash and slices
- 1/2 tsp apple cider vinegar
- 1 tbsp parmesan cheese, grated
- 1 tsp olive oil

- 1/4 tsp pepper
- 1/4 tsp salt

Directions:
1. Add all ingredients to the bowl and toss well.
2. Serve and enjoy.

Nutritional Value (Amount per Serving):
Calories 155; Fat 10 g; Carbohydrates 11 g; Sugar 2.5 g; Protein 10 g; Cholesterol 10 mg

Spinach Salad

Preparation Time: 5 minutes; Cooking Time: 5 minutes; Serve: 2
Ingredients:
- 8 oz fresh spinach, washed
- 2 tsp sesame seeds, toasted
- 1 tsp soy sauce
- 1 1/2 tsp olive oil
- 2 garlic cloves, minced
- 1 green onion, chopped
- 1/4 tsp salt

Directions:
1. Blanch spinach in boiling water for 30 seconds.
2. Rinse spinach in cold water.
3. Squeeze out excess water of spinach.
4. In a bowl, add green onion, oil, garlic clove, sesame seeds, salt, and soy sauce.
5. Add spinach into the bowl and mix well.
6. Serve and enjoy.

Nutritional Value (Amount per Serving):
Calories 81; Fat 5 g; Carbohydrates 6 g; Sugar 1 g; Protein 4 g; Cholesterol 0 mg

Cabbage Salad

Preparation Time: 10 minutes; Cooking Time: 15 minutes; Serve: 6
Ingredients:
- 2 lbs red cabbage, shred
- 1 1/2 tbsp fresh dill, chopped
- 4 oz butter
- 1 orange juice
- 1 tbsp vinegar
- 1/4 tsp pepper
- 1 tsp salt

Directions:
1. Heat butter in the pan over medium heat.
2. Add cabbage cook for 10-15 minutes. Season with pepper and salt.
3. Add orange juice, and vinegar. Stir well and simmer for 5 minutes.
4. Remove pan from heat.
5. Serve and enjoy.

Nutritional Value (Amount per Serving):
Calories 400; Fat 40 g; Carbohydrates 12 g; Sugar 7 g; Protein 3 g; Cholesterol 102 mg

Zucchini Parmesan Salad

Preparation Time: 10 minutes; Cooking Time: 15 minutes; Serve: 2
Ingredients:
- 1 green zucchini, spirilized using slicer
- 3 tbsp parmesan cheese, grated

- 1 tsp fresh lemon zest, grated
- 1 yellow zucchini, spirilized using slicer
- 1 1/2 tbsp fresh lemon juice
- 1 1/2 tbsp olive oil
- Pepper
- Salt

Directions:
1. In mixing bowl, whisk together olive oil, lemon zest, pepper, salt, and lemon juice.
2. Add zucchini and cheese and toss well.
3. Serve and enjoy.

Nutritional Value (Amount per Serving):
Calories 122; Fat 11 g; Carbohydrates 7 g; Sugar 3 g; Protein 2 g; Cholesterol 0 mg

Kale Salad

Preparation Time: 10 minutes; Cooking Time: 20 minutes; Serve: 2
Ingredients:
- 2 cups kale, chopped
- 1 avocado, peel and cut into cubes
- 2 tbsp olive oil
- 1/2 orange juice
- 1/2 lime juice
- 2 1/2 tbsp pine nuts
- 1/4 tsp pepper
- 1/2 tsp sea salt

Directions:
1. Boil water in large stock pot.
2. Add salt and kale into the pot and cook for 10-20 minutes.
3. Drain kale well and set aside to cool.
4. Add kale, avocado, and pine nuts into the mixing bowl and toss well. Season with pepper and salt.
5. In a small bowl, whisk together oil, orange juice, and lime juice and pour over salad.
6. Serve and enjoy.

Nutritional Value (Amount per Serving):
Calories 380; Fat 35 g; Carbohydrates 10 g; Sugar 2 g; Protein 5 g; Cholesterol 0 mg

Lettuce Avocado Salad

Preparation Time: 10 minutes; Cooking Time: 10 minutes; Serve: 4
Ingredients:
- 2 garlic cloves, minced
- 12 cups romaine lettuce, chopped
- 3 tbsp hemp seeds
- 2 tbsp water
- 3 tbsp fresh lemon juice
- 1 ripe avocado
- 2 tsp Dijon mustard
- 1 tbsp capers
- 1 tbsp caper brine
- Pepper
- Salt

Directions:
1. Add avocado, pepper, salt, mustard, capers, caper brine, garlic, water, and lemon juice in a blender and blend until smooth.
2. Pour avocado mixture and hemp seeds in large mixing bowl and mix well.
3. Add chopped romaine lettuce in a bowl and toss well.
4. Serve and enjoy.

Nutritional Value (Amount per Serving):

Calories 165; Fat 12 g; Carbohydrates 5 g; Sugar 4 g; Protein 7 g; Cholesterol 0 mg

Feta Cucumber Salad

Preparation Time: 10 minutes; Cooking Time: 5 minutes; Serve: 4
Ingredients:

- 2 cups cucumbers, chopped
- 1/2 cup fresh mint, chopped
- 1 tbsp lime juice
- 2 avocados, peeled and chopped
- 1/2 cup feta cheese, crumbled
- 1/4 tsp salt
- 2 tbsp olive oil

Directions:

1. In a bowl, add chopped cucumbers and salt and set aside for 15-20 minutes.
2. Drain cucumber well and place in large bowl.
3. Add remaining ingredients and mix well.
4. Serve and enjoy.

Nutritional Value (Amount per Serving):
Calories 330; Fat 31 g; Carbohydrates 12 g; Sugar 2 g; Protein 5 g; Cholesterol 16 mg

Avocado Egg Salad

Preparation Time: 10 minutes; Cooking Time: 5 minutes; Serve: 4
Ingredients:

- 6 eggs, hard-boiled, peel and diced
- 1 avocado, peel and chopped
- 1 cucumber, peel and chopped
- ¼ tsp garlic powder
- ¼ tsp onion powder
- 1/2 tsp paprika
- 1/4 cup mayonnaise
- Salt

Directions:

1. Add all ingredients into the large mixing bowl and toss well.
2. Serve and enjoy.

Nutritional Value (Amount per Serving):
Calories 265; Fat 21 g; Carbohydrates 10 g; Sugar 3 g; Protein 10 g; Cholesterol 250 mg

Strawberry Arugula Salad

Preparation Time: 10 minutes; Cooking Time: 10 minutes; Serve: 2
Ingredients:

- 5 strawberries, sliced
- 2 cups arugula
- 1 avocado, cut into chunks
- 1 tbsp olive oil
- 7.5 oz halloumi cheese, cut into cubes
- For dressing:
- 1 tbsp mint leaves, chopped
- 2 tbsp olive oil
- 1 tbsp fresh lime juice
- 1 tbsp basil leaves, chopped
- ½ tsp pepper
- ½ tsp salt

Directions:

1. In a small bowl, mix together all dressing ingredients and set aside.
2. Heat tablespoon of oil in a pan over medium heat.
3. Add cheese to the pan and cook until lightly golden brown.
4. In a large bowl, add arugula, avocado, strawberries, and halloumi cheese and mix well.
5. Pour dressing over salad and toss well.
6. Serve and enjoy.

Nutritional Value (Amount per Serving):
Calories 250; Fat 25 g; Carbohydrates 6 g; Sugar 3 g; Protein 4 g; Cholesterol 2 mg

Celery Cauliflower Egg Salad

Preparation Time: 10 minutes; Cooking Time: 15 minutes; Serve: 8
Ingredients:
- 1 cauliflower head, cut into small pieces
- 1/4 cup dill pickles, chopped
- 2 green onions, sliced
- 4 eggs, hard-boiled, peeled, and chopped
- ½ cup celery, chopped
- ½ cup radishes, sliced
- For dressing:
- ½ tsp garlic powder
- ½ tsp black pepper
- ½ tsp seasoning salt
- 1 tbsp mustard
- 1 cup mayonnaise

Directions:
1. Boil cauliflower until tender, about 8-10 minutes. Drain well and transfer in large bowl.
2. Add eggs, onions, dill pickles, radishes, and celery to the bowl and mix well.
3. In a small bowl, whisk together all dressing ingredients and pour over salad and toss well.
4. Cover and place in fridge.
5. Serve chilled and enjoy.

Nutritional Value (Amount per Serving):
Calories 160; Fat 13 g; Carbohydrates 10 g; Sugar 3 g; Protein 4 g; Cholesterol 90 mg

Mozzarella Cauliflower Salad

Preparation Time: 10 minutes; Cooking Time: 5 minutes; Serve: 6
Ingredients:
- 1 cauliflower head, cut into florets
- 8 oz mozzarella cheese, crumbled
- 2 cups cherry tomatoes, halved
- 3 tbsp mayonnaise
- 3 tbsp basil pesto

Directions:
1. Add cauliflower florets into the boiling water and boil for 5 minutes. Drain well and place in large bowl.
2. Add remaining ingredients into the bowl and toss well.
3. Serve and enjoy.

Nutritional Value (Amount per Serving):
Calories 155; Fat 12 g; Carbohydrates 6 g; Sugar 3 g; Protein 9 g; Cholesterol 30 mg

Curried Cabbage Salad

Preparation Time: 10 minutes; Cooking Time: 5 minutes; Serve: 4

Ingredients:

- ½ medium head cabbage, shredded
- ½ tsp ginger powder
- 2 tsp sesame seeds
- ¼ cup tamari sauce
- ½ tsp cumin
- 1 tsp curry powder
- ¼ cup olive oil
- 1 fresh lemon juice
- 1/3 cup unsweetened desiccated coconut

Directions:

1. Add all ingredients into the large mixing bowl and toss well.
2. Place in fridge for 1 hour.
3. Serve and enjoy.

Nutritional Value (Amount per Serving):

Calories 195; Fat 16 g; Carbohydrates 11 g; Sugar 6 g; Protein 3 g; Cholesterol 0 mg

Asparagus Salad

Preparation Time: 10 minutes; Cooking Time: 10 minutes; Serve: 4

Ingredients:

- 1/2 lb asparagus, trimmed and cut into pieces
- 7.5 oz cherry tomatoes, halved

For dressing:

- 1 tbsp water
- 2 tbsp olive oil
- 1 tbsp vinegar
- 1/4 tsp garlic and herb seasoning blend
- 1 tbsp onion, minced
- 1 garlic clove, minced

Directions:

1. Add 1 tablespoon of water and asparagus in baking dish and cover with cling film and microwave for 2 minutes.
2. Remove asparagus from dish and place into a ice water until cool.
3. Add asparagus and tomatoes into a mixing bowl.
4. In a small bowl, mix together all remaining ingredients and pour over asparagus mixture.
5. Toss well and serve.

Nutritional Value (Amount per Serving):

Calories 82; Fat 7 g; Carbohydrates 5 g; Sugar 2 g; Protein 2 g; Cholesterol 0 mg

Chapter 8: Brunch & Dinner

Olive Cheese Omelet

Preparation Time: 10 minutes; Cooking Time: 5 minutes; Serve: 4
Ingredients:

- 4 large eggs
- 2 oz cheese
- 12 olives, pitted
- 2 tbsp butter
- 2 tbsp olive oil
- 1 tsp herb de Provence
- 1/2 tsp salt

Directions:

1. Add all ingredients except butter in a bowl whisk well until frothy.
2. Melt butter in a pan over medium heat.
3. Pour egg mixture onto hot pan and spread evenly.
4. Cover and cook for 3 minutes.
5. Turn omelet to other side and cook for 2 minutes more.
6. Serve and enjoy.

Nutritional Value (Amount per Serving):

Calories 250; Fat 23 g; Carbohydrates 2 g; Sugar 1 g; Protein 10 g; Cholesterol 216 mg

Cheese Almond Pancakes

Preparation Time: 10 minutes; Cooking Time: 10 minutes; Serve: 4
Ingredients:

- 4 eggs
- 1/4 tsp cinnamon
- 1/2 cup cream cheese
- 1/2 cup almond flour
- 1 tbsp butter, melted

Directions:

1. Add all ingredients into the blender and blend until combined.
2. Melt butter in a pan over medium heat.
3. Pour 3 tablespoons of batter per pancake and cook for 2 minutes on each side.
4. Serve and enjoy.

Nutritional Value (Amount per Serving):

Calories 271; Fat 25 g; Carbohydrates 5 g; Sugar 1 g; Protein 10.8 g; Cholesterol 203 mg

Cauliflower Frittata

Preparation Time: 10 minutes; Cooking Time: 5 minutes; Serve: 1
Ingredients:

- 1 egg
- 1/2 tbsp onion, diced
- ¼ cup cauliflower rice
- 1 tbsp olive oil
- 1/4 tsp turmeric
- Pepper
- Salt

Directions:

1. Add all ingredients except oil into the bowl and mix well to combine.
2. Heat oil in a pan over medium heat.
3. Pour the mixture into the hot oil pan and cook for 3-4 minutes or until lightly golden brown.
4. Serve and enjoy.

Nutritional Value (Amount per Serving):
Calories 196; Fat 19 g; Carbohydrates 3 g; Sugar 1 g; Protein 7 g; Cholesterol 165 mg

Basil Tomato Frittata

Preparation Time: 10 minutes; Cooking Time: 15 minutes; Serve: 2
Ingredients:

- 5 eggs
- 1 tbsp olive oil
- 7 oz can artichokes
- 1 garlic clove, chopped
- 1 onion, chopped
- 1/2 cup cherry tomatoes
- 2 tbsp fresh basil, chopped
- 1/4 cup feta cheese, crumbled
- 1/4 tsp pepper
- 1/4 tsp salt

Directions:
1. Heat oil in a pan over medium heat.
2. Add garlic and onion and sauté for 4 minutes.
3. Add artichokes, basil, and tomatoes and cook for 4 minutes.
4. Beat eggs in a bowl and season with pepper and salt.
5. Pour egg mixture into the pan and cook for 5-7 minutes.
6. Serve and enjoy.

Nutritional Value (Amount per Serving):
Calories 325; Fat 22 g; Carbohydrates 14 g; Sugar 6.2 g; Protein 20 g; Cholesterol 425 mg

Chia Spinach Pancakes

Preparation Time: 10 minutes; Cooking Time: 5 minutes; Serve: 6
Ingredients:

- 4 eggs
- ½ cup coconut flour
- 1 cup coconut milk
- ¼ cup chia seeds
- 1 cup spinach, chopped
- 1 tsp baking soda
- ½ tsp pepper
- ½ tsp salt

Directions:
1. Whisk eggs in a bowl until frothy.
2. Combine together all dry ingredients and add in egg mixture and whisk until smooth. Add spinach and stir well.
3. Greased pan with butter and heat over medium heat.
4. Pour 3-4 tablespoons of batter onto the pan and make pancake.
5. Cook pancake until lightly golden brown from both the sides.
6. Serve and enjoy.

Nutritional Value (Amount per Serving):
Calories 111; Fat 7.2 g; Carbohydrates 6 g; Sugar 0.4 g; Protein 6.3 g; Cholesterol 110 mg

Feta Kale Frittata

Preparation Time: 10 minutes; Cooking Time: 2 Hour 10 minutes; Serve: 8
Ingredients:

- 8 eggs, beaten
- 4 oz feta cheese, crumbled
- 6 oz bell pepper, roasted and diced
- 5 oz baby kale
- 1/4 cup green onion, sliced
- 2 tsp olive oil

Directions:

1. Heat olive oil in a pan over medium-high heat.
2. Add kale to the pan and sauté for 4-5 minutes or until softened.
3. Spray slow cooker with cooking spray.
4. Add cooked kale into the slow cooker.
5. Add green onion and bell pepper into the slow cooker.
6. Pour beaten eggs into the slow cooker and stir well to combine.
7. Sprinkle crumbled feta cheese.
8. Cook on low for 2 hours or until frittata is set.
9. Serve and enjoy.

Nutritional Value (Amount per Serving):
Calories 150; Fat 9 g; Carbohydrates 10 g; Sugar 5 g; Protein 10 g; Cholesterol 175 mg

Protein Muffins

Preparation Time: 10 minutes; Cooking Time: 15 minutes; Serve: 12
Ingredients:

- 8 eggs
- 2 scoop vanilla protein powder
- 8 oz cream cheese
- 4 tbsp butter, melted

Directions:

1. In a large bowl, combine together cream cheese and melted butter.
2. Add eggs and protein powder and whisk until well combined.
3. Pour batter into the greased muffin pan.
4. Bake at 350 F for 25 minutes.
5. Serve and enjoy.

Nutritional Value (Amount per Serving):
Calories 149; Fat 12 g; Carbohydrates 2 g; Sugar 0.4 g; Protein 8 g; Cholesterol 115 mg

Healthy Waffles

Preparation Time: 10 minutes; Cooking Time: 10 minutes; Serve: 4
Ingredients:

- 8 drops liquid stevia
- 1/2 tsp baking soda
- 1 tbsp chia seeds
- 1/4 cup water
- 2 tbsp sunflower seed butter
- 1 tsp cinnamon
- 1 avocado, peel, pitted and mashed
- 1 tsp vanilla
- 1 tbsp lemon juice
- 3 tbsp coconut flour

Directions:

1. Preheat the waffle iron.

2. In a small bowl, add water and chia seeds and soak for 5 minutes.
3. Mash together sunflower seed butter, lemon juice, vanilla, stevia, chia mixture, and avocado.
4. Mix together cinnamon, baking soda, and coconut flour.
5. Add wet ingredients to the dry ingredients and mix well.
6. Pour waffle mixture into the hot waffle iron and cook on each side for 3-5 minutes.
7. Serve and enjoy.

Nutritional Value (Amount per Serving):
Calories 220; Fat 17 g; Carbohydrates 13 g; Sugar 1.2 g; Protein 5.1 g; Cholesterol 0 mg

Cheese Zucchini Eggplant

Preparation Time: 10 minutes; Cooking Time: 2 hours; Serve: 8
Ingredients:
- 1 eggplant, peeled and cut in 1-inch cubes
- 1 ½ cup spaghetti sauce
- 1 onion, sliced
- 1 medium zucchini, cut into 1-inch pieces
- 1/2 cup parmesan cheese, shredded

Directions:
1. Add all ingredients into the crock pot and stir well.
2. Cover and cook on high for 2 hours.
3. Stir well and serve.

Nutritional Value (Amount per Serving):
Calories 47; Fat 1.2 g; Carbohydrates 8 g; Sugar 4 g; Protein 2.5 g; Cholesterol 2 mg

Coconut Kale Muffins

Preparation Time: 10 minutes; Cooking Time: 30 minutes; Serve: 8
Ingredients:
- 6 eggs
- 1/2 cup unsweetened coconut milk
- 1 cup kale, chopped
- ¼ tsp garlic powder
- ¼ tsp paprika
- 1/4 cup green onion, chopped
- Pepper
- Salt

Directions:
1. Preheat the oven to 350 F.
2. Add all ingredients into the bowl and whisk well.
3. Pour mixture into the greased muffin tray and bake in oven for 30 minutes.
4. Serve and enjoy.

Nutritional Value (Amount per Serving):
Calories 92; Fat 7 g; Carbohydrates 2 g; Sugar 0.8 g; Protein 5 g; Cholesterol 140 mg

Blueberry Muffins

Preparation Time: 10 minutes; Cooking Time: 25 minutes; Serve: 12
Ingredients:
- 2 eggs
- ½ tsp vanilla
- 1/2 cup fresh blueberries
- 1 tsp baking powder

- 6 drops stevia
- 1 cup heavy cream

Directions:
1. Preheat the oven to 350 F.
2. Add eggs to the mixing bowl and whisk until well mix.
3. Add remaining ingredients to the eggs and mix well to combine.

Nutritional Value (Amount per Serving):

Calories 190; Fat 18 g; Carbohydrates 6 g; Sugar 1.4 g; Protein 5.4 g; Cholesterol 55 mg

Coconut Bread

Preparation Time: 10 minutes; Cooking Time: 35 minutes; Serve: 12

Ingredients:
- 6 eggs
- 1 tbsp baking powder
- 2 tbsp swerve
- 1/2 cup ground flaxseed
- 1/2 cup coconut flour
- 1/2 tsp cinnamon
- 1 tsp xanthan gum
- 1/3 cup unsweetened coconut milk
- 1/2 cup olive oil
- 1/2 tsp salt

Directions:
1. Preheat the oven to 375 F.
2. Add eggs, milk, and oil into the stand mixer and blend until combined.
3. Add remaining ingredients and blend until well mixed.
4. Pour batter in greased loaf pan.
5. Bake in oven for 40 minutes.
6. Slice and serve.

Nutritional Value (Amount per Serving):

Calories 150; Fat 13.7 g; Carbohydrates 6 g; Sugar 3 g; Protein 3.9 g; Cholesterol 82 mg

Pumpkin Muffins

Preparation Time: 10 minutes; Cooking Time: 25 minutes; Serve: 10

Ingredients:
- 4 eggs
- 1/2 cup pumpkin puree
- 1 tsp pumpkin pie spice
- 1/2 cup almond flour
- 1 tbsp baking powder
- 1 tsp vanilla
- 1/3 cup coconut oil, melted
- 2/3 cup swerve
- 1/2 cup coconut flour
- 1/2 tsp sea salt

Directions:
1. Preheat the oven to 350 F.
2. In a large bowl, stir together coconut flour, pumpkin pie spice, baking powder, swerve, almond flour, and sea salt.
3. Stir in eggs, vanilla, coconut oil, and pumpkin puree until well combined.
4. Pour batter into the greased muffin tray and bake in oven for 25 minutes.
5. Serve and enjoy.

(From the first recipe at top right:)
- 2 cups almond flour
- 1/4 cup butter, melted

4. Pour batter into greased muffin tray and bake in oven for 25 minutes.
5. Serve and enjoy.

Nutritional Value (Amount per Serving):

Calories 150; Fat 13 g; Carbohydrates 8g; Sugar 2 g; Protein 5 g; Cholesterol 75 mg

Broccoli Nuggets

Preparation Time: 10 minutes; Cooking Time: 15 minutes; Serve: 4
Ingredients:

- 2 egg whites
- 2 cups broccoli florets
- 1/4 cup almond flour
- 1 cup cheddar cheese, shredded
- 1/8 tsp salt

Directions:

1. Preheat the oven to 350 F.
2. Add broccoli in bowl and mash using masher.
3. Add remaining ingredients to the broccoli and mix well.
4. Drop 20 scoops onto baking tray and press lightly down.
5. Bake in preheated oven for 20 minutes.
6. Serve and enjoy.

Nutritional Value (Amount per Serving):

Calories 145; Fat 10.4 g; Carbohydrates 4 g; Sugar 1.1 g; Protein 10.5 g; Cholesterol 30 mg

Cheesy Spinach Quiche

Preparation Time: 10 minutes; Cooking Time: 7 Hours; Serve: 6
Ingredients:

- 8 eggs
- 2 cups fresh spinach
- 1/2 cup feta cheese, crumbled
- 1/2 cup parmesan cheese, shredded
- 1/4 cup cheddar cheese, shredded
- 3 garlic cloves, minced
- 2 cups unsweetened almond milk
- 1/4 tsp salt

Directions:

1. In a large bowl, whisk together eggs and almond milk.
2. Add spinach, parmesan cheese, feta cheese, garlic, and salt and stir well to combine.
3. Spray crock potwith cooking spray.
4. Pour egg mixture into the crock pot.
5. Sprinkle shredded cheddar cheese over the top of egg mixture.
6. Cover and cook on low for 7 hours.

Nutritional Value (Amount per Serving):

Calories 365; Fat 32.5 g; Carbohydrates 7 g; Sugar 4 g; Protein 16.1 g; Cholesterol 249 mg

Vegetable Quiche

Preparation Time: 10 minutes; Cooking Time: 30 minutes; Serve: 6
Ingredients:

- 8 eggs
- 1 onion, chopped
- 1 cup Parmesan cheese, grated
- 1 cup unsweetened coconut milk
- 1 cup tomatoes, chopped
- 1 cup zucchini, chopped
- 1 tbsp butter
- 1/2 tsp pepper

- 1 tsp salt

Directions:
1. Preheat the oven to 400 F.
2. Melt butter in a pan over medium heat then add onion and sauté until onion soften.
3. Add tomatoes and zucchini to pan and sauté for 4 minutes.
4. Beat eggs with cheese, milk, pepper and salt in a bowl.
5. Pour egg mixture over vegetables and bake in oven for 30 minutes.
6. Slices and serve.

Nutritional Value (Amount per Serving):
Calories 25; Fat 16.7 g; Carbohydrates 8 g; Sugar 4 g; Protein 22 g; Cholesterol 257 mg

Coconut Porridge

Preparation Time: 10 minutes; Cooking Time: 5 minutes; Serve: 6

Ingredients:
- 1 cup unsweetened shredded coconut
- 1/4 tsp cinnamon
- 1 tsp vanilla
- 2 cups unsweetened coconut milk
- 1/4 cup psyllium husks
- 1/4 cup coconut flour
- 28 drops liquid stevia
- 1/4 tsp nutmeg
- 2 2/3 cups water

Directions:
1. Add coconut in pot and toast over medium-high heat.
2. Add water and coconut milk and stir well. Cover and bring to boil.
3. When it begins to boiling then remove from heat.
4. Add remaining ingredients and stir well.
5. Serve and enjoy.

Nutritional Value (Amount per Serving):
Calories 140; Fat 8 g; Carbohydrates 15 g; Sugar 1 g; Protein 1 g; Cholesterol 0 mg

Baked Eggplant Zucchini

Preparation Time: 10 minutes; Cooking Time: 40 minutes; Serve: 6

Ingredients:
- 3 medium zucchini, sliced
- 1/4 cup parsley, chopped
- 1/4 cup basil, chopped
- 1 cup cherry tomatoes, halved
- 1 medium eggplant, sliced
- 1 tbsp olive oil
- 3 oz parmesan cheese, grated
- 3 garlic cloves, minced
- 1/4 tsp pepper
- 1/4 tsp salt

Directions:
1. Preheat the oven to 350 F.
2. In a bowl, add cherry tomatoes, eggplant, zucchini, olive oil, garlic, cheese, basil, pepper, and salt toss well until combined.
3. Transfer eggplant mixture into greased baking dish.
4. Bake in oven for 35 minutes.
5. Garnish withparsley and serve.

Nutritional Value (Amount per Serving):
Calories 110; Fat 5.8 g; Carbohydrates 11 g; Sugar 4.8 g; Protein 7 g; Cholesterol 11 mg

Cheese Broccoli Bread

Preparation Time: 10 minutes; Cooking Time: 25 minutes; Serve: 5
Ingredients:

- 5 eggs, lightly beaten
- 2 tsp baking powder
- 4 tbsp coconut flour
- 1 cup broccoli florets, chopped
- 1 cup cheddar cheese, shredded

Directions:

1. Preheat the oven to 350 F.
2. Add all ingredients into the bowl and mix well.
3. Pour egg mixture into the prepared loaf pan and bake in oven for 30 minutes.
4. Slice and serve.

Nutritional Value (Amount per Serving):

Calories 210; Fat 12 g; Carbohydrates 8 g; Sugar 1 g; Protein 12 g; Cholesterol 188 mg

Shrimp Green Beans

Preparation Time: 10 minutes; Cooking Time: 10 minutes; Serve: 4
Ingredients:

- 1 lb shrimp, peeled and deveined
- 1 ½ tbsp soy sauce
- 2 tbsp olive oil
- 1/2 lb green beans, trimmed
- Salt

Directions:

1. Heat oil in a pan over medium-high heat.
2. Add beans to the pan and sauté for 5-6 minutes.
3. Remove pan from heat and set aside.
4. Add shrimp in the same pan and sauté for 2-3 minutes each side.
5. Return beans to the pan.
6. Add soy sauce and stir well and cook shrimp is completely cooked.
7. Season with salt. Serve.

Nutritional Value (Amount per Serving):

Calories 215; Fat 10 g; Carbohydrates 6 g; Sugar 1 g; Protein 27 g; Cholesterol 15 mg

Easy Asparagus Quiche

Preparation Time: 10 minutes; Cooking Time: 60 minutes; Serve: 6
Ingredients:

- 14 asparagus spears, cut ends and halved
- 5 eggs, beaten
- 1 cup unsweetened almond milk
- 1 cup cheddar cheese, shredded
- 1/4 tsp salt

Directions:

1. Preheat the oven to 350 F.
2. In a bowl, beat together eggs, thyme, white pepper, almond milk, and salt.
3. Arrange asparagus in greased quiche dish then pour egg mixture over asparagus.
4. Sprinkle cheese on top and bake for 60 minutes.
5. Slices and serve.

Nutritional Value (Amount per Serving):

Calories 224; Fat 17 g; Carbohydrates 6 g; Sugar 2 g; Protein 10 g; Cholesterol 150 mg

Cheese Mushroom Spinach Quiche

Preparation Time: 10 minutes; Cooking Time: 45 minutes; Serve: 6

Ingredients:

- 4 eggs
- 8 oz mushrooms, sliced
- 1/4 cup parmesan cheese, grated
- 2 oz feta cheese, crumbled
- 1 cup unsweetened almond milk
- 10 oz frozen spinach, thawed
- 1/2 cup mozzarella cheese, shredded
- 1 garlic clove, minced
- Pepper
- Salt

Directions:

1. Preheat the oven to 350 F.
2. Add garlic, mushrooms, pepper and salt in a pan and sauté for 5 minutes.
3. Greased 9-inch pie dish with cooking spray.
4. Add spinach in dish then places sautéed mushroom over spinach.
5. Sprinkle crumbled feta cheese on top.
6. In a bowl, whisk together eggs, parmesan cheese, and almond milk.
7. Pour egg mixture over spinach and mushroom then sprinkle mozzarella cheese.
8. Bake in oven for 45 minutes.
9. Slice and serve.

Nutritional Value (Amount per Serving):

Calories 220; Fat 16 g; Carbohydrates 7 g; Sugar 2 g; Protein 13 g; Cholesterol 141 mg

Zucchini Carrot Patties

Preparation Time: 10 minutes; Cooking Time: 5 minutes; Serve: 4

Ingredients:

- 1 egg, lightly beaten
- 1/2 cup carrot, grated
- 1 cup zucchini, grated
- 2 tsp coconut oil
- 1/3 cup mozzarella cheese, shredded
- 1/2 cup parmesan cheese, grated
- 1/4 tsp pepper
- 1 tsp salt

Directions:

1. Add all ingredients except oil into the bowl and mix until well combined.
2. Heat oil in a pan over medium-high heat.
3. Drop tablespoon of zucchini mixture on a hot pan and cook for 2 minutes on each side.
4. Serve and enjoy.

Nutritional Value (Amount per Serving):

Calories 102; Fat 6 g; Carbohydrates 2.5 g; Sugar 1 g; Protein 7 g; Cholesterol 55 mg

Tomato Zucchini Frittata

Preparation Time: 10 minutes; Cooking Time: 20 minutes; Serve: 4

Ingredients:

- 8 eggs
- 1 tbsp basil, chopped
- 2 tbsp olive oil
- 1 cup feta cheese, crumbled
- 1/2 cup olives, pitted and halved
- 1 cup grape tomatoes, cut in half
- 1 medium zucchini, sliced
- 1/2 tsp Italian seasoning
- 2 garlic cloves, minced
- Pepper
- Salt

Directions:
1. Heat the oven grill to medium heat.
2. Heat oil in a pan. Add zucchini and sauté until lightly golden.
3. Add garlic, Italian seasoning, and olives and cook for 1 minute.
4. In a bowl, whisk together eggs, pepper, and salt.
5. Stir in feta cheese.
6. Add tomatoes to a pan and pour egg mixture.
7. Turn heat to low and cook for 5-8 minutes.
8. Transfer pan to the oven and bake until frittata is set.
9. Garnish with basil and serve.

Nutritional Value (Amount per Serving):
Calories 320; Fat 25 g; Carbohydrates 7 g; Sugar 4 g; Protein 17 g; Cholesterol 360 mg

Italian Basil Tomato Omelet

Preparation Time: 10 minutes; Cooking Time: 5 minutes; Serve: 1
Ingredients:
- 2 eggs
- 2 oz mozzarella cheese
- 1 tbsp water
- 1 tomato, cut into thin slices
- 5 fresh basil leaves
- 1 tbsp butter
- Pepper
- Salt

Directions:
1. In a small bowl, whisk together eggs and water.
2. Melt butter in a pan over medium heat.
3. Pour egg mixture in pan and cook for 30 seconds.
4. Spread tomatoes, basil, and cheese on top of the omelet. Season with pepper and salt.
5. Cook for 2 minutes.
6. Serve and enjoy.

Nutritional Value (Amount per Serving):
Calories 401; Fat 30.4 g; Carbohydrates 6 g; Sugar 2 g; Protein 28 g; Cholesterol 389 mg

Curried Spinach

Preparation Time: 10 minutes; Cooking Time: 10 minutes; Serve: 6
Ingredients:
- 15 oz frozen spinach, thawed and squeeze out all liquid
- 2 tsp curry powder
- 1 tsp lemon zest
- 14 oz coconut milk
- 1/2 tsp salt

Directions:
1. Heat pan over medium heat.

2. Curry powder and few tablespoons of coconut milk and cook for a minute.
3. Add spinach, lemon zest, salt, and remaining milk. Stir well.
4. Cook spinach mixture until thickened.
5. Serve and enjoy.

Nutritional Value (Amount per Serving):

Calories 165; Fat 15 g; Carbohydrates 7 g; Sugar 2 g; Protein 3 g; Cholesterol 0 mg

Tofu Scramble

Preparation Time: 10 minutes; Cooking Time: 10 minutes; Serve: 4

Ingredients:

- 1 lb firm tofu, drained
- 1 cup mushrooms, sliced
- 1 garlic clove, minced
- 1 bell pepper, diced
- 1 tomato, diced
- 1 small onion, diced
- Pinch of turmeric
- ¼ tsp onion powder
- 1/2 tsp pepper
- 1/2 tsp salt

Directions:

1. Heat pan over medium heat.
2. Add tomato, mushrooms, garlic, onion and bell pepper and sauté for 5 minutes.
3. Crumble tofu and add in a pan and stir with vegetables.
4. Add turmeric, onion powder, pepper, and salt. Stir well.
5. Cook for 5 minutes.
6. Serve and enjoy.

Nutritional Value (Amount per Serving):

Calories 102; Fat 5 g; Carbohydrates 8 g; Sugar 3 g; Protein 11 g; Cholesterol 0 mg

Cheese Herb Frittata

Preparation Time: 10 minutes; Cooking Time: 3 Hours; Serve: 6

Ingredients:

- 8 eggs
- 4 cups baby arugula
- 1/2 tsp dried oregano
- 1/3 cup unsweetened almond milk
- 3/4 cup feta cheese, crumbled
- 1/2 cup onion, sliced
- 1 1/2 cups red peppers, roasted and chopped
- Pepper
- Salt

Directions:

1. Spray slow cooker with cooking spray.
2. In a mixing bowl, whisk eggs, oregano, and almond milk. Season with pepper and salt.
3. Add red peppers, onion, arugula, and cheese into the slow cooker.
4. Pour egg mixture over the vegetables.
5. Cover and cook on low for 3 hours.
6. Serve and enjoy.

Nutritional Value (Amount per Serving):

Calories 175; Fat 13 g; Carbohydrates 6 g; Sugar 3 g; Protein 11 g; Cholesterol 230 mg

Easy Broccoli Omelet

Preparation Time: 10 minutes; Cooking Time: 10 minutes; Serve: 2
Ingredients:

- 4 eggs
- 1 cup broccoli, chopped and cooked
- 1 tbsp olive oil
- 1 tbsp parsley, chopped
- ¼ tsp garlic powder
- ¼ tsp onion powder
- 1/4 tsp pepper
- 1/2 tsp salt

Directions:

1. In a bowl, whisk eggs with onion powder, garlic powder, pepper, and salt.
2. Heat oil in a pan over medium heat.
3. Pour broccoli and eggs mixture into the pan and cook until set.
4. Turn omelet to other side and cook until lightly golden brown.
5. Garnish with chopped parsley and serve.

Nutritional Value (Amount per Serving):
Calories 202; Fat 16 g; Carbohydrates 4 g; Sugar 2 g; Protein 12 g; Cholesterol 325 mg

Leek Mushroom Frittata

Preparation Time: 10 minutes; Cooking Time: 35 minutes; Serve: 4
Ingredients:

- 6 eggs
- 1 cup leeks, sliced
- 6 oz mushrooms, sliced
- Pepper
- Salt

Directions:

1. Preheat the oven to 350 F.
2. Spray pan with cooking spray and heat over medium heat.
3. Add mushrooms, leeks, and salt in a pan sauté for 6 minutes.
4. Whisk eggs in a bowl with pepper and salt.
5. Transfer sautéed mushroom and leek mixture into the greased baking dish.
6. Pour egg mixture over mushroom.
7. Bake in oven for 40 minutes.
8. Serve and enjoy.

Nutritional Value (Amount per Serving):
Calories 115; Fat 7 g; Carbohydrates 5 g; Sugar 2 g; Protein 10 g; Cholesterol 245 mg

Broccoli Cream Cheese Quiche

Preparation Time: 10 minutes; Cooking Time: 140 minutes; Serve: 8
Ingredients:

- 9 eggs
- 8 oz cream cheese
- 1/4 tsp onion powder
- 3 cups broccoli, cut into florets
- 2 cups cheddar cheese, shredded and divided
- 1/4 tsp pepper
- 3/4 tsp salt

Directions:

1. Add broccoli into the boiling water and cook for 3 minutes. Drain well and set aside to cool.
2. Whisk eggs, cream cheese, onion powder, pepper, and salt in mixing bowl.
3. Spray slow cooker with cooking spray.
4. Add cooked broccoli into the slow cooker then sprinkle half cup cheese.
5. Pour egg mixture over broccoli and cheese mixture.
6. Cover and cook on high for 2 hours and 15 minutes.
7. Sprinkle remaining cheese on top.
8. Cover for 10 minutes or until cheese melted.
9. Serve and enjoy.

Nutritional Value (Amount per Serving):
Calories 295; Fat 24 g; Carbohydrates 4 g; Sugar 2 g; Protein 15 g; Cholesterol 245 mg

Vanilla Banana Pancakes

Preparation Time: 5 minutes; Cooking Time: 5 minutes; Serve: 6
Ingredients:
- 2 eggs
- 1/8 tsp baking powder
- 1 large banana, mashed
- 2 tbsp vanilla protein powder
- ½ tsp vanilla

Directions:
1. Heat pan over medium heat.
2. Meanwhile, add all ingredients into the bowl and mix well until combined.
3. Spray pan with cooking spray.
4. Pour 3 tablespoons of batter onto the hot pan to make a pancake.
5. Cook a pancake for 30-40 seconds.
6. Turn to other side and cook for 30 seconds.
7. Serve and enjoy.

Nutritional Value (Amount per Serving):
Calories 75; Fat 2 g; Carbohydrates 5 g; Sugar 2 g; Protein 12 g; Cholesterol 54 mg

Mozzarella Zucchini Quiche

Preparation Time: 10 minutes; Cooking Time: 40 minutes; Serve: 6
Ingredients:
- 3 eggs
- 1 cup mozzarella, shredded
- 15 oz ricotta
- 1 onion, chopped
- 2 medium zucchini, sliced
- 1/2 tsp dried oregano
- 1/2 tsp dried basil
- 1 tbsp olive oil
- Pepper
- Salt

Directions:
1. Preheat the oven to 350 F.
2. Sauté zucchini over low heat.
3. Add onion and cook for 10 minutes.
4. Add pepper and seasoning to zucchini mixture.
5. Beat eggs, and then add in mozzarella and ricotta.
6. Fold in onions and zucchini.
7. Pour egg mixture into the greased pie dish and bake in oven for 30 minutes.
8. Serve and enjoy.

Nutritional Value (Amount per Serving):

Calories 180; Fat 12 g; Carbohydrates 8 g; Sugar 2 g; Protein 13 g; Cholesterol 105 mg

Zucchini Breakfast Casserole

Preparation Time: 10 minutes; Cooking Time: 25 minutes; Serve: 6

Ingredients:

- 2 eggs
- 1 tbsp garlic, minced
- 1/2 cup onion, diced
- 4 cup zucchini, grated
- 1/2 cup cheddar cheese, shredded
- 1 cup mozzarella cheese, shredded
- 1/2 cup parmesan cheese, grated
- 1/2 tsp salt

Directions:

1. Preheat the oven to 375 F.
2. Add zucchini and salt into the colander and set aside for 10 minutes.
3. Squeeze out all liquid from zucchini.
4. Combine together zucchini, cheddar cheese, mozzarella cheese, 1/2 parmesan cheese, eggs, garlic, and onion and pour into the greased baking dish.
5. Bake in oven for 25 minutes.
6. Serve and enjoy.

Nutritional Value (Amount per Serving):

Calories 145; Fat 9 g; Carbohydrates 4 g; Sugar 2 g; Protein 12 g; Cholesterol 75 mg

Bacon Egg Muffins

Preparation Time: 10 minutes; Cooking Time: 25 minutes; Serve: 12

Ingredients:

- 12 eggs
- 2 tbsp fresh parsley, chopped
- ½ tsp mustard powder
- 1/3 cup heavy cream
- 2 green onion, chopped
- 4 oz cheddar cheese, shredded
- 8 bacon slices, cooked and crumbled
- Pepper
- Salt

Directions:

1. Preheat the oven to 375 F.
2. In a mixing bowl, whisk together eggs, mustard powder, heavy cream, pepper, and salt.
3. Divide cheddar cheese, onions, and bacon into the muffin tray cups.
4. Pour egg mixture into the muffin cups.
5. Bake in oven for 25 minutes.
6. Serve and enjoy.

Nutritional Value (Amount per Serving):

Calories 115; Fat 9 g; Carbohydrates 1 g; Sugar 1 g; Protein 8 g; Cholesterol 175 mg

Zucchini Ham Quiche

Preparation Time: 10 minutes; Cooking Time: 40 minutes; Serve: 6

Ingredients:

- 8 eggs
- 1 cup cheddar cheese, shredded

- 1 cup zucchini, shredded and squeezed
- 1 cup ham, cooked and diced
- ½ tsp dry mustard
- ½ cup heavy cream
- Pepper
- Salt

Directions:
1. Preheat the oven to 375 F.
2. Combine ham, cheddar cheese, and zucchini in a pie dish.
3. In a bowl, whisk together eggs, heavy cream, and seasoning. Pour egg mixture over ham mixture.
4. Bake in oven for 40 minutes.
5. Serve and enjoy.

Nutritional Value (Amount per Serving):
Calories 234; Fat 18 g; Carbohydrates 2 g; Sugar 1 g; Protein 17 g; Cholesterol 264 mg

Italian Casserole

Preparation Time: 10 minutes; Cooking Time: 35 minutes; Serve: 4
Ingredients:
- 2 eggs
- 2/3 cup parmesan cheese, grated
- 2/3 cup chicken broth
- 1 lb Italian sausage
- 4 egg whites
- 4 tsp pine nuts, minced
- ¼ cup roasted red pepper, sliced
- ¼ cup pesto sauce
- 1/8 tsp pepper
- ¼ tsp sea salt

Directions:
1. Preheat the oven to 400 F.
2. Add sausage in pan and cook until golden brown. Drain excess oil and spread it into the greased casserole dish.
3. Whisk remaining ingredients except pine nuts in a bowl and pour over sausage.
4. Bake in oven for 35 minutes.
5. Garnish with pine nuts and serve.

Nutritional Value (Amount per Serving):
Calories 630; Fat 49 g; Carbohydrates 3 g; Sugar 2 g; Protein 40 g; Cholesterol 200 mg

Coconut Chicken Casserole

Preparation Time: 10 minutes; Cooking Time: 35 minutes; Serve: 8
Ingredients:
- 2 ½ lbs chicken breasts, boneless and cubed
- 12 oz roasted red peppers, drained and chopped
- 8 garlic cloves
- 2/3 cup mayonnaise
- 5 zucchini, cut into cubes
- 1 tsp xanthan gum
- 1 tbsp tomato paste
- 5.4 oz coconut cream
- 1 tsp salt

Directions:
1. Preheat the oven to 400 F.
2. Add zucchini and chicken to a casserole dish. Cover dish with foil.
3. Bake in oven for 25 minutes. Stir well and cook for 10 minutes more.
4. Meanwhile, in a bowl, stir together remaining ingredients.

5. Pour bowl mixture over chicken and zucchini and broil on high for 5 minutes.

6. Serve and enjoy.

Nutritional Value (Amount per Serving):

Calories 236; Fat 15 g; Carbohydrates 12 g; Sugar 6 g; Protein 17 g; Cholesterol 49 mg

Healthy Carrot Noodles

Preparation Time: 10 minutes; Cooking Time: 10 minutes; Serve: 3

Ingredients:

- 5 medium carrots
- 3 garlic cloves, chopped
- 1/4 cup fresh spring onions, chopped
- 1/2 cup basil leaves
- 1 cup fresh parsley
- 3 tbsp red chili pepper flakes, crushed
- 2/3 cup olive oil
- 1/4 cup vinegar
- Salt

Directions:

1. Add red chili flakes, oil, vinegar, garlic, spring onions, basil, and parsley in a blender and blend until smooth. Pour paste into a mixing bowl.
2. Add water and salt in a pot and bring to boil.
3. Peel carrots and using slicer make noodles.
4. Add carrot noodles in boiling water and blanch for 2 minutes.
5. Add cooked noodles in large bowl and toss well with paste.
6. Serve and enjoy.

Nutritional Value (Amount per Serving):

Calories 451; Fat 46 g; Carbohydrates 13 g; Sugar 5 g; Protein 1 g; Cholesterol 0 mg

Grape Tomato Frittata

Preparation Time: 10 minutes; Cooking Time: 10 minutes; Serve: 2

Ingredients:

- 6 eggs
- 1 tbsp butter
- 3.5 oz grape tomatoes, halved
- 2/3 cup feta cheese, crumbled
- 1 tbsp fresh basil, chopped
- 1 tbsp fresh chives, chopped
- 1 small onion, chopped
- ¼ tsp garlic powder
- ¼ tsp onion powder
- Pepper
- Salt

Directions:

1. Preheat the broiler to 400 F.
2. Melt butter in a pan over medium-high heat.
3. Add onion and sauté until lightly browned.
4. In a bowl, whisk together eggs, garlic powder, onion powder, basil, chives, pepper, and salt.
5. Pour egg mixture into a pan.
6. Top with grape tomatoes and crumbled cheese.
7. Place pan under the broiler and cook for 5-7 minutes.
8. Serve and enjoy.

Nutritional Value (Amount per Serving):

Calories 396; Fat 30 g; Carbohydrates 8 g; Sugar 6 g; Protein 25 g; Cholesterol 552 mg

Cauliflower Chili

Preparation Time: 10 minutes; Cooking Time: 25 minutes; Serve: 4

Ingredients:

- 2 cups cauliflower rice
- 1 cup mushrooms, quartered
- 1/2 small onion, chopped
- 1 tbsp olive oil
- 1/4 tsp paprika
- 1 tsp cumin powder
- 1/2 cup tomatoes, chopped
- 1 tbsp tomato paste
- 2 garlic cloves, chopped
- 2 tsp chili powder
- 1/2 tsp black pepper
- 1/2 tsp salt

Directions:

1. Heat olive oil in a saucepan over medium heat.
2. Add onion and garlic and sauté for 5 minutes.
3. Add cauliflower rice and mushrooms and cook for 10 minutes.
4. Add spices and stir for minute.
5. Add tomatoes and tomato paste. Stir well.
6. Cover and cook for 10 minutes.
7. Stir well and serve.

Nutritional Value (Amount per Serving):

Calories 65; Fat 4 g; Carbohydrates 7.4 g; Sugar 3 g; Protein 2 g; Cholesterol 0 mg

Fluffy Spinach Quiche

Preparation Time: 10 minutes; Cooking Time: 35 minutes; Serve: 6

Ingredients:

- 10 eggs
- 1 cup unsweetened coconut milk
- 1 tbsp butter
- 1 cup fresh spinach
- 1/4 cup fresh green onion, minced
- 1 cup cheddar cheese, shredded
- 1 cup heavy cream
- 1/4 tsp pepper
- 1/4 tsp salt

Directions:

1. Preheat the oven to 350 F.
2. In a bowl, whisk together eggs, cream, coconut milk, pepper, and salt.
3. Pour egg mixture into the greased pan then sprinkle with spinach, green onion, and cheese.
4. Bake in oven for 35 minutes.
5. Serve and enjoy.

Nutritional Value (Amount per Serving):

Calories 360; Fat 33 g; Carbohydrates 4 g; Sugar 2 g; Protein 16 g; Cholesterol 324 mg

Creamy Broccoli Casserole

Preparation Time: 10 minutes; Cooking Time: 20 minutes; Serve: 4

Ingredients:

- 1 cup mozzarella cheese, grated
- 1/2 cup sour cream
- 3 cups broccoli florets
- 1/2 cup heavy cream
- Pepper
- Salt

Directions:

1. Preheat the oven to 350 F.
2. Add broccoli florets to the greased baking dish.
3. Pour sour cream and cream over broccoli florets. Stir well.
4. Top with cheese and cook in oven for 20 minutes.
5. Serve and enjoy.

Nutritional Value (Amount per Serving):

Calories 202; Fat 17 g; Carbohydrates 4 g; Sugar 2 g; Protein 10 g; Cholesterol 49 mg

Dijon Cauliflower Casserole

Preparation Time: 10 minutes; Cooking Time: 15 minutes; Serve: 6

Ingredients:

- 1 cauliflower head, cut into florets and boil
- 2 oz cream cheese
- 1 cup heavy cream
- 1 tsp garlic powder
- 2 cups cheddar cheese, shredded
- 2 tsp Dijon mustard
- 1/2 tsp pepper
- 1/2 tsp salt

Directions:

1. Preheat the oven to 375 F.
2. Add cream in a small saucepan and bring to simmer, stir well.
3. Add mustard and cream cheese and stir until thickens.
4. Remove from heat and add 1 cup shredded cheese and seasoning and stir well.
5. Place boiled cauliflower florets into the greased baking dish.
6. Pour saucepan mixture over cauliflower florets.
7. Sprinkle remaining cheese on top of cauliflower mixture.
8. Bake in oven for 15 minutes.
9. Serve and enjoy.

Nutritional Value (Amount per Serving):

Calories 265; Fat 24 g; Carbohydrates 4 g; Sugar 2 g; Protein 12 g; Cholesterol 75 mg

Cheese Mushroom Pie

Preparation Time: 10 minutes; Cooking Time: 60 minutes; Serve: 6

Ingredients:

- 4 eggs
- 2 tbsp parmesan cheese, grated
- 10 oz fresh spinach
- 2 tsp olive oil
- 1 tsp garlic, minced
- 8 oz mushrooms, sliced
- 1/2 cup mozzarella cheese, shredded
- 1/4 tsp nutmeg
- 1/2 tsp pepper
- 1/2 cup heavy cream
- 16 oz cottage cheese
- 1 tsp salt

Directions:
1. Preheat the oven to 350 F.
2. Heat oil in a pan over medium heat.
3. Add mushrooms and garlic in a pan and sauté until tender.
4. Add spinach, nutmeg, pepper, and salt and cook until spinach is wilted.
5. Drain spinach and mushrooms mixture.
6. Sprinkle parmesan cheese into the 9-inch pie dish.
7. In a bowl, whisk together eggs, cottage cheese, and cream and stir well.
8. Add mushroom and spinach mixture and stir well.
9. Pour mushroom and spinach mixture into a pie dish and bake in oven for 50 minutes.
10. Slice and serve.

Nutritional Value (Amount per Serving):
Calories 195; Fat 11 g; Carbohydrates 6 g; Sugar 2 g; Protein 19 g; Cholesterol 130 mg

Spicy Egg Scrambled

Preparation Time: 10 minutes; Cooking Time: 5 minutes; Serve: 1
Ingredients:
- 2 large eggs
- 2 jalapeno pepper, chopped
- 1 tsp olive oil
- 1/4 tsp onion powder
- 1/4 tsp garlic powder
- 1 oz cream cheese
- 1/4 tsp pepper
- 1/4 tsp salt

Directions:
1. Heat oil in a pan over medium heat.
2. Add jalapeno pepper in a pan and sauté until softened.
3. Add eggs to the pan and stir until scramble.
4. Remove pan from heat.
5. Add cream cheese and spices and stir well.
6. Serve and enjoy.

Nutritional Value (Amount per Serving):
Calories 290; Fat 25 g; Carbohydrates 4 g; Sugar 2 g; Protein 15 g; Cholesterol 402 mg

Coconut Pumpkin Risotto

Preparation Time: 10 minutes; Cooking Time: 10 minutes; Serve: 4
Ingredients:
- 1/2 cup unsweetened coconut milk
- 1 1/2 cups vegetable broth
- 1 cup pumpkin, grated
- 4 cups cauliflower rice
- 1 tbsp olive oil
- 2 garlic cloves, minced
- Pepper
- Salt

Directions:
1. Heat olive oil in a pan over medium heat.
2. Add garlic, cauliflower, and pumpkin in a pan and cook until softened.
3. Add coconut milk and broth and cook until done. Season with pepper and salt.
4. Serve and enjoy.

Nutritional Value (Amount per Serving):
Calories 165; Fat 12 g; Carbohydrates 12 g; Sugar 5 g; Protein 5 g; Cholesterol 0 mg

Coconut Cauliflower Chowder

Preparation Time: 10 minutes; Cooking Time: 15 minutes; Serve: 4
Ingredients:

- 1 cauliflower head, chopped
- 1 cup unsweetened coconut milk
- 4 cups vegetable stock
- 2 celery stalk, chopped
- 1 onion, chopped
- 2 garlic cloves, minced
- 1/2 tsp coriander powder
- 1 tsp turmeric
- 1 1/4 tsp ground cumin
- 2 tbsp olive oil
- Pepper
- Salt

Directions:

1. Heat oil in a saucepan over medium-high heat.
2. Add celery, onion, and garlic and sauté for 5 minutes.
3. Add cauliflower and stir well and cook for 4-5 minutes.
4. Add stock, coconut milk, coriander, turmeric, and cumin and stir well. Bring to boil.
5. Turn heat to low and simmer for 15 minutes. Season with pepper and salt.
6. Serve and enjoy.

Nutritional Value (Amount per Serving):
Calories 235; Fat 22 g; Carbohydrates 10 g; Sugar 5 g; Protein 3 g; Cholesterol 0 mg

Cauliflower Cheese Grits

Preparation Time: 10 minutes; Cooking Time: 2 Hours; Serve: 8
Ingredients:

- 6 cups cauliflower rice
- 1/2 cup vegetable broth
- 1 cup cream cheese
- 1/2 tsp pepper
- 1 tsp salt

Directions:

1. Add all ingredients to the crock pot and stir well combine.
2. Cover slow cooker with lid and cook on low for 2 hours.
3. Stir well and serve.

Nutritional Value (Amount per Serving):
Calories 122; Fat 10 g; Carbohydrates 5 g; Sugar 2 g; Protein 4 g; Cholesterol 30 mg

Roasted Pepper Quiche

Preparation Time: 10 minutes; Cooking Time: 40 minutes; Serve: 6
Ingredients:

- 8 egg whites
- 1 cup gruyere cheese, shredded
- 1/4 cup onion, diced
- 2 cups spinach, steamed and squeeze out excess liquid
- 1 garlic cloves, minced
- 4 pieces roasted red peppers, sliced
- 1/2 cup cherry tomatoes, halved
- 1/2 cup unsweetened coconut milk
- Pepper
- Salt

Directions:
1. Preheat the oven to 350 F.
2. Add garlic and onion and sauté for minutes.
3. In a bowl, whisk together egg whites, cheese, and coconut milk.
4. Add sautéed onion and garlic into the egg mixture and stir well.
5. Layer tomatoes, roasted peppers, and spinach in a pie dish. Pour egg mixture over the vegetables.
6. Bake in oven for 40 minutes.
7. Serve and enjoy.

Nutritional Value (Amount per Serving):
Calories 155; Fat 10 g; Carbohydrates 4 g; Sugar 2 g; Protein 12 g; Cholesterol 20 mg

Flax Pumpkin Muffins

Preparation Time: 5 minutes; Cooking Time: 5 minutes; Serve: 2
Ingredients:
- 1 egg
- 2 tbsp swerve
- 2 tbsp ground flaxseed
- 2 tbsp almond flour
- 1 1/2 tsp pumpkin spice
- 1/4 tsp baking powder
- 2 tbsp pumpkin puree

Directions:
1. Grease two ramekins with butter.
2. In a bowl, mix together pumpkin puree and egg.
3. In separate bowl, mix together almond flour, pumpkin spice, baking powder, swerve, and ground flaxseed.
4. Pour pumpkin and egg mixture into the almond flour mixture and mix well.
5. Pour mixture into the prepared ramekins and microwave for 1-2 minutes.
6. Serve and enjoy.

Nutritional Value (Amount per Serving):
Calories 130; Fat 9 g; Carbohydrates 8 g; Sugar 1 g; Protein 5 g; Cholesterol 80 mg

Coconut Protein Porridge

Preparation Time: 5 minutes; Cooking Time: 5 minutes; Serve: 2
Ingredients:
- 3 tbsp flaxseed meal
- 2 tbsp coconut flour
- 1 1/2 cups unsweetened coconut milk
- 2 tbsp protein powder

Directions:
1. In a bowl, mix together coconut flour, protein powder, and flaxseed meal.
2. Add to a saucepan along with milk and cook over medium heat.
3. Once mixture thickens then removes from heat.
4. Serve and enjoy.

Nutritional Value (Amount per Serving):
Calories 120; Fat 6 g; Carbohydrates 10.5 g; Sugar 1 g; Protein 5 g; Cholesterol 0 mg

Kale Egg Scrambled

Preparation Time: 10 minutes; Cooking Time: 5 minutes; Serve: 1

Ingredients:

- 2 eggs, lightly beaten
- 1 1/2 tsp turmeric
- 1 cup kale, chopped
- 1 tbsp butter
- 1 tsp garlic powder
- Pepper
- Salt

Directions:

1. Melt butter in a pan over medium heat.
2. Add kale in the pan and cook until wilted then add eggs and stir until scrambled.
3. Add remaining ingredients and stir for 1-2 minutes.
4. Serve and enjoy.

Nutritional Value (Amount per Serving):

Calories 280; Fat 20 g; Carbohydrates 10 g; Sugar 1 g; Protein 14 g; Cholesterol 355 mg

Sausage Egg Muffins

Preparation Time: 10 minutes; Cooking Time: 25 minutes; Serve: 12

Ingredients:

- 6 eggs
- ½ cup mozzarella cheese
- 1 cup egg whites
- 1 lb ground pork sausage
- 3/4 cup cheddar cheese
- 2 tbsp onion, minced
- ½ red pepper, diced
- Pepper
- Salt

Directions:

1. Preheat the oven to 350 F.
2. Brown sausage in pan over medium heat.
3. Divide red pepper, cooked sausages, cheese, and onion into each muffin cups.
4. In a large bowl, whisk together egg whites, egg, pepper, and salt.
5. Pour egg mixture into each muffin cups.
6. Bake in oven for 20-25 minutes.
7. Serve and enjoy.

Nutritional Value (Amount per Serving):

Calories 185; Fat 14 g; Carbohydrates 2 g; Sugar 1 g; Protein 14 g; Cholesterol 116 mg

Healthy Cinnamon Flax Muffin

Preparation Time: 5 minutes; Cooking Time: 5 minutes; Serve: 1

Ingredients:

- 1 egg, lightly beaten
- 1/2 tsp ground cinnamon
- ¼ cup ground flaxseed
- 1 tsp butter, melted
- 2 tsp swerve
- ½ tsp baking powder

Directions:

1. Grease mug with butter.
2. Add all ingredients to the mug and mix well.
3. Place mug in microwave and microwave for 45 seconds.
4. Serve and enjoy.

Nutritional Value (Amount per Serving):
   Calories 250; Fat 16 g; Carbohydrates 10 g; Sugar 1 g; Protein 11 g; Cholesterol 175 mg

Chapter 9: Desserts & Drinks

Cinnamon Almond Balls

Preparation Time: 10 minutes; Cooking Time: 5 minutes; Serve: 12
Ingredients:

- 1 tsp cinnamon
- 3 tbsp erythritol
- 1 ¼ cup almond flour
- 1 cup peanut butter
- Pinch of salt

Directions:

1. Add all ingredients into the mixing bowl and mix well.
2. Cover and place bowl in fridge for 30 minutes.
3. Make small bite size ball from mixture and serve.

Nutritional Value (Amount per Serving):

Calories 160; Fat 12 g; Carbohydrates 5 g; Sugar 1 g; Protein 6 g; Cholesterol 0 mg

Choco Frosty

Preparation Time: 5 minutes; Cooking Time: 5 minutes; Serve: 4
Ingredients:

- 1 tsp vanilla
- 8 drops liquid stevia
- 2 tbsp unsweetened cocoa powder
- 1 tbsp almond butter
- 1 cup heavy cream

Directions:

1. Add all ingredients into the mixing bowl and beat with immersion blender until soft peaks form.
2. Place in refrigerator for 30 minutes.
3. Add frosty mixture into the piping bag and pipe in serving glasses.
4. Serve and enjoy.

Nutritional Value (Amount per Serving):

Calories 240; Fat 25 g; Carbohydrates 4 g; Sugar 3 g; Protein 3 g; Cholesterol 43 mg

Cheesecake Fat Bombs

Preparation Time: 10 minutes; Cooking Time: 10 minutes; Serve: 24
Ingredients:

- 8 oz cream cheese
- 1 ½ tsp vanilla
- 2 tbsp erythritol
- 4 oz coconut oil
- 4 oz heavy cream

Directions:

1. Add all ingredients into the mixing bowl and beat using immersion blender until creamy.
2. Pour batter into the mini cupcake liner and place in refrigerator until set.
3. Serve and enjoy.

Nutritional Value (Amount per Serving):

Calories 90; Fat 9.8 g; Carbohydrates 1.4 g; Sugar 0.1 g; Protein 0.8 g; Cholesterol 17 mg

Matcha Ice Cream

Preparation Time: 5 minutes; Cooking Time: 5 minute; Serve: 2
Ingredients:
- ½ tsp vanilla
- 2 tbsp swerve
- 1 tsp matcha powder
- 1 cup heavy whipping cream

Directions:
1. Add all ingredients into the glass jar.
2. Seal jar with lid and shake for 4-5 minutes until mixture double.
3. Place in refrigerator for 3-4 hours.
4. Serve chilled and enjoy.

Nutritional Value (Amount per Serving):
Calories 215; Fat 22 g; Carbohydrates 3.8 g; Sugar 0.2 g; Protein 1.2 g; Cholesterol 82 mg

Moist Avocado Brownies

Preparation Time: 10 minutes; Cooking Time: 35 minutes; Serve: 9
Ingredients:
- 2 avocados, mashed
- 2 eggs
- 1 tsp baking powder
- 2 tbsp swerve
- 1/3 cup chocolate chips, melted
- 4 tbsp coconut oil, melted
- 2/3 cup unsweetened cocoa powder

Directions:
1. Preheat the oven to 325 F.
2. In a mixing bowl, mix together all dry ingredients.
3. In another bowl, mix together avocado and eggs until well combined.
4. Slowly add dry mixture to the wet along with melted chocolate and coconut oil. Mix well.
5. Pour batter in greased baking pan and bake for 30-35 minutes.
6. Slice and serve.

Nutritional Value (Amount per Serving):
Calories 207; Fat 18 g; Carbohydrates 11 g; Sugar 3.6 g; Protein 3.8 g; Cholesterol 38 mg

Mix Berry Sorbet

Preparation Time: 10 minutes; Cooking Time: 10 minutes; Serve: 1
Ingredients:
- ½ cup raspberries, frozen
- ½ cup blackberries, frozen
- 1 tsp liquid stevia
- 6 tbsp water

Directions:
1. Add all ingredients into the blender and blend until smooth.
2. Pour blended mixture into the container and place in refrigerator until harden.
3. Serve chilled and enjoy.

Nutritional Value (Amount per Serving):

Calories 63; Fat 0.8 g; Carbohydrates 14 g; Sugar 6 g; Protein 1.7 g; Cholesterol 0 mg

Chia Almond Pudding

Preparation Time: 5 minutes; Cooking Time: 5 minutes; Serve: 4
Ingredients:

- 2 tbsp almonds, toasted and crushed
- 1/3 cup chia seeds
- ½ tsp vanilla
- 4 tbsp erythritol
- ¼ cup unsweetened cocoa powder
- 2 cups unsweetened almond milk

Directions:

1. Add almond milk, vanilla, sweetener, and cocoa powder into the blender and blend until well combined.
2. Pour blended mixture into the bowl.
3. Add chia seeds and whisk for 1-2 minutes.
4. Pour pudding mixture into the serving bowls and place in fridge for 1-2 hours.
5. Top with crushed almonds and serve.

Nutritional Value (Amount per Serving):
Calories 170; Fat 12 g; Carbohydrates 12 g; Sugar 1 g; Protein 7 g; Cholesterol 35 mg

Chia Raspberry Pudding

Preparation Time: 5 minutes; Cooking Time: 5 minutes; Serve: 2
Ingredients:

- ¼ tsp vanilla
- ¾ cup unsweetened almond milk
- 1 tbsp erythritol
- 2 tbsp proteins collagen peptides
- ¼ cup chia seeds
- ½ cup raspberries, mashed

Directions:

1. Add all ingredients into the bowl and stir until well combined.
2. Place in refrigerator for overnight.
3. Serve chilled and enjoy.

Nutritional Value (Amount per Serving):
Calories 102; Fat 6 g; Carbohydrates 13 g; Sugar 1.4 g; Protein 4 g; Cholesterol 0 mg

Chocolate Chia Pudding

Preparation Time: 5 minutes; Cooking Time: 5 minutes; Serve: 3
Ingredients:

- ½ cup chia seeds
- ½ tsp vanilla
- 1/3 cup unsweetened cocoa powder
- 1 ½ cups unsweetened coconut milk

Directions:

1. Add all ingredients into the mixing bowl and whisk well.
2. Place bowl in refrigerator for overnight.
3. Serve chilled and enjoy.

Nutritional Value (Amount per Serving):
Calories 138; Fat 9.4 g; Carbohydrates 10.3 g; Sugar 0.3 g; Protein 6 g; Cholesterol 0 mg

Choco Peanut Cookies

Preparation Time: 10 minutes; Cooking Time: 10 minutes; Serve: 24

Ingredients:

- 1 cup peanut butter
- 1 tsp baking soda
- 2 tsp vanilla
- 1 tbsp butter, melted
- 2 eggs
- 2 tbsp unsweetened cocoa powder
- 2/3 cup erythritol
- 1 1/3 cups almond flour

Directions:

1. Preheat the oven to 350 F.
2. Add all ingredients into the mixing bowl and stir to combine.
3. Make 2-inch balls from mixture and place on greased baking tray and gently press down each ball with fork.
4. Bake in oven for 8-10 minutes.
5. Serve and enjoy.

Nutritional Value (Amount per Serving):

Calories 110; Fat 9 g; Carbohydrates 9 g; Sugar 1.3 g; Protein 4.6 g; Cholesterol 15 mg

Chocolate Macaroon

Preparation Time: 10 minutes; Cooking Time: 20 minutes; Serve: 20

Ingredients:

- 1 tsp vanilla
- ¼ cup coconut oil
- 2 eggs
- 1/3 cup unsweetened coconut, shredded
- 1/3 cup erythritol
- ½ tsp baking powder
- ¼ cup unsweetened cocoa powder
- 3 tbsp coconut flour
- 1 cup almond flour
- Pinch of salt

Directions:

1. Add all ingredients into the mixing bowl and mix until well combined.
2. Make small balls from mixture and place on greased baking tray.
3. Bake at 350 F for 15-20 minutes.
4. Serve and enjoy.

Nutritional Value (Amount per Serving):

Calories 80; Fat 7 g; Carbohydrates 6.5 g; Sugar 0.5 g; Protein 2.3 g; Cholesterol 16 mg

Mocha Ice-Cream

Preparation Time: 10 minutes; Cooking Time: 10 minutes; Serve: 2

Ingredients:

- ¼ tsp xanthan gum
- 1 tbsp instant coffee
- 2 tbsp unsweetened cocoa powder
- 15 drops liquid stevia
- 2 tbsp erythritol
- ¼ cup heavy cream
- 1 cup unsweetened coconut milk

Directions:

1. Add all ingredients except xanthan gum into the blender and blend until smooth.
2. Add xanthan gum and blend until mixture is slightly thickened.
3. Pour mixture into the ice cream maker and churn according to machine instructions.
4. Serve chilled and enjoy.

Nutritional Value (Amount per Serving):
Calories 88; Fat 8 g; Carbohydrates 14 g; Sugar 0.1 g; Protein 1.4 g; Cholesterol 21 mg

Quick Mug Brownie

Preparation Time: 5 minutes; Cooking Time: 1 minutes; Serve: 1
Ingredients:
- 2 eggs
- 1 tbsp heavy cream
- 1 scoop protein powder
- 1 tbsp erythritol
- ¼ tsp vanilla

Directions:
1. Add all ingredients into the mug and mix well.
2. Place mug in microwave and microwave for 1 minute.
3. Serve and enjoy.

Nutritional Value (Amount per Serving):
Calories 305; Fat 16 g; Carbohydrates 7 g; Sugar 1.8 g; Protein 33 g; Cholesterol 412 mg

Protein Peanut Butter Ice Cream

Preparation Time: 5 minutes; Cooking Time: 5 minutes; Serve: 2
Ingredients:
- 5 drops liquid stevia
- 2 tbsp heavy cream
- 2 tbsp peanut butter
- 2 tbsp protein powder
- ¾ cup cottage cheese

Directions:
1. Add all ingredients into the blender and blend until smooth.
2. Pour blended mixture into the container and place in refrigerator for 30 minutes.
3. Serve chilled and enjoy.

Nutritional Value (Amount per Serving):
Calories 222; Fat 15 g; Carbohydrates 7 g; Sugar 2 g; Protein 16 g; Cholesterol 27 mg

Fruit Salad

Preparation Time: 5 minutes; Cooking Time: 5 minutes; Serve: 2
Ingredients:
- 1 tsp erythritol
- 1 tsp lemon juice
- 1 sage leaf, chopped
- 1 tbsp blueberries
- ¼ cup strawberries, sliced
- ½ cup raspberries
- ½ cup blackberries

Directions:

1. Add all ingredients into the bowl and toss well.
2. Serve and enjoy.

Nutritional Value (Amount per Serving):
   Calories 40; Fat 0.5 g; Carbohydrates 11 g; Sugar 7 g; Protein 1 g; Cholesterol 0 mg

Blackberry Pops

Preparation Time: 10 minutes; Cooking Time: 10 minutes; Serve: 6
Ingredients:
- 1 tsp liquid stevia
- ½ cup water
- 1 fresh sage leaf
- 1 cup blackberries

Directions:
1. Add all ingredients into the blender and blend until smooth.
2. Pour blended mixture into the ice pop molds and place in refrigerator for overnight.
3. Serve and enjoy.

Nutritional Value (Amount per Serving):
   Calories 10; Fat 0.1 g; Carbohydrates 2.3 g; Sugar 1.2 g; Protein 0.3 g; Cholesterol 0 mg

Avocado Peanut Butter Fat Bombs

Preparation Time: 10 minutes; Cooking Time: 10 minutes; Serve: 6
Ingredients:
- 1 tbsp swerve
- 1 avocado, peeled, pitted, and chopped
- 1 cup peanut butter
- 3 tbsp heavy cream
- ½ cup butter, melted
- ½ cup coconut oil, meleted

Directions:
1. Add all ingredients into the blender and blend until smooth.
2. Pour mixture into the mini cupcake liner and place in refrigerator until set.
3. Serve and enjoy.

Nutritional Value (Amount per Serving):
   Calories 640; Fat 64 g; Carbohydrates 11 g; Sugar 4 g; Protein 11 g; Cholesterol 51 mg

Peanut Butter Mousse

Preparation Time: 5 minutes; Cooking Time: 5 minutes; Serve: 2
Ingredients:
- 1 tsp vanilla
- 1 tsp swerve
- 1 tbsp peanut butter
- ½ cup heavy whipping cream

Directions:
1. Add all ingredients into the bowl and whisk until soft peaks form.
2. Pipe into serving bowls and serve.

Nutritional Value (Amount per Serving):
   Calories 260; Fat 25 g; Carbohydrates 3 g; Sugar 1 g; Protein 3 g; Cholesterol 80 mg

Raspberry Mousse

Preparation Time: 5 minutes; Cooking Time: 10 minutes; Serve: 6
Ingredients:

- ½ tsp vanilla
- 1 cup heavy cream
- ¼ cup erythritol
- 8 oz cream cheese
- 2 tbsp water
- 1 cup raspberries

Directions:

1. Add berries, water, cream cheese, and sweetener into the blender and blend until smooth.
2. Add heavy cream in a large bowl and beat using hand mixer until soft peaks form.
3. Add berry mixture into the whipped cream and fold well.
4. Pour mixture into the serving glasses and place in refrigerator for 1 hour.
5. Serve and enjoy.

Nutritional Value (Amount per Serving):
Calories 279; Fat 27 g; Carbohydrates 5 g; Sugar 3 g; Protein 3 g; Cholesterol 92 mg

Cheesecake Mousse

Preparation Time: 5 minutes; Cooking Time: 5 minutes; Serve: 6
Ingredients:

- 1 cup heavy whipping cream
- ½ tsp vanilla
- 1/3 cup erythritol
- 8 oz cream cheese

Directions:

1. In a large bowl, beat heavy cream until soft peaks form.
2. Add cream cheese, sweetener, and vanilla into the blender and blend until smooth.
3. Pour cream cheese mixture into the heavy cream and fold well.
4. Place in refrigerator for 2 hours.
5. Serve chilled and enjoy.

Nutritional Value (Amount per Serving):
Calories 270; Fat 27 g; Carbohydrates 3 g; Sugar 1 g; Protein 3 g; Cholesterol 95 mg

Blueberry Pops

Preparation Time: 10 minutes; Cooking Time: 10 minutes; Serve: 6
Ingredients:

- ½ cup blueberries
- ¼ tsp xanthan gum
- ½ cup unsweetened coconut milk
- ¼ cup sour cream
- ¼ cup swerve
- 2 tbsp protein powder
- ¾ cup water

Directions:

1. Add all ingredients into the blender and blend until smooth.
2. Pour blended mixture into the popsicle mold and place in refrigerator for overnight.
3. Serve and enjoy.

Nutritional Value (Amount per Serving):

Calories 35; Fat 2 g; Carbohydrates 3 g; Sugar 2 g; Protein 2.2 g; Cholesterol 6 mg

Strawberry Pops

Preparation Time: 5 minutes; Cooking Time: 5 minutes; Serve: 6
Ingredients:

- ¼ tsp xanthan gum
- ½ cup strawberries
- 2 tbsp MCT oil
- ¼ cup swerve
- 1 cup unsweetened coconut milk

Directions:

1. Add all ingredients into the blender and blend until smooth.
2. Pour blended mixture into the popsicle mold and place in refrigerator for overnight.
3. Serve and enjoy.

Nutritional Value (Amount per Serving):
Calories 95; Fat 9.6 g; Carbohydrates 3.2 g; Sugar 1.9 g; Protein 0 g; Cholesterol 0 mg

Strawberry Cheese Popsicles

Preparation Time: 5 minutes; Cooking Time: 5 minutes; Serve: 12
Ingredients:

- 2 cups strawberries, sliced
- 1 ½ tsp lemon zest
- 1 tbsp lemon juice
- ¼ tsp vanilla
- 1/3 cup swerve
- 1 cup cream
- 8 oz cream cheese

Directions:

1. Add all ingredients into the blender and blend until smooth.
2. Pour blended mixture into the Popsicle mold and place in refrigerator for overnight.
3. Serve and enjoy.

Nutritional Value (Amount per Serving):
Calories 87; Fat 7 g; Carbohydrates 3 g; Sugar 1.7 g; Protein 1.8 g; Cholesterol 25 mg

Chocolate Bars

Preparation Time: 10 minutes; Cooking Time: 35 minutes; Serve: 24
Ingredients

- 5 eggs
- 1 cup walnuts, chopped
- ¼ cup coconut flour
- 2 tsp vanilla
- ½ cup butter
- 8.5 oz cream cheese
- 2 cups erythritol
- 1 cup unsweetened chocolate chips
- 1 ½ tsp baking powder
- 1 cup almond flour
- Pinch of salt

Directions:

1. Preheat the oven to 350 F.
2. In a bowl, beat together butter, sweetener, vanilla, and cream cheese until smooth.
3. Add eggs and beat until well combined.
4. Add remaining ingredients and stir gently to combine.
5. Transfer mixture to the greased cookie sheet and spread evenly.
6. Bake in oven for 35 minutes.
7. Allow to cool completely.
8. Slice and serve.

Nutritional Value (Amount per Serving):
Calories 205; Fat 19 g; Carbohydrates 5 g; Sugar 0.4 g; Protein 5.5 g; Cholesterol 43 mg

Cheese Cake

Preparation Time: 10 minutes; Cooking Time: 45 minutes; Serve: 8
Ingredients:
- 2 eggs
- ¼ cup coconut flour
- 14.5 oz ricotta
- ½ cup erythritol
- Pinch of salt

Directions:
1. Preheat the oven to 350 F.
2. In a bowl whisk eggs.
3. Add remaining ingredients and mix until well combined.
4. Pour batter in greased baking pan.
5. Bake in oven for 45 minutes.
6. Allow to cool completely.
7. Slice and serve.

Nutritional Value (Amount per Serving):
Calories 90; Fat 5 g; Carbohydrates 3 g; Sugar 0.3 g; Protein 7 g; Cholesterol 3 mg

Chocolate Fat Bomb

Preparation Time: 5 minutes; Cooking Time: 10 minutes; Serve: 10
Ingredients:
- ½ cup unsweetened cocoa powder
- ½ cup almond butter
- ½ cup of coconut oil
- 1 tbsp stevia
- ½ tbsp sea salt

Directions:
1. Melt coconut oil and almond butter in a saucepan and over medium heat.
2. Add cocoa powder and stevia and stir well.
3. Turn off the heat and let it cool for 5 minutes.
4. Pour saucepan mixture in silicone candy mold and place in the refrigerator until set.
5. Serve and enjoy.

Nutritional Value (Amount per Serving):
Calories 105; Fat 11 g; Carbohydrates 2.5 g; Sugar 0.1 g; Protein 1 g; Cholesterol 9 mg

Choco Butter Fat Bomb

Preparation Time: 5 minutes; Cooking Time: 5 minutes; Serve: 8

Ingredients:
- 8 drops stevia
- 1/4 cup coconut oil
- 1/4 cup cocoa butter

Directions:
1. Melt together coconut oil and cocoa butter in a pan over low heat.
2. Remove from heat and stir in sweetener.
3. Pour mixture into the silicone mold and refrigerate until set.
4. Serve and enjoy.

Nutritional Value (Amount per Serving):
Calories 120; Fat 13 g; Carbohydrates 0 g; Sugar 0 g; Protein 0 g; Cholesterol 9 mg

White Chocó Fat Bomb

Preparation Time: 5 minutes; Cooking Time: 5 minutes; Serve: 12
Ingredients:
- 1/2 cup cocoa butter
- 1/4 cup erythritol
- 1 tsp vanilla
- 1 scoop vanilla protein powder
- Pinch of salt

Directions:
1. Add cocoa butter in a pan and heat over medium-low heat until melted.
2. Remove from heat and add remaining ingredients and stir well to combine.
3. Pour mixture into the silicone molds and refrigerate until set.
4. Serve and enjoy.

Nutritional Value (Amount per Serving):
Calories 90; Fat 9 g; Carbohydrates 0.1 g; Sugar 0.1 g; Protein 2 g; Cholesterol 16 mg

Blackberry Ice Cream

Preparation Time: 5 minutes; Cooking Time: 30 minutes; Serve: 8
Ingredients:
- 1 cup blackberries
- 1 egg yolks
- ½ cup erythritol
- 1 ½ cup heavy whipping cream

Directions:
1. Add all ingredients to the bowl and blend until well combined.
2. Pour ice cream mixture into the ice cream maker and churn ice cream according to the machine instructions.
3. Serve chilled and enjoy.

Nutritional Value (Amount per Serving):
Calories 90; Fat 9 g; Carbohydrates 2.4 g; Sugar 0.9 g; Protein 1.1 g; Cholesterol 5 mg

Coconut Popsicle

Preparation Time: 5 minutes; Cooking Time: 5 minutes; Serve: 12
Ingredients:
- 2 cans unsweetened coconut milk
- 1/2 cup peanut butter

- 1 tsp liquid stevia
- Pinch of salt

Directions:

1. Add all ingredients into the blender and blend until smooth.
2. Pour mixture into the molds and place in the refrigerator for overnight.
3. Serve and enjoy.

Nutritional Value (Amount per Serving):

Calories 176; Fat 17 g; Carbohydrates 4 g; Sugar 2 g; Protein 3 g; Cholesterol 10 mg

Easy Strawberry Yogurt

Preparation Time: 5 minutes; Cooking Time: 5 minutes; Serve: 8
Ingredients:
- 3 1/2 cups frozen strawberries
- 1 tsp liquid stevia
- 1 tbsp fresh lemon juice
- 1/2 cup plain yogurt

Directions:

1. Add all ingredients into the blender and blend until yogurt is smooth.
2. Serve immediately and enjoy.

Nutritional Value (Amount per Serving):

Calories 35; Fat 0.9 g; Carbohydrates 7 g; Sugar 5 g; Protein 1 g; Cholesterol 4 mg

Delicious Custard

Preparation Time: 10 minutes; Cooking Time: 10 minutes; Serve: 4
Ingredients:
- 2 ½ cups heavy cream
- 2 tbsp fresh lime juice
- ¼ cup fresh lemon juice
- ½ cup Swerve
- ½ tsp orange extract
- Pinch of salt

Directions:

1. Boil heavy cream and sweetener in a saucepan for 5-6 minutes. Stir constantly.
2. Turn off the heat and add orange extract, lime juice, lemon juice, and salt and mix well.
3. Pour custard mixture into ramekins and place in refrigerator for 6 hours.
4. Serve chilled and enjoy.

Nutritional Value (Amount per Serving):

Calories 265; Fat 27 g; Carbohydrates 2.8 g; Sugar 0.5 g; Protein 1.7 g; Cholesterol 17 mg

Creamy Peanut Butter Mousse

Preparation Time: 5 minutes; Cooking Time: 5 minutes; Serve: 5
Ingredients:
- ¼ cup erythritol
- 2 tbsp peanut butter powder
- ¾ cup heavy cream
- 3.5 oz cream cheese, softened
- ¼ cup peanut butter

Directions:

1. Add all ingredients in a large bowl and beat using a hand mixer until creamy.

2. Pipe mousse into serving glasses and place in the refrigerator for 1-2 hours.
3. Serve chilled and enjoy.

Nutritional Value (Amount per Serving):
Calories 215; Fat 20 g; Carbohydrates 5 g; Sugar 1 g; Protein 7 g; Cholesterol 10 mg

Easy Berry Jam

Preparation Time: 10 minutes; Cooking Time: 20 minutes; Serve: 6
Ingredients:
- 1 3/4 cups fresh raspberries
- 1 1/2 cup fresh blackberries
- 2 tbsp water
- 1 1/2 cups fresh blueberries
- 16 drops stevia
- 3 tbsp chia seeds

Directions:
1. Add water and berries in a saucepan and bring to boil over medium heat.
2. Cook berries until soften.
3. Mash the berries using fork until getting desired consistency.
4. Add sweetener and chia seed and mix well.
5. Serve and enjoy.

Nutritional Value (Amount per Serving):
Calories 70; Fat 2 g; Carbohydrates 12 g; Sugar 5 g; Protein 2 g; Cholesterol 0 mg

Lemon Ginger Detox Drink

Preparation Time: 10 minutes; Cooking Time: 5 minutes; Serve: 6
Ingredients:
- 2 tbsp lemon juice
- 4 tbsp fresh ginger, chopped
- 4 tbsp lemon zest
- 64 oz water

Directions:
1. Add ginger, lemon zest, and water in a large saucepan and bring to boil.
2. Remove from heat and cover and set aside for 4 hours.
3. Strain water into the container.
4. Add lemon juice and stir well.
5. Serve and enjoy.

Nutritional Value (Amount per Serving):
Calories 16; Fat 0.3 g; Carbohydrates 3.5 g; Sugar 0.5 g; Protein 0.5 g; Cholesterol 0 mg

Perfect Electrolyte Drink

Preparation Time: 5 minutes; Cooking Time: 5 minutes; Serve: 3
Ingredients:
- 24 oz water
- 1 tsp lemon juice
- 2 oz aloe vera juice
- 1/3 tsp sea salt

Directions:
1. Mix together all ingredients.
2. Serve immediately or chilled.

Nutritional Value (Amount per Serving):

Calories 1; Fat0 g; Carbohydrates 0.2 g; Sugar 0 g; Protein 0 g; Cholesterol 0 mg

Apple Cider Detox Drink

Preparation Time: 5 minutes; Cooking Time: 5 minutes; Serve: 1
Ingredients:

- 1 tsp cinnamon
- 1 tbsp fresh lemon juice
- 1 tbsp apple cider vinegar
- 8 oz warm water

Directions:

1. Mix together all ingredients and serve immediately.

Nutritional Value (Amount per Serving):

Calories 12; Fat 0.2 g; Carbohydrates 2.3 g; Sugar 0.4 g; Protein 0.2 g; Cholesterol 0 mg

Creamiest Bulletproof Coffee

Preparation Time: 5 minutes; Cooking Time: 1 minute; Serve: 1
Ingredients:

- 1 tsp MCT oil
- 1 tbsp butter, unsalted
- 8 oz brewed coffee
- Pinch of cinnamon

Directions:

1. Add all ingredients into the blender and blend until frothy.
2. Serve and enjoy.

Nutritional Value (Amount per Serving):

Calories 140; Fat 15 g; Carbohydrates 0 g; Sugar 0 g; Protein 0 g; Cholesterol 31 mg

Hot Chocolate

Preparation Time: 5 minutes; Cooking Time: 5 minutes; Serve: 1
Ingredients:

- 1/8 tsp vanilla
- 1 cup boiling water
- 1 tbsp butter, unsalted
- 1 tbsp unsweetened cocoa powder

Directions:

1. Add all ingredients into the blender and blend until frothy.
2. Serve and enjoy.

Nutritional Value (Amount per Serving):

Calories 116; Fat 12 g; Carbohydrates 3 g; Sugar 0.2 g; Protein 1.2 g; Cholesterol 31 mg

Thick & Creamy Milkshake

Preparation Time: 5 minutes; Cooking Time: 5 minutes; Serve: 2
Ingredients:

- 1 tsp vanilla
- ½ cup heavy whipping cream
- 11 oz coconut milk

Directions:

1. Add all ingredients into the blender and blend until smooth and creamy.
2. Garnish with fresh berries and serve.

Nutritional Value (Amount per Serving):

Calories 498; Fat 48 g; Carbohydrates 9 g; Sugar 5 g; Protein 4 g; Cholesterol 41 mg

Simple Keto Coffee

Preparation Time: 5 minutes; Cooking Time: 5 minutes; Serve: 1

Ingredients:

- ¼ tsp liquid stevia
- 1 tbsp butter
- 12 oz brewed coffee

Directions:

1. Add all ingredients into the blender and blend until frothy.
2. Serve and enjoy.

Nutritional Value (Amount per Serving):

Calories 105; Fat 11 g; Carbohydrates 0 g; Sugar 0 g; Protein 0.5 g; Cholesterol 30 mg

Quick Ice Latte

Preparation Time: 5 minutes; Cooking Time: 5 minutes; Serve: 2

Ingredients:

- 2 keto butter coffee shake
- ½ tsp vanilla
- 8 oz prepared coffee
- Ice cubes

Directions:

1. Mix together vanilla and coffee and pour into two glasses.
2. Add ice cubes both the glasses.
3. Stir in keto butter coffee shake and serve.

Nutritional Value (Amount per Serving):

Calories 205; Fat 1 g; Carbohydrates 3 g; Sugar 1 g; Protein 10 g; Cholesterol 43 mg

Healthy Golden Latte

Preparation Time: 5 minutes; Cooking Time: 5 minutes; Serve: 1

Ingredients:

- 2 tsp vanilla
- ½ tsp cinnamon
- ½ tsp ground ginger
- 1 tsp turmeric
- 2 tsp MCT oil
- 1 cup unsweetened almond milk

Directions:

1. Heat almond milk in a saucepan until just warm. Remove from heat and let it cool for 2-3 minutes.
2. Once almond milk is cold then transfer in blender along with remaining ingredients and blend until frothy.
3. Serve and enjoy.

Nutritional Value (Amount per Serving):

Calories 165; Fat 13 g; Carbohydrates 6 g; Sugar 1.2 g; Protein 1.3 g; Cholesterol 0 mg

Perfect Peppermint Mocha

Preparation Time: 5 minutes; Cooking Time: 5 minutes; Serve: 1
Ingredients:

- 1 tbsp chocolate creamer
- ¼ tsp peppermint extract
- 14 oz strong coffee

Directions:

1. Add all ingredients into the blender and blend until frothy.
2. Serve and enjoy.

Nutritional Value (Amount per Serving):

Calories 7; Fat 0.1 g; Carbohydrates 0.1 g; Sugar 0.1 g; Protein 0.5 g; Cholesterol 0 mg

Fat Bomb Coffee

Preparation Time: 5 minutes; Cooking Time: 5 minutes; Serve: 1
Ingredients:

- 1 tbsp MCT oil
- 1/8 tsp liquid stevia
- 3 tbsp heavy whipping cream
- ¼ cup macadamia nuts, roasted
- 8 oz hot coffee

Directions:

1. Add all ingredients into the blender and blend until smooth and creamy.
2. Serve and enjoy.

Nutritional Value (Amount per Serving):

Calories 515; Fat 55 g; Carbohydrates 5 g; Sugar 1 g; Protein 4 g; Cholesterol 60 mg

Pumpkin Spice Latte

Preparation Time: 5 minutes; Cooking Time: 5 minutes; Serve: 1
Ingredients:

- 1 cup brewed coffee
- 2 tbsp coconut cream
- ½ tsp pumpkin spice stevia
- ½ tsp pumpkin spice
- ½ tbsp MCT oil

Directions:

1. Add all ingredients into the blender and blend until frothy.
2. Serve and enjoy.

Nutritional Value (Amount per Serving):

Calories 165; Fat 17 g; Carbohydrates 2 g; Sugar 1 g; Protein 1 g; Cholesterol 43 mg

Ginger Lemonade

Preparation Time: 5 minutes; Cooking Time: 5 minutes; Serve: 4
Ingredients:

- 1/3 cup erythritol
- 4 cups water
- 2 tbsp ginger, grated
- 2 lemon juice

- Ice

Directions:
1. Add sweetened, lemon juice and ginger in a pitcher.
2. Add water and stir well.

Nutritional Value (Amount per Serving):
Calories 15; Fat 0.4 g; Carbohydrates 18 g; Sugar 0.6 g; Protein 0.4 g; Cholesterol 0 mg

Protein Coffee

Preparation Time: 5 minutes; Cooking Time: 5 minutes; Serve: 1

Ingredients:
- 6 oz brewed coffee
- 1 tbsp unsweetened cocoa powder
- 1 scoop protein powder
- 2 tbsp heavy whipping cream
- 1 tbsp coconut oil

Directions:
1. Add all ingredients into the blender and blend until frothy.
2. Serve and enjoy.

Nutritional Value (Amount per Serving):
Calories 355; Fat 27 g; Carbohydrates 7.5 g; Sugar 1 g; Protein 24 g; Cholesterol 105 mg

Choco Almond Breakfast Drink

Preparation Time: 5 minutes; Cooking Time: 5 minutes; Serve: 2

Ingredients:
- 1 scoop chocolate protein powder
- 1 tbsp unsweetened cocoa powder
- 1 tbsp almond butter
- 2 cups hot water

Directions:
1. Add all ingredients into the blender and blend for minute.
2. Serve immediately and enjoy.

Nutritional Value (Amount per Serving):
Calories 83; Fat 5 g; Carbohydrates 4 g; Sugar 0.9 g; Protein 7 g; Cholesterol 10 mg

Chapter 10: 30-Day Meal Plan

Day 1

- Breakfast-Simple Egg Muffins
- Lunch-Mexican Cauliflower Rice
- Dinner-Baked Chicken Fajitas

Day 2

- Breakfast-Cauliflower Breakfast Casserole
- Lunch-Almond Celery Soup
- Dinner-Salmon Patties

Day 3

- Breakfast-Almond Porridge
- Lunch-Feta Zucchini Arugula Salad
- Dinner-Juicy & Tender Baked Pork Chops

Day 4

- Breakfast-Spinach Quiche
- Lunch-Balsamic Zucchini Noodles
- Dinner-Baked Chicken Wings

Day 5

- Breakfast-Simple Egg Tomato Scramble
- Lunch-Yogurt Cucumber Soup
- Dinner-Garlic Shrimp

Day 6

- Breakfast-Kale Muffins
- Lunch-Cucumber Yogurt Egg Salad
- Dinner-Chicken with Spinach Broccoli

Day 7

- Breakfast-Cauliflower Frittata
- Lunch-Cauliflower Broccoli Rice
- Dinner-Avocado Shrimp Salad

Day 8

- Breakfast-Cinnamon Flaxseed Muffin
- Lunch-Creamy Cauliflower Soup
- Dinner-Grilled Cilantro Lime Pork Chops

Day 9

- Breakfast-Asparagus Quiche
- Lunch-Dill Cucumber Salad
- Dinner-Delicious Bacon Chicken

Day 10

- Breakfast-Pecan Porridge
- Lunch-Cheesy Cauliflower Broccoli Risotto
- Dinner-Flavorful Pork Chops

Day 11

- Breakfast-Chia Vanilla Pudding
- Lunch-Tasty Creamy Spinach
- Dinner-Mexican Chicken

Day 12

- Breakfast-Squash Casserole
- Lunch-Bacon Chicken Salad
- Dinner-Buttery Shrimp

Day 13

- Breakfast-Almond Pancakes
- Lunch-Zucchini Soup
- Dinner-Chicken Casserole

Day 14

- Breakfast-Creamy Egg Scrambled
- Lunch-Cauliflower Mash
- Dinner-Baked Salmon

Day 15

- Breakfast-Olive Cheese Omelet
- Lunch-Roasted Broccoli
- Dinner-Shrimp & Broccoli

Day 16

- Breakfast-Cheese Almond Pancakes
- Lunch-Stir Fried Broccoli with Mushroom
- Dinner-Stuffed Jalapenos

Day 17

- Breakfast-Cauliflower Frittata

- Lunch-Flavors Zucchini Gratin
- Dinner-Asian Garlic Chicken

Day 18

- Breakfast-Basil Tomato Frittata
- Lunch-Delicious Pumpkin Risotto
- Dinner-Thyme Oregano Pork Roast

Day 19

- Breakfast-Chia Spinach Pancakes
- Lunch-Ginger Carrot Soup
- Dinner-Rosrmary Garlic Pork Chops

Day 20

- Breakfast-Easy Cheese Omelet
- Lunch-Coconut Squash Soup
- Dinner-Creamy Chicken Mushrooms

Day 21

- Breakfast-Feta Kale Frittata
- Lunch-Cheese Mushroom Shrimp Soup
- Dinner-Pan Fry Pork Chops

Day 22

- Breakfast-Protein Muffins
- Lunch-Beef Veggie Soup
- Dinner-Cheese Bacon Chicken

Day 23

- Breakfast-Healthy Waffles
- Lunch-Basil Broccoli Soup
- Dinner-Simple Grilled Pork Tenderloin

Day 24

- Breakfast-Coconut Kale Muffins
- Lunch-Basil Tomato Soup
- Dinner-Grilled Ranch Pork Chops

Day 25

- Breakfast-Blueberry Muffins
- Lunch-Garlic Leek Onion Soup
- Dinner-Delicious Minced Pork

Day 26

- Breakfast-Pumpkin Muffins
- Lunch-Pumpkin Cranberry Salad
- Dinner-Cinnamon Olive Pork Chops

Day 27

- Breakfast-Broccoli Nuggets
- Lunch-Avocado Watermelon Salad
- Dinner-Spinach Shrimp Alfredo

Day 28

- Breakfast-Cheesy Spinach Quiche
- Lunch-Mushroom Pepper Tomato Salad
- Dinner-Shrimp Scampi

Day 29

- Breakfast-Vegetable Quiche
- Lunch-Chicken Broccoli Cranberry Salad
- Dinner-Crab Cakes

Day 30

- Breakfast-Coconut Porridge
- Lunch-Egg Apple Spinach Salad
- Dinner- Creamy Herb Chicken

Conclusion

This book is perfect for keto diet beginners, you will get everything in this book not only preparing recipes but also, we have seen how the ketogenic diet is different from other diet and what are the health benefits of the diet in detail with enjoying different types of delicious and healthy keto recipes.

In this book, you will get 550 delicious and healthy keto recipes that are delicious and easy to prepare.

Made in the USA
Columbia, SC
16 March 2020